The Singing Book

The Singing Book

Meribeth Bunch
Cynthia Vaughn

W. W. Norton & Company
New York London

W. W. Norton & Company has been independent since its founding in 1923, when William Warder Norton and Margaret D. Herter Norton first published lectures delivered at the People's Institute, the adult education division of New York City's Cooper Union. The Nortons soon expanded their program beyond the Institute, publishing books by celebrated academics from America and abroad. By mid-century, the two major pillars of Norton's publishing program—trade books and college texts—were firmly established. In the 1950s, the Norton family transferred control of the company to its employees, and today—with a staff of 400 and a comparable number of trade, college, and professional titles published each year—W. W. Norton & Company stands as the largest and oldest publishing house owned wholly by its employees.

Printed in the United States of America
First Edition

Manufacturing by RR Donnelley
Book design by Maura Rosenthal/Mspace
Production Manager: JoAnn Simony

Cover illustration: André Masson. *Street Singer*. 1941. The Museum of Modern Art, New York, NY. Purchase (158.1942). Digital Image © The Museum of Modern Art/Licensed by SCALA/Art Resource, NY. © 2003 Artists Rights Society (ARS), New York/ADAGP, Paris.

Editor: Maribeth Payne
Managing Editor—College: Marian Johnson
Assistant Editor: Allison Benter
Copy Editor: Patterson Lamb
Project Editor: Kathryn Talalay
Editorial Assistant: Allison Courtney Fitch

Library of Congress Cataloging-in-Publication Data

Bunch, Meribeth, 1938–
The singing book/Meribeth Bunch and Cynthia Vaughn.
p. cm.
Includes bibliographical references (p.) and index.

ISBN 0-393-97994-6 (pbk.)

1. Singing—Instruction and study. 2. Singing—Physiological aspects. I. Vaughn, Cynthia. II. Title.

MT820.B86 2004
783—dc22 2003066238

Every effort has been made to contact the copyright holders of each selection. Rights holders of any selection not credited should contact W. W. Norton & Company, 500 Fifth Avenue, New York, NY 10110, for a correction to be made in the next reprinting of our work.

W. W. Norton & Company, Inc., 500 Fifth Avenue, New York, N.Y. 10110
www.wwnorton.com

W. W. Norton & Company Ltd., Castle House,
75/76 Wells Street, London W1T 3QT

3 4 5 6 7 8 9 0

Contents

PART III: HOW THE VOICE WORKS

Preface

The Singing Book brings a new sense of adventure and fun to class voice. This book is designed to help the beginning singer develop fundamental habits of singing that are both healthful and easy. Using the principles outlined here, singers will be able to perform in any style they wish, not just classical. The concepts in *The Singing Book* lay the foundations for a new generation of healthy and confident singers.

The book is based on a multi-dimensional approach that includes a balanced use of mental, physical, and imaginative methods for performance. Mental approaches include techniques for visualization, focusing for success, and basic knowledge of how the voice works. The physical components have the two-fold goal of focusing both the body and the mind through exercises that create balanced right-left brain functioning and that work with effective concepts of postural and physical awareness. Finally, creativity and imagination are encouraged throughout the process. Students are urged to experiment with vocal improvisations, to visualize scenes, to develop characters based on the song texts, and even to sing the book aloud as they read.

Key to this multi-dimensional approach is the concept of *co-responsibility,* which is emphasized and implemented through numerous sections labeled *Finding out for yourself* . . . . When students are given permission to experiment with both efficient *and* inefficient ways of singing in order to see and hear for themselves the habits that produce the best results, learning time is halved. The *Finding out* exercises can be performed in groups or alone with a video camera. The use of a video camera for teaching and feedback is a powerful learning tool. However, it is not always practical in a class situation. The exercises in *Finding out* sections are designed to give the singer an idea of what a video session might produce.

The book is divided into three sections. Part I teaches students to sing comfortably and easily; Part II contains over sixty songs with comprehensive, interesting annotations and appropriate translations; and Part III gives a detailed description of how the vocal mechanism works.

The book is organized in a way that gives the singer a chance to explore his or her own voice first and then begin singing without too many intellectual restrictions. By reading and working through the exercises in Part I, students will learn to focus their bodies and minds. Part I also includes easy physical warm-ups, suggestions for imaginative ways of learning songs, and easy vocal improvisations using everyday conversation. Finally, the first part of this book teaches students to handle performance jitters and to focus on confident performances.

Part II of *The Singing Book* contains an anthology of over sixty songs, demonstrating a wide range of moods, rhythms, and tempos that are suitable for both men and women and that range from easy to challenging. A variety of world folk music, spirituals, patriotic songs, and rounds encourage healthy vocal technique, while two examples of improvisation encourage creativity and individuality. Unison group songs and rounds offer beginning singers an opportunity to sing together before stepping out of their comfort zones and singing alone or in a duet. Representative art songs in a variety of languages from the Renaissance, Baroque, Romantic, and Modern eras are included in the anthology as well as songs from musical theater, television, film, and jazz standards. Annotations at the beginning of Part II provide students with interesting background materials and performance suggestions for each of the songs.

When more in-depth knowledge is needed, teachers and students can turn to Part III, which contains detailed text and illustrations relating to the logic and construction of the vocal mechanism. Part III also provides information on vocal problems and instructions on how to keep a healthy voice.

Supplementing the text is a 2-CD set that gives students three listening options for learning and practicing the songs. Each song in the anthology is recorded in "split-track," with the melody and guide rhythm on one track and piano accompaniment on the other track. Using a computer or any stereo equipped with balance controls, students can adjust the speaker balance to hear either the melody/rhythm or piano accompaniment alone, or to hear both tracks played together. (Stereos without balance controls will play both tracks simultaneously.) Using the recordings will enable students to learn the music and become comfortable with the accompaniments before performing the songs in class.

Another excellent resource is *The Singing Book* Web site (wwnorton.com/web/singing). Here, students and teachers can transpose and print sheet music in alternate keys for all of the folk songs, hymns, spirituals, and several art songs from the anthology.

Class voice is an excellent introduction to the art of singing, which will prove to be fun, imaginative, exciting, and satisfying to students and teachers alike. Often, class voice becomes one of those required courses that students consider boring and instructors consider a chore. In many instances, the course is handled in the same way that many classical private studios are—as a kind of private lesson in a group format without regard to the various styles of singing and the varied interests and abilities of those required to take class voice. This book represents the antithesis of that philosophy.

We invite you to enjoy the journey of learning to sing and perform.

Meribeth Bunch Dayme and Cynthia Vaughn

Acknowledgments

No book of this scope can be written without incorporating information and feedback from every teacher, student, and mentor we have ever had. So to every one of you, thank you. We know that there is nothing new under the sun, that most information is just a new arrangement of existing knowledge. This book is no different.

To everyone who has reviewed the manuscript, we have appreciated your comments and input. Special thanks go to Rita Farrell and Jane Vukovic, who gave us editorial suggestions and helpful encouragement. Thanks also to the "Diction Divas" Candace Magner and Yvonne deChance, and to Jeson Yan, Alex Pudov, and Noemi Lugo for Chinese, Russian, and Spanish translations.

We would also like to thank the editorial staff at W. W. Norton & Company for their expertise and help. It has been an honor to work with them on this project. Maribeth Payne was instrumental in getting this project off the ground, and Allison Benter, Kathryn Talalay, and Courtney Fitch have been great facilitators. The Norton team has given us invaluable help and support.

Cynthia and Meribeth thank each other as well. It has been quite a team effort to put this book together. There have been many hours spent chatting on the Internet and transcontinental phone calls and many e-mails with attachments sent into the wee hours of the night.

Our thanks would not be complete without acknowledging the dedication and talent of Beryl Maile, the illustrator, our arrangers, Scarlett Antaloczy and Frank Ponzio, and pianist Cynthia Lee Fox. They worked to tight deadlines with wonderful, positive attitudes.

Putting *The Singing Book* together took a huge team of dedicated and skilled people. The combined experience, education, and wisdom of everyone concerned is greatly appreciated. Many thanks to everyone.

INTRODUCTION

Getting Started

Let's get right to the heart of the matter: Singing is fun, joyful, imaginative, exciting, and satisfying. It includes a variety of styles such as classical, musical theater, pop, jazz, rap, soul, and much, much more. This book is designed to help you enjoy using your voice easily, healthily, and happily. Along the way, you will develop a clear understanding of how the voice works and what it means to perform with purpose and a message in a number of the vocal styles listed above.

Any sustained sound that you make with your voice can be considered singing whether in the shower, in your car with the windows up, or on the karaoke stage. (Even your un-hums and ums and ers have a certain singing quality to them.) In those situations there is no one to tell you how to do it, and your analytical-critical left brain that wants to stop the sound before you begin is strangely absent.

Singing easily and healthily involves a balance of creativity, spontaneity, and knowledge of basic, healthy principles. This balance is important because much of your learning has been dedicated to analytical-critical thinking and data-specific information. For singing, it is important to balance the intellect with feeling, emotion, and intuition. The left brain is usually in charge of intellectual thinking and the right brain in charge of intuition and spontaneity. For singing and performance, a balanced use of the right and left brain is necessary. Therefore, here are three principles that are important to your approach to singing.

Humans Are Meant to Sing

We "sing" all the time without realizing it. Listen to ordinary conversation and you will hear many musical sounds scattered throughout. There are many sustained sounds in every language. These form the basis of a natural way to move into singing. The sound *hummm,* often a response to conversation, could be considered a short hum, the basis for the beginning of a warm-up for many singers.

Preconceptions about *singing* often get in singers' way and stop them from making any sustained sound without criticizing it. These preconceptions include everything from ideas that only highly trained singers perform in public to self-judgments about the quality of the voice as heard from the inside rather than the sounds heard by the audience. *Somehow we have the idea that "singing" has to be perfect rather than fun and enjoyable.* Yet we go about our normal day having "sung" quite often.

VOCABULARY AND LEARNING

When in doubt, always think positively. There is increasing evidence that positive thinking and the vocabulary you use set you up to succeed. Words and phrases like *I am capable of doing this, I can do this, I will do my best* will create an atmosphere in which you can reach your potential.

Unhelpful words that are best eliminated from your spoken and mental vocabulary include *right* and *wrong, should* and *ought, control* and *hold.* These words inhibit spontaneity, creativity, and intuition, and they set up an internal radio of nonstop comment and negativity in our brains. These and many more thought forms tend to lower the immune system temporarily. So, for this class, discard them; in fact, establish fines for their use, and give bonuses for using *enjoy* and *imagination*: the "e" and "i" words.

With that in mind, here is a crazy way to begin using this text. *Rather than just sitting and reading these words, sing them!* Now go back to the beginning of the chapter and sing everything you have just read in any way you wish. There are no "wrong" notes because you are making up the tune. Do this in class by having a "sung" conversation with a partner. When you can't think of something to sing, hum until you are ready. You can now say you have learned the basics of improvisation. Your assignment for the duration of your vocal study is to sing, rather than read silently, all the text in this book.

Finding out for yourself . . .

When you read the last paragraph, did you think any of the following: "I can't do this, it is too childish," "People will think I'm nuts," or "I should be doing proper singing—something more sophisticated and classical"? These are good examples of an approach that is analytical-critical, creativity inhibiting, and under the control of a dominant left brain. However, if you said, "This sounds crazy and fun" or "What an imaginative way to begin singing" or any number of other positive things, then your inner child and your right brain thought it must be worth doing.

You can find out how your body reacts to positive and negative thoughts by using the following test with a partner. Person A is to stand and think thoughts like "I shouldn't be singing this way," "I can't do this," and "this is silly." Person B tests Person A's stability using two fingers to gently push on A's sternum (chest bone). Normally you will find that A cannot maintain his or her balance while thinking the negative thoughts. Now perform the same test using the following thoughts: "This is fun," "I am excited about doing this," "I am strong and centered in myself." The body will remain strong and unable to be pushed off center. Now that you know what negative thoughts do to your body, you can begin to understand what they do to your singing as well.

Technique Serves the Message

A vocally healthy, good technique is considered basic to singing well, whatever the style. This idea cannot be stressed enough. Many students become so involved with the technical aspects, however, that they forget about the message in the words and music. Yet singers who are good on stage are completely involved in the music and the audience adores them. Those who are only technically proficient complain about the poor technique of popular singers but are themselves somewhat boring. The truth is that you can do both—be completely involved and have good technique—and both are essential. A good technique provides the ease and freedom for your imagination and creativity to capture your audience. When you concentrate too much on your voice and how you sound, the message that comes across to the audience is "I am being very diligent about my singing." The message of the song and the music is then lost and the audience becomes bored very quickly.

Now that you have begun to use your creativity and imagination, it is important to have a pleasant, healthy voice. There are some key principles involved. You will probably need to change some old habits. That will take thought. However, this is part of the balance mentioned earlier.

The sections that follow are deliberately simple with minimal information given to allow you to experience your voice for yourself. More specific details of how the voice works are located in Part III. You may *sing* Part III any time you choose. First get started with Part I and Part II, the songs, and then find out how your voice works and how to keep it healthy in Part III.

PART I

The First Steps to Singing Easily

The singing voice is a combination of mind, body, imagination, and spirit all working together. That is the context in which this text is written. Singing easily requires physical ease, awareness, imagination, and enjoyment.

Finding out for yourself . . .

Begin this process by asking yourself this question: "In the best of all possible worlds, how would I like my voice described?" If someone heard you sing and were to describe your voice to others, what would you like said about it? Make a list of the characteristics that are important to you. (For example, this list might include adjectives such as *warm, clear, bright,* and so on.) By knowing how you wish to sound, you can begin to make it happen.

Chapter One

Healthy Singing

Vocal ease and health go hand in hand. They are the basis for a long-lasting technique and a beautiful sound. Your technique is the support or the framework for everything you want to do with your voice. Three basic principles of technique are presented here: physical balance, breathing, and presence.

Physical Balance

The first principle of healthy singing is good physical balance. Instrumentalists will tell you that the most wonderful technique in the world will not help when their instruments are unbalanced or misshapen. This is doubly true of the human voice whose instrument is the body. It is the equivalent of having a house built on shaky foundations with crooked walls. Those who can sing well, easily, and healthily despite posturally unbalanced and misshapened bodies are exceptional. Unfortunately, the characteristics of admired singers most copied are the faults and exaggerations, because they are usually the most obvious to the student with limited knowledge. These faults include poking the head forward to "sing to the audience," holding the body in a stiff and artificial manner, and adopting the super casual look of a pop singer.

As you are used to your current habits of standing and sitting, you may find that the suggestions that follow feel awkward at first. When you are aligned well (ears in line with shoulders and hips) for the first time, your body will tell you that your balance is now not correct (see following Box). Use a mirror or a video to tell you how it really looks. Persist, and you will find that your muscles will adjust very quickly to a new way of standing and sitting.

As you know, how we *think* we look and how we actually look can be very different. It is important that you test for yourself what is said in this text. Here are some observations for you to make in a group or for yourself with the help of a video recording.

Figure 1.1: Good posture

Finding out for yourself . . .

First, how are you standing presently? Get a partner to coach someone to duplicate your posture exactly. After that person is standing or sitting exactly like you, notice what your profile is like. Get that person to describe how it feels to adopt your stance while you move around him or her to see how you look. (It is very effective to look at a side view of yourself with a video camera.)

Choose a few lines from any song and, with a partner, experiment with what happens to your singing, your body, and your tone quality when you do the following:

1. Sing with your weight on your heels.
2. Sing with an overly arched back.
3. Sing with your weight on your toes.

Now "superglue" your feet to the floor and reach for the ceiling with the crown of your head (that area where your cowlick sits near the back), don't adjust your chin up or down, keep your knees gently loose, and balance your weight evenly between the balls of your feet and your heels. The balance is correct when you can rise up on your toes by pushing through the feet without adjusting any other part of the body. You may find you have to move your weight more forward than you thought. Remember that the feet are superglued so the full foot will remain on the floor with your weight more forward. (This is a beginning and it does not matter if you are not perfect at it yet.)

4. Compare this final version with those in 1, 2, and 3 above. As awkward as it may feel, sing your phrases in this position. You will find the voice now is a more efficient instrument to sing/play.

Efficient physical balance ensures that the parts of your instrument are aligned and in position to work together to produce a free sound. This means that your lungs, your voice box (larynx), and your throat (vocal tract) are all in a line and in a position of maximum efficiency for singing (see Figure 1.1).

BREATHING EASILY

The second principle is that breathing for singing needs to be accomplished easily and deeply. Notice that the word *deeply* is used. No one said to take a big breath. Deep and big are not the same. Deep, in this case, refers to the lower half of your body (including the abdomen and the lower ribs in the back) where you feel expansion on inhalation. You can take in a lot or a small amount of air as long as you feel the response deeply in your body.

Ideally, imagine you have a large tube from your mouth to your lower abdomen that forms a channel for your air. This tube does not change shape during the breathing process and nothing in the upper chest is disturbed. There is no gasping and no noise that comes from the mouth or throat and no extra movement of the shoulders or chest. Any visible action of breathing is seen in the lower abdomen and the lower ribs at the back (see Figure 1.2). Pay attention to your posture because when the back is overly arched (swaybacked), the lower ribs are not able to respond and it is difficult to get a deep breath. (A thorough discussion of breathing is in Chapter 8).

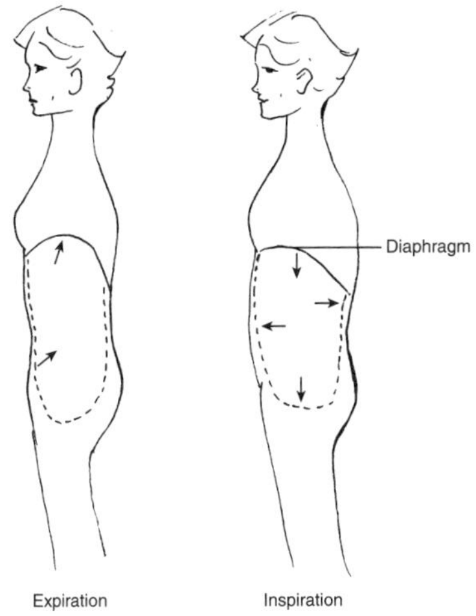
Diaphragm
Expiration
Inspiration

Figure 1.2: Deep breathing

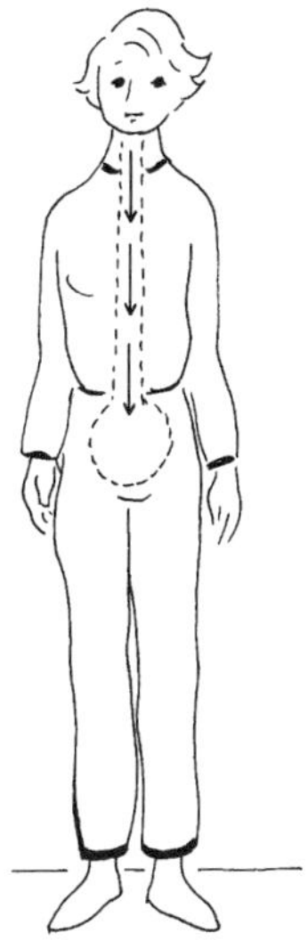

Figure 1.3: Imagery for deep breathing

Finding out for yourself . . .

This is an experiment in efficient and inefficient breathing and how it can affect your singing. Note: Let your partner do the listening. You cannot sing and listen at the same time. Your job is to do the "feeling." Sing a line or two of a song immediately after breathing in the manner below:

1. Take a huge breath letting your shoulders and chest rise.
2. Take a breath with a slouched posture.
3. Take a breath with an overly arched back.
4. Breathe with efficient physical alignment.
5. Breathe and feel as if you have an imaginary pipeline to the lower abdomen (see Figure 1.3).

Never stop breathing. This may sound ridiculous to you. However, notice what you do the next time you "stop" to think. There is a good chance that you also stop the process of inhaling and exhaling. Mental and physical hesitation can cause us to stop breathing for the moment. It's all about flow, and in singing, especially airflow. When you gasp or grab a breath, the body wants to lock it in; there is a momentary pause, and the voice tends to seize up just when you want to sing. So, go with the flow.

STAYING PRESENT

The third principle is to stay present at all times. Being present implies that you are aware of what is happening around you while you are singing. This does not mean the same thing as being distracted. Presence is a state of being centered, of having a quiet alertness. In performance, this state acts as a powerful magnet to draw an audience to you. It enables you to be in touch with the music, yourself, and your audience. At the same time, it has a profound effect on your physical state and the freedom of your performance.

Presence is the first step to the development of a listening body and mind. You can tell the state of someone's presence by his or her alignment and the eyes. People who are present and aware seem to be able to see anything in the room without its being obvious. They use peripheral vision rather than a stare and they are *seeing* rather than *looking*. We need to do the same thing when we sing. Singing with the eyes looking up at the ceiling or down at the floor tends to focus the singer and the music inward rather than allowing it to fill the space around. This inhibits the freedom of the body and the participation of the audience.

Finding out for yourself . . .

(It is taken for granted that your posture is exemplary.) Have your partner note the differences (or use a video) when you sing a few lines of any song (the same lines each time) in the following ways:

1. With glaring eyes
2. With soft seeing eyes
3. Staring at the far wall or a person
4. With eyes looking heavenward (do not raise the head)
5. With eyes looking down (do not lower the head)
6. Using peripheral vision (seeing everything around you with calm eyes)
7. Using peripheral vision and being the "dot" in the middle of a circle that encompasses the whole audience (so that your awareness is 360 degrees)

No matter what you are singing or practicing, always stay fully present in the room. Do not take a mental vacation. Developing presence is an essential part of performance and doing so is important from the first moment you begin to sing—even during your vocal warm-ups. Warming up with your mind a thousand miles away will do nothing for your singing.

CHAPTER TWO

Preparing to Sing

Preparing to sing is like preparing to participate in a sport. Every part of us needs to be available and ready to respond. The mind and body need equal attention from the very beginning. By beginning with focusing the mind, your body will be alerted to the need for action.

FOCUSING

Top athletes and competitors are taught to focus or visualize their goals before they ever set foot on the playing field. Research has shown that good visualization can be almost as effective as the actual physical practice. Certainly one key to being centered, remaining in the present and in charge of your practice and performance, is the ability to visualize what you want to happen. This can include anything from physical elements of your technique to positive attitudes about performance (including exams).

Here is an easy, short way to focus. Do this at the beginning of every practice session—and for that matter before you study any subject. You can do this even while waiting for a bus.

Finding out for yourself . . .

Note: For those of you who are used to moving and fidgeting, you may find it difficult to sit still for a minute. Start with thirty seconds instead (see Figure 2.1).

With your eyes open . . .

1. Sit (or stand) with two feet flat on the floor. Imagine that you have superglue attached to the bottoms of your feet. Everything is still. Nothing is twitching or moving.
2. Place your hands on something flat or your thighs. Imagine that you have superglue attached to the palms of your hands. Again, nothing is moving (except your breath).

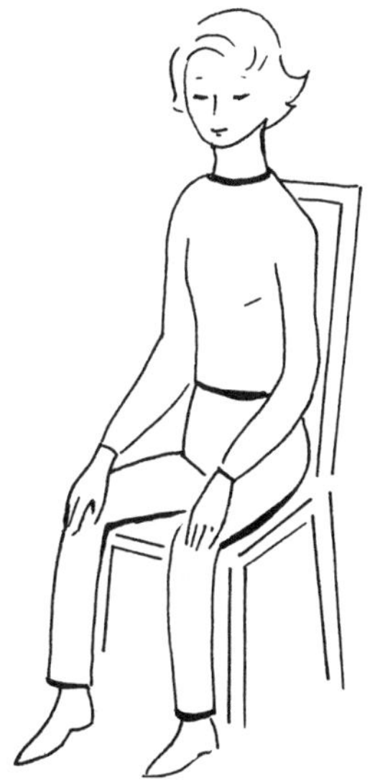

Figure 2.1: Being still

3. Sit in this complete stillness for one minute. You may find that you begin to feel a different kind of energy and that your thoughts begin to slow down. Enjoy this strange feeling. It will calm you and enable you to clear your mind of all the inner voice debris that gets in your way.
4. Observe your breathing. Ideally, you will feel as if you are breathing in air from the bottom of the chair. Deep breathing has nothing to do with a big breath or the volume of air you take in. It has to do with a feeling of depth in the body. You can imagine that you are breathing in from the top of your spine to the very bottom of it. To breathe out you reverse the procedure. Deep breathing at its best is barely noticeable.
5. Now visualize yourself creating an atmosphere in which you remain focused and able to do your best.

Focusing is the first step to readying your mind and body for the tasks ahead. The second step is to get the body moving in ways that will benefit your voice.

MOVEMENT

Here are some gentle physical warm-ups. They take less than two minutes to perform and are to be done at an easy slow pace and in a centered manner. These exercises consist of stretches and coordinated movements to free the body and get both sides of your brain working together. In all cases pay attention to your postural alignment.

Rib stretches

The idea here is to give the ribs and waist a good stretch. The exercise is to be done slowly for the best effect. During these movements make sure the head is over the shoulders and not poked forward (see Figure 2.2).

Figure 2.2: Rib stretches

a. Interlock your fingers and turn the palms outward.

b. Push your palms outward toward the ceiling until your arms are fully stretched.

c. Bend your elbows and bring the palms (still facing outward) toward the top of your head. Push the palms out and up to the right. Bring them back again and push them out to the left.

d. Repeat the exercise. This time as you do it, bend the knees as you bring the palms toward your body and straighten the knees when the palms and arms are fully stretched. You will find that when your arms are fully extended to the left or right the ribs get a nice stretch.

Cross crawl*

This exercise is similar to marching in place. You alternately move one arm to touch the opposite leg (knee) as you march. It is like walking and swinging your arms as you go. You would normally do it using alternating arm and leg (right leg up and left arm forward, then left leg up and right arm forward). As you touch the opposite knee, maintain your good spinal alignment (see Figure 2.3). You may do this exercise while singing if you wish. However, ten times for each side would be enough.

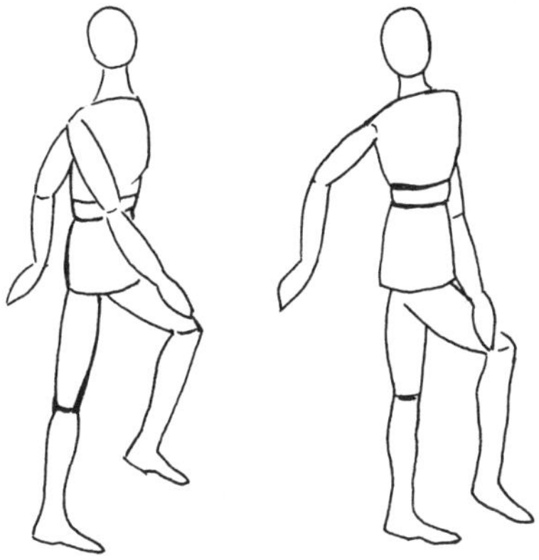

Figure 2.3: Cross crawl

Lazy 8's

This helps you focus and relax the eyes, neck, and shoulders.

Note: Keep the spine aligned and do not lean forward from the waist while you do this exercise.

Begin with either arm outstretched forward. Draw in the air an eight on its side (∞), beginning in the middle and moving up to either the right or left to make the pattern (Figure 2.4). It is important that your first movement be up!

As you draw the eight slowly, smoothly, and evenly, carefully follow your fingertips with your eyes. Alternate left and right arms.

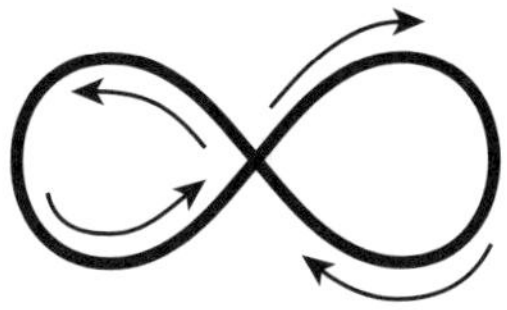

Figure 2.4: Lazy 8's

*The Cross crawl, Lazy 8's, and Energy yawn are Brain-gym exercises based on studies by Paul E. Denison and Gail E. Denison.

This exercise can also be done with both arms outstretched, palms together. And for more variety you can do this slowly with your nose, making the largest possible movement.

Repeat any of the above patterns ten times (see Figure 2.4).

Energy yawn

Figure 2.5: Energy yawn

Somehow this exercise always helps people sing better. You can repeat it any time your jaw feels tight. If jaw tension is one of your problem areas, do this exercise several times during a practice session or several times during the day. Be sure to keep your head over your shoulders. There is a tendency to poke the head forward in this exercise.

Open your mouth as if you are yawning. While maintaining the yawning position, strongly massage the area near the cheek bone above your back teeth (see Figure 2.5). Do this three times.

WARMING UP YOUR VOICE

Now that you have warmed up your body and gotten both sides of your brain working, it is time to give the muscles of your voice some special attention. The vocal warm-ups suggested here do not have to be done as scales. By playing and experimenting with sound, you can discover interesting ways of covering a wide range of pitches while relaxing the jaw, lips, and tongue.

Note: During all of the exercises below be sure to check your posture, levels of awareness, and presence. Here are some options for you:

1. Lip trills or "motor boats" going from the middle of your voice and as high as you can go, and then from the middle of your voice and as low as you can go.

2. Sirens up and down—not missing any pitches. This means lots of sliding up and down on an "ng" sound. You may also use a comfortable vowel sound for this.

3. Tongue trills or "raspberries" up and down in the same manner as numbers 1 and 2. (This is the same as a continual rolled r.)

4. Use any of the above methods to sing the melodies of your songs.

5. Using vowels and other vocal sounds, improvise by starting with a rhythm or melody. Just let it develop in any way it wishes to go. Sometimes you can go on and on—especially in the shower. There is no rule that says you must sing anything recognizable for a warm-up.

Note: When you are using scales as warm-up material, vary the rhythm and beat so that you are not practicing the same way every time. That way lies boredom because when you are on automatic pilot, you lose presence and awareness of what you are doing.

Reminder: Singing this text is also a type of warm-up.

For those of you who want more ideas for warm-ups, see Appendix C at the back of the book.

Chapter Three

Selecting Music to Sing

If you are new to voice classes, printed music can look like strange hieroglyphics and you may not feel ready to choose your own songs. (See Appendix D for the fundamentals of reading music.) At this stage of your vocal education, your teacher can choose the music best suited to you until you are able to read music and can choose for yourself. Help is also available on the CDs that come with this text. They contain the melodies, rhythms, and accompaniments of all the songs in this text, some of which may already be familiar to you.

There are some things you need to know about songs that will help you choose your music wisely. To do this, you will need to suspend your own perceptions of the limits of your voice at this point in time. Remember, you are in this class to improve your voice and expand its capabilities. While studying singing, you have the potential to extend your vocal range, quality, and expression. Therefore, choosing a particular song may help you to sing smoothly or legato, extend your current pitch range, or bring out your personality and expression. What follows are some of the considerations you and/or your teacher may use when choosing a song.

Range and Tessitura

The range of the song includes the highest and lowest notes to be sung. However, it is the *tessitura*, or where the average or median of the pitches lies, that can often determine the difficulty of a song. For example suppose the highest note is an F5 and the lowest G3 (see Figure 3.1). There may be only one of those F's or one of those G's and the rest of the song may include mostly medium-range pitches. That song would be much easier than one that has many notes at the top or the bottom of the range throughout.

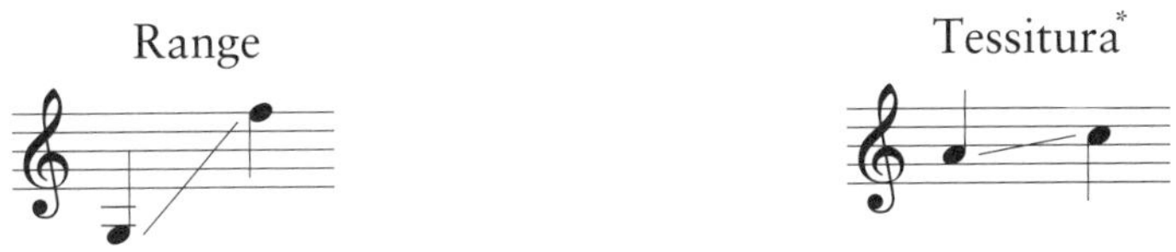
Range
Tessitura*

* Refer to Appendix D for location of notes on the keyboard.

Figure 3.1: Range and tessitura

MELODY

Some melodies are smooth and meant to be sung in a very connected manner (*legato*), such as ballads or love songs. Others are full of detached and sharp, accented notes (*staccato*). Teachers often assign specific styles to help beginning singers develop a versatile technique. Good singers can sing various melodic styles with ease.

TEXT

The words and how fast or slow they have to be pronounced are another important consideration. Slow songs place emphasis on singing the vowels well while fast songs with lots of words get the tongue and lips moving. Rap is certainly a way of teaching singers how to articulate well and say words very quickly. Patter songs, such as "Modern Major-General" (p. 229), are also fun and helpful diction songs.

Fluency in several languages opens up the possibilities for much more music. Singing in a foreign language can often eradicate some poor speech habits in English. It is fun to learn songs in languages other than English, and several are included with this text.

RHYTHM

Rhythms can be simple or complex. Hymns have simple rhythms and much of the popular music of today has complex rhythms. Mastering basic rhythms is the first priority. Your teacher will know when you are ready to tackle a song with tricky rhythms.

DO YOU LIKE IT?

Finally, it is important for you to enjoy the music you are singing. After you have learned and lived with a song for several weeks, you may decide you do not like it. Perceived difficulty or seeing a note that looks or sounds too high is not a good reason for disliking a piece of music. However, if the song continues to irritate you, find one you do like. The world is full of good music.

Finding out for yourself . . .

The CD accompanying this book offers a fine way to hear the music. First listen to the melody and then the accompaniment. This will give you an excellent opportunity to decide how much you like the song.

Chapter Four

Learning Music Efficiently

After you have selected the songs you wish to sing, your imagination is going to play a key role in learning your music and performing. Approach each song as if you are the director of a play. You choose the characters and know each one intimately (eye color, hair, height, weight, type of clothes, etc.); you design the set and costumes and be responsible for choosing every color and piece of material that appears on the stage. When you take this approach, your imagination will supply all the vocal color you need naturally and fill in the picture for the audience. Do this before you ever begin to learn the music. Take the text to each song you are singing and write a thorough description of each character. There is a worksheet, Appendix A, that will help you do this. It will give you the appropriate questions for setting the scene for each song you sing.

First, the Words

Your text is your message, and it is important. First, learn the words in their own natural rhythm and dramatize them as prose or poetry until they make complete sense to someone else. Do not be tempted to learn the tune yet. As an optional exercise, make a copy of your text and use colored pens to illustrate the various vocal colors you would like to include in your interpretation. For example, one phrase might be colored blue and the next a cream yellow. This stimulation of your imagination will help you when you begin to sing the song.

Second, the Rhythm

Everything has its own rhythm. All you have to do is tap into it. If instead you try to "make" the rhythm, that will only cause your body to tense and you will get slower and slower. What is meant by *make*? Well, think about this. You do not make your heart beat; it just beats. Your breathing has its own pattern, and each organ in your body has its own vibration as well. You can consider rhythm as the underlying heartbeat of the music. You do not make it happen; it is just there. First, there is the natural rhythm of the text alone, and second, there is the basic rhythm set by the composer. Each language has its own rhythm, as well. Stop and listen to someone speak French, German, English, or Chinese. When people learn a foreign language, it is not the pronunciation that usually trips them up; it is the rhythm of the language.

Physical rhythm, or the pulse, is the foundation of music. Using your whole body to feel the rhythm is very useful at this point. There is nothing wrong with dancing your song to learn it.

Finding out for yourself . . .

Rhythmic exercises

1. First, tap into the pulse of a song by walking or marching and clapping loudly the basic beat of the song. Do not bother with the exact rhythm yet; just get the feel of the music. You can do this with the rhythm and melody tracks on the CD.

2. Next, begin to singsong or chant the actual rhythm of the song on one pitch using any syllable such as [la] or [du] to this basic beat. Then singsong the words of the song, on one pitch, to the rhythm while walking and clapping. Do not allow your left brain to trap you into lacking courage or to stop where you perceive a mistake; just keep walking and clapping. Be aware that when you feel insecure, your body will want to hesitate. By walking and clapping you will be able to overcome this tendency. This is why it is not helpful to tap a toe or finger (they are too small and can be bullied easily by your analytical brain). The moment you become unsure, the tapping will stop. Please do not stop until the end of the song! Don't worry about being perfect.

3. A way of checking that you know the rhythm is to singsong it in a staccato manner using any syllable such as [ha] or [la] or [ti] or [hi]. This means that each note is short and sharp and totally disconnected from the note before. Rhythmic mistakes show up quickly when you do this because you are filling in with silence rather than sound.

4. Here is one you can do after you have learned the melody. Sing to your own pulse. Find the pulse in your wrist or on your neck. While keeping your finger lightly on your pulse sing a familiar song. Make sure you stay in touch with your own inner beat while singing. If you find you cannot feel your pulse, you have probably allowed physical tension to interfere.

Third, the Melody

With the words and rhythm firmly in place, you can learn the melody with confidence. The melody is available for you on the CD. First, feel the melody and the phrasing by moving your arms and hands to the shape of it. Next, while continuing to follow the phrasing with your arms, use a vocally easy syllable such as [pa], [la], [di], or [lu] to sing the melody. This makes singing the melody easier, and it also acts as a vocal warm-up. When you are confident of the notes or pitches, add the words.

Finally, Putting It All Together

All the pieces are now in place and you are finally ready to put everything together. If you have worked to assimilate this time-consuming process, you will find that your musicianship is more accurate. That is because you have built in imagination and expression and are not stumbling or stopping and starting because of inaccurate words or rhythms. This process is one that builds confidence at each step.

CHAPTER FIVE

Practice Habits

Consistency is the key word here. A little every day is the best approach to singing. Vocal muscles need intelligent and varied repetition for you to create healthy singing habits. It would be ideal for you to spend thirty to forty-five minutes practicing per day. However, ten minutes is better than nothing. At the beginning, it does more harm than good for you to sing more than forty-five minutes. Therefore, singing is not something you can cram the day before a class.

You do not have to be in a studio to practice. You can do loads of work away from a piano or CD. Visualization can be done anywhere. The words can be learned and recited in your room, on street corners, even in front of theater students who may later expect you to reciprocate.

Once you have learned the words and rhythm, you can think or inwardly say or sing your words in rhythm as you walk across campus or down the street. Interestingly, you have to stay on beat because your walk is steady.

Practicing in a Small Room

Almost every singer who practices in small rooms sings too softly. The reason for this is that the ear will constantly adjust the sound to the room it is in. Think of it this way—if you are singing *piano,* or softly, in a small room, and you were to sing at that same dynamic level on a stage, you would not be heard. Your practice room "soft" would become triply soft in a large space. Because your habitual dynamic levels would be soft, you would find that singing in a much larger situation would cause you to strain and push your voice in larger spaces. Translated, this means that a good target to reach for when practicing in small spaces is a medium volume.

Checklist for Practice Session

1. Spend thirty seconds to one minute focusing.
2. Check your posture.
3. Make sure you are seeing peripherally and are fully aware and present during the entire session.
4. Do two minutes of physical warm-up using the stretching and Brain-gym exercises.

5. Do five minutes of vocal warm-up, including an easy song to sing as an exercise.

6. Vary the remaining time between learning new music and rehearsing songs you know. It is important vocally and mentally to practice songs that are in the learning stage, the developing stage, and the performance-ready stage.

7. Your imagination is also needed in a practice session to make the words of a song take shape. Here is a way to encourage it. As you sing your song, use your hands to fully illustrate the text. In other words, be a ham and enjoy it. The rule is very strict: Your hands must draw a picture. For example, when you are singing about a "long road," you must allow your hand to indicate a very long road; when singing about a person, indicate where that person is and what he or she looks like. Pretend your audience is wearing earplugs and needs to see the song mimed. Be thorough in your visual presentation. You will be surprised at how quickly the song will come to life.

8. Never leave the studio without singing one song with full involvement with the message, as if you are performing before an audience of thousands. This means that you are not allowed to stop yourself in the middle if it isn't going the way you want. You must continue. Besides, if you are paying that much attention to the technique, you have forgotten the message.

CHAPTER SIX

Performing

Nothing is more satisfying than the supportive energy of a live audience willing you to be wonderful. This is why many singers do their best with an audience. Note that your perception of your performance and the audience's perception of your performance may be entirely different.

You have a memory of having sung a song many times. Each one of these times is firmly entrenched in your mind. What's more, you have compared all of these times and put each one on a scale of best and worst (see Figure 6.1).

Figure 6.1: Your memory bank of singing the song

|_|_|_|_|_|_|_|_|_|_|_|_|_{_|_}_|_|_|_|_|_|_|_|_|

Audience's perception

Worst ——————————————→ Best

The audience's perception of your singing = {_|_} Wonderful!

Each vertical mark represents a time you have sung the song. The box represents the time the audience heard you sing. They think it is wonderful. However, you are remembering all the times you have sung it and it does not satisfy your "best."

You have the dubious privilege of knowing where each performance fits on this scale. Your audience does not. They have heard it once or twice at most. They are judging you on a limited knowledge and may perceive it to have been sung wonderfully. Meanwhile, on your scale you may have sung it somewhere near mediocre. You must honor their perception of your singing. The best reply to *"You were wonderful"* is *"Thank you."* Whatever your thoughts are about your performance, *keep them to yourself.* For you to turn around and say, *"Oh, no, I can do it so much better,"* or *"That was terrible!"* is the equivalent of saying *"You do not know what you are talking about."* The fact is, they know their own taste and appreciation. Respect that! You may well be able to sing it better, but a musically unsophisticated audience may not know that. Your self-criticism does not increase the listener's pleasure or understanding.

We often give the audience credit for knowing everything that is going on inside us as we sing. So many times when singers see a video of themselves, they say "I was going through hell, and yet I look so calm and in control." But there may be a difference between how you think you sound and look, and how you actually sound and look. Remember this!

Finding out for yourself . . .

Positive thoughts from the audience help the singer enormously. When singing for your classmates or peers, experiment with the following:

Have someone sing a song for the class. While he or she is singing, have the class mentally send positive thoughts of support and care for the person performing. *Will* that person to sing well. *Note:* Do not tell the singer what you are doing.

Now do the opposite. While that person is singing, ask the class to send critical negative thoughts.

Ask the singer about the differences in performing in each situation.

Always send positive caring thoughts to the person singing. No mental criticism allowed. It is not helpful to you or the performer.

NERVES

Of course you want to be confident when you perform. Confidence comes with the process of disciplined practice and attention to learning combined with positive thinking. Believe it or not, one way of becoming confident is to pretend you are. "Fake it until you make it" is not a bad adage when it comes to performing in public. The audience does not usually see your perceived wobbly legs and knotted stomach. It is worth repeating here: "How you perceive yourself and how others see you are very different."

When people are nervous, it means that they are thinking about themselves more than the message or the music. This is usually the time the words are forgotten. At no time do you want to call attention to yourself by thinking thoughts such as "Is this OK? " or "Oops, I sang a wrong rhythm." Focus on the message of the music and communicating with your audience. By working through the worksheet in Appendix A, you will have a strong basis for remembering the words and delivering a meaningful message.

By using the focusing technique you learned earlier, you can see yourself on stage or in performance being comfortable, remembering the words, and being fully involved with the message.

PRESENCE

This topic has been discussed earlier. However, it can never be stressed enough. Your presence is a combination of your physical balance, seeing as you sing, your desire to be there, the music, and the message of the music. Remember you are sharing that with the audience at all times. You and your sound are the drop that creates ripples going out in all directions so that you fill the entire space.

THE MESSAGE

Before you sing, ask yourself: "What is the one thing I would like my audience to take away from this performance?" It could be many things. It is up to you to choose one as the "bottom line." (An example: *I would like to create an atmosphere in which the members of my audience go away feeling better for having come to hear me.*) Having an underlying goal for your whole performance will help you be comfortable with your audience and will help you believe you have something to offer them.

Never forget that each song has its own message. Your careful preparation of the text, your full involvement in its message, and your presence all contribute to a compelling performance.

PART II

Improvisations and Songs

- Improvisation
- Patriotic Songs, Unison Songs, and Rounds
- Folk Songs, Spirituals, and Hymns
- Theater, Film, and Television Songs
- Popular and Jazz Standards
- Art Songs and Arias

Men and women have used music and song to express and lift their spirits, energies, and emotions for as long as we know. Songs have been used to develop religious fervor, to create energy for work, to urge men to war, to serenade loved ones, and to lull babies to sleep. Whenever we express our thoughts and words through music, the effect is many times more powerful. Singing "I love you" on a high note can certainly magnify the intensity and meaning of the words beyond any stated declaration of them.

The oral tradition of handing down songs has existed for thousands of years and continues today. Children are taught the songs their parents and grandparents were taught. We sing many of these "folk" songs today. Part II devotes a whole section to this type of song. In fact, Part II contains the widest possible variety of songs, which in turn provides a basis for expressing yourself in music. The improvisations give you the freedom to experiment with your voice and to be creative with the music. Annotations are included to help you understand the context of each song and to aid your interpretations. The accompanying CDs make it easy to learn your music, while the Student Web site allows you to listen to many of the songs in various keys and to print a copy of that song as performance-ready sheet music.

Many of the songs in this book are timeless and have a history of inspiring people to sing. There are tunes you "can't get out of your head," which is why many of them have been sung for decades. You can sing these songs anywhere, even to your computer. Years ago, before electronic diversions of CDs, MP3s, radios, TVs, and computers, people gathered around the piano to sing for their entertainment. Today this happens formally in choirs and informally in karaoke bars, at football games, or at Christmas, when groups gather to sing carols.

The late, great American folk singer Burl Ives remarked "Now songs are, roughly, of two kinds: The songs sung at us . . . and the songs sung by us." This book is all about "the songs sung by us." The songs that follow will help your vocal development, but they were chosen for their beauty, fun, tradition, and inspiration. You are encouraged to use these songs to explore and improve your unique vocal instrument and to discover a wealth of traditional and popular solo vocal repertoire.

Improvisation

Improvisation is a creative, spontaneous process with no set rules or text. You have already begun to improvise music by singing this book and having sung conversations with partners. Jazz and pop styles are full of improvisation. So is much of the Baroque music of Bach and Handel—it is just incorporated into the composed music. In fact, there is a tradition of classical singers improvising during the seventeenth and eighteenth centuries as well as today in contemporary music.

The key to improvisation is allowing yourself to give voice without *any* self-criticism. Yes, you will sing clinkers—just call them contemporary music. Here are some ways to begin:

1. Listen to the CD improvisations and hum along with any pitches you like. Let your ear, not your intellect, guide you.
2. If you are a little timid, just add a note and hold it until you sense it is time to change it.
3. Where there are long notes on the recording sing notes to fill in the gaps with syllables like [ta], [la], [ti], or [du].
4. Change your hums to vowel sounds or to something like Dooby-doo.
5. Be really daring and choose a familiar nursery rhyme tune to sing on top of the CD accompaniment.
6. Improvise with your favorite recording.
7. For the truly brave—record yourself singing along with your CD and then play it back.

Just as instrumentalists have "jam" sessions, so can singers. You have some class exercises that begin to address this. Now it is up to you to go bravely into the unknown and make "child's play" with music. When you learned to walk, everyone was proud of your first step. Be the same with yourself in regard to improvisation.

Ballad (Major Key)

Scarlett Antaloczy

(Intro) ♩ = 80
D
Em7
D/F♯
G
mf
D
Em7
D/F♯
G
Bm
F♯m7
Em7
A7sus4
A7

13
D
Em7
D/F♯
G
17
Bm
F♯m7
Em7
A7sus4
A7
21
Bm
G
Bm
G♯ø7
C♯7
25
F♯m
G
F♯m
A7sus4
A7
rit.

29
D
Em7
D/F♯
G
33
Bm
F♯m7
Em7
36
A7
rit.
D

Swingin' in Minor Blues

Scarlett Antaloczy

(Intro) ♩ = 144
Swing
D7(♯9)
G7
Cm
Gm7
(finger-snap on 2 & 4)
Cm7
Dm7(♭5)
Cm/E♭
Dm7(♭5)
Cm
Gm7
Cm
Cm7
Dm7(♭5)
Cm
Dm7(♭5)
Cm
Gm7
Cm

13
Fm7 Gm7 Fm7/A♭ Gm Fm Cm Fm
17
Cm7 Dm7(♭5)/C Cm Dm7(♭5) Cm Gm7 Cm
21
D7(♯9) G7 Cm Gm7 Cm
25
(walking bass line)
Cm7 Dm7(♭5) Cm7 Dm7(♭5) Cm Gm7 Cm

29
Cm7 Dm7(♭5) Cm7 Dm7(♭5) Cm7 Gm7 Cm
33
Fm7 Gm7 Fm7/A♭ Gm7 Fm Cm/E♭ Fm
37
C pedal
Cm7 Dm7(♭5)/C Cm Dm7(♭5) Cm Gm7 Cm
41
(yeah!)
D7(♯9) G7 Cm Gm7 Cm

Patriotic Songs, Unison Songs, and Rounds

Patriotic Songs

Patriotic songs were usually written after some big event, like the pride of winning a battle, for instance, or seeing something so beautiful that the love for one's country just welled up into a song. For months after the September 11, 2001, terrorist attacks in New York, Washington, D.C., and Pennsylvania, you could frequently hear patriotic songs in concerts and on radio and TV. Singing and hearing "God Bless America" and "The Star Spangled Banner" was a way of encouraging and uniting people after a national tragedy.

Unison Songs and Rounds

Single line melodies were the earliest type of song. It must have been interesting to be there when the first person came in late in a song and it actually sounded all right. That is how one might imagine rounds began. It is fun to imagine that you can come in at almost any time and still make nice music with other people. This is why rounds are so much fun and satisfying for group singing. Also people are comfortable because if they did not learn the song on the first go, they have plenty of repeats to catch up.

My Country 'Tis of Thee (p. 37)

The Reverend Samuel French Smith wrote the words of this well-known patriotic song, while the tune was "borrowed" from an old English manuscript called *Thesaur's Musicus of 1744*. (Throughout the history of music you will find many borrowed tunes.) "My Country 'Tis of Thee" is a favorite choir audition song because the melody begins and ends on the same note. Choir directors want to see if the singer can maintain the key from the beginning to the end.

America the Beautiful (p. 38)

Katherine Lee Bates wrote these lyrics after visiting Colorado's Pike's Peak, creating a song that evokes the emotion produced by the beauty that is prevalent across the United States. The Reverend Samuel Ward set the poem to music. Though Bates and Ward never met, their song became immensely popular. Elvis Presley, Ray Charles, and many other artists have recorded the song. Opera singer Denyce Graves sang a particularly stirring and heartfelt rendition at the National Prayer Service after September 11, 2001.

There's Music in the Air (p. 39)

Sentimental songs were extremely popular in the Victorian era when poetry on the topics of love, joy, angels, and death reflected the ideals of the time. The memorable tunes and repeated phrases of these songs appealed to all social classes and were played in fashionable homes, in music halls, and by hurdy-gurdy musicians on the streets. The words to "There's Music in the Air" were written by hymnist Fanny J. Crosby and the music by George Friederick Wurzel whose pen name was "George F. Root."

The Frog in the Bog (p. 40)

Look at this whimsical musical tongue twister as an interesting challenge or as a kind of rap. Start slow enough that every word is clear, and then try singing faster and faster. You may have to return to your childhood, but it is great fun to play with these words! Even serious composers weren't serious all the time. H. Worthington Loomis's non-silly songs include "The Foggy, Foggy Dew" and a setting of Shakespeare's "Hark, Hark, the Lark."

Gaudeamus Igitur (p. 41)

The Latin words to this rousing song were written by a German university student in 1723. "Let's rejoice while we are young!" was his motto. In 1781, C. W. Kindlebein adapted ten verses of the drinking song and set them to a familiar Finnish melody. This version of the song became so well known on campuses that the great German composer Johannes Brahms used the tune in his *Academic Festival Overture* for orchestra. "Gaudeamus Igitur" is still popular with men's glee clubs and a capella student choirs. (For word-for-word translations and IPA symbols, see page 309.)

Banana Boat Song (p. 42)

Work songs were created by laborers to ease the rigors of their work and to keep everyone working at the same pace. Railroad songs, sailing songs, and harvesting songs are all examples of work songs. American singer, composer, and civil rights activist Harry Belafonte spent his childhood in Jamaica and his version of "Banana Boat Song" became one of the biggest hits during the 1950s calypso craze. The song originated in Port Antonio, Jamaica, where men and women sang as they loaded banana boats, and it has been recorded by groups ranging from the Kinks to the Royal Philharmonic.

Music Alone Shall Live (p. 42)
Oh, How Lovely Is the Evening (p. 43)

Rounds and folk dances such as Germany's "Die Musici" and "O wie wohl is mir am Abend" were extremely popular in England during the seventeenth and eighteenth centuries. A round, or "circular canon," consists of two or more musical phrases of equal length. Two, three, four or more singers enter the song at various times to create their own harmonies. Singers circle back to the beginning and repeat the song as many times as they wish. Early rounds were not written down but were spread by composers and troubadours traveling from town to town, and even from country to country. While the melodies of many rounds remained relatively intact over the centuries, the words changed freely. You can discover the same tune set to English, Latin, or foreign texts, ranging from sacred to secular to downright indecent topics. Singing and drinking (not necessarily in that order) were the tradition of "Catch Clubs" in Victorian England, which featured humorous, bawdy rounds known as "catches." The rounds sung, however, on "ladie's night" were on more delicate subjects such as blind mice, rowing boats, music, and lovely evenings.

Babylon (p. 44)

This round, by American composer William Billings, is a setting of Psalm 137, a lament for the Jewish people who were exiled from their homeland. Billings, a Boston tanner's apprentice by trade, became well known for his sacred music after the publication of his *New England Psalm Singer* in 1770. Two hundred years later, Babylon became a metaphor for Vietnam, when singer/songwriter Don McLean featured Billings' round on his classic American rock album *American Pie*.

Dona Nobis Pacem (p. 45)
Ego Sum Pauper (p. 45)

These two ancient Latin rounds were influenced by sacred liturgy and chants. Tunes were borrowed freely from Catholic canonic chants were often sung outside the church by ordinary people. Some Latin rounds used liturgical lyrics, such as "dona nobis pacem" or "alleluia." Others, such as "Ego Sum Pauper," used secular words about everyday situations like poverty, marriage, and unrequited love. There are reports of Latin rounds as early as 1065, but the first printed collections of Middle English and Latin rounds and songs were published by Thomas Ravenscroft around 1600. The oldest Ravenscroft round is "Sumer is icumin" ("Summer is a-coming"). The best-known Ravenscroft round is "Dona Nobis Pacem," which is attributed to the sixteenth-century composer Palestrina.

Ah, Poor Bird (p. 46)
Shalom, Chaverim (p. 46)
Ah, Poor Bird/Shalom (p. 47)

These modern rounds most likely evolved from the same tune. Though "Shalom, Chaverim" is an Israeli folk song and "Ah! Poor Bird" is an American round, both songs have similar melodies and harmonic structure. After you learn each song separately, try combining them as a duet, using the English version of the Hebrew song. The songs fit like a glove musically, and even the words make sense: "Farewell my friends . . . take thy flight . . . We'll meet again."

Three Alleluia Rounds (p. 48)

If you are tempted to dismiss rounds as simple children's songs, then consider that many of the leading classical composers wrote rounds and canons. (Canons are similar to rounds, except both voices end at the same time instead of repeating continuously.) Purcell, Haydn, Mozart, Beethoven, Mendelssohn, Schubert, and Brahms all wrote rounds. Here, the first "Alleluia" example is a simple two-part round by Mozart. The second Mozart "Alleluia" round is much more challenging and uses melodic material that Mozart later recycled for his solo motet *Exsultate, Jubilate* for soprano and chamber orchestra. Mozart may also have "borrowed" some tunes from fellow composer William Boyce, who is said to have remarked, "Mozart takes ordinary things and turns them into pearls." The final "Alleluia" round by William Boyce is no mere child's play, however, and it will challenge the most accomplished singers. Though rounds and canons lost their popularity during the nineteenth century, modern composers such as David Diamond, Vincent Persechetti, and Randall Thompson have all composed rounds.

My Country 'Tis of Thee

Words by Samuel F. Smith

Music by Henry Carey

For background and performance notes, see page 34.

♩ = 80
1 G D G G
My coun - try 'tis of thee, Sweet land of lib - er - ty, Of thee I sing.
7 G D7
Land where my fa - thers died, Land of the Pil - grims' pride,
11 G C G C G D7 G
From ev - 'ry___ moun - tain side, Let___ free - dom ring!

America the Beautiful

Words by Katherine Lee Bates

Music by Samuel A. Ward

For background and performance notes, see page 34.

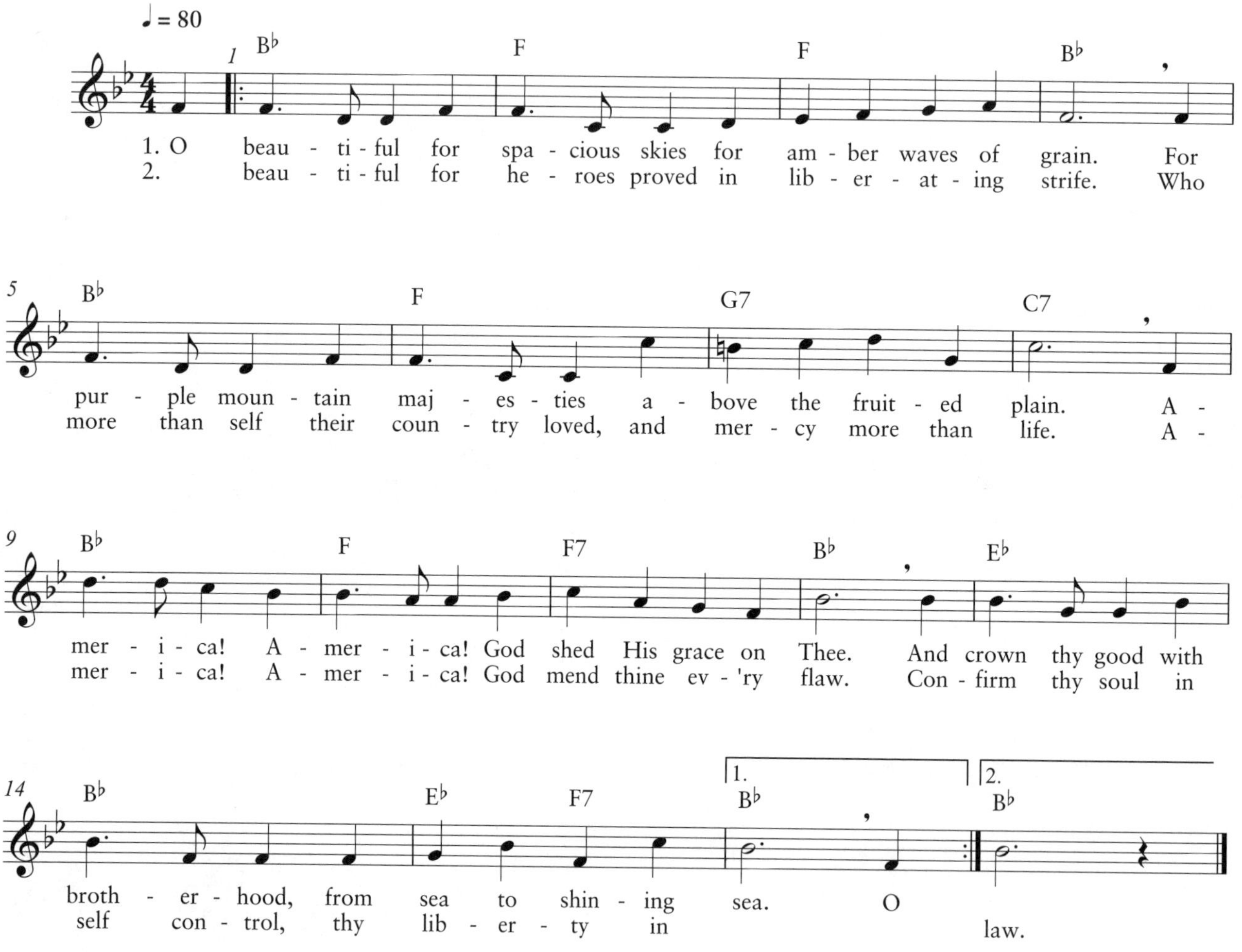
♩ = 80
B♭ F F B♭
1. O beau - ti - ful for spa - cious skies for am - ber waves of grain. For
2. beau - ti - ful for he - roes proved in lib - er - at - ing strife. Who
B♭ F G7 C7
pur - ple moun - tain maj - es - ties a - bove the fruit - ed plain. A -
more than self their coun - try loved, and mer - cy more than life. A -
B♭ F F7 B♭ E♭
mer - i - ca! A - mer - i - ca! God shed His grace on Thee. And crown thy good with
mer - i - ca! A - mer - i - ca! God mend thine ev - 'ry flaw. Con - firm thy soul in
B♭ E♭ F7 1. B♭ 2. B♭
broth - er - hood, from sea to shin - ing sea. O
self con - trol, thy lib - er - ty in law.

There's Music in the Air

Words by Fanny Crosby

Music by George F. Root

For background and performance notes, see page 34.

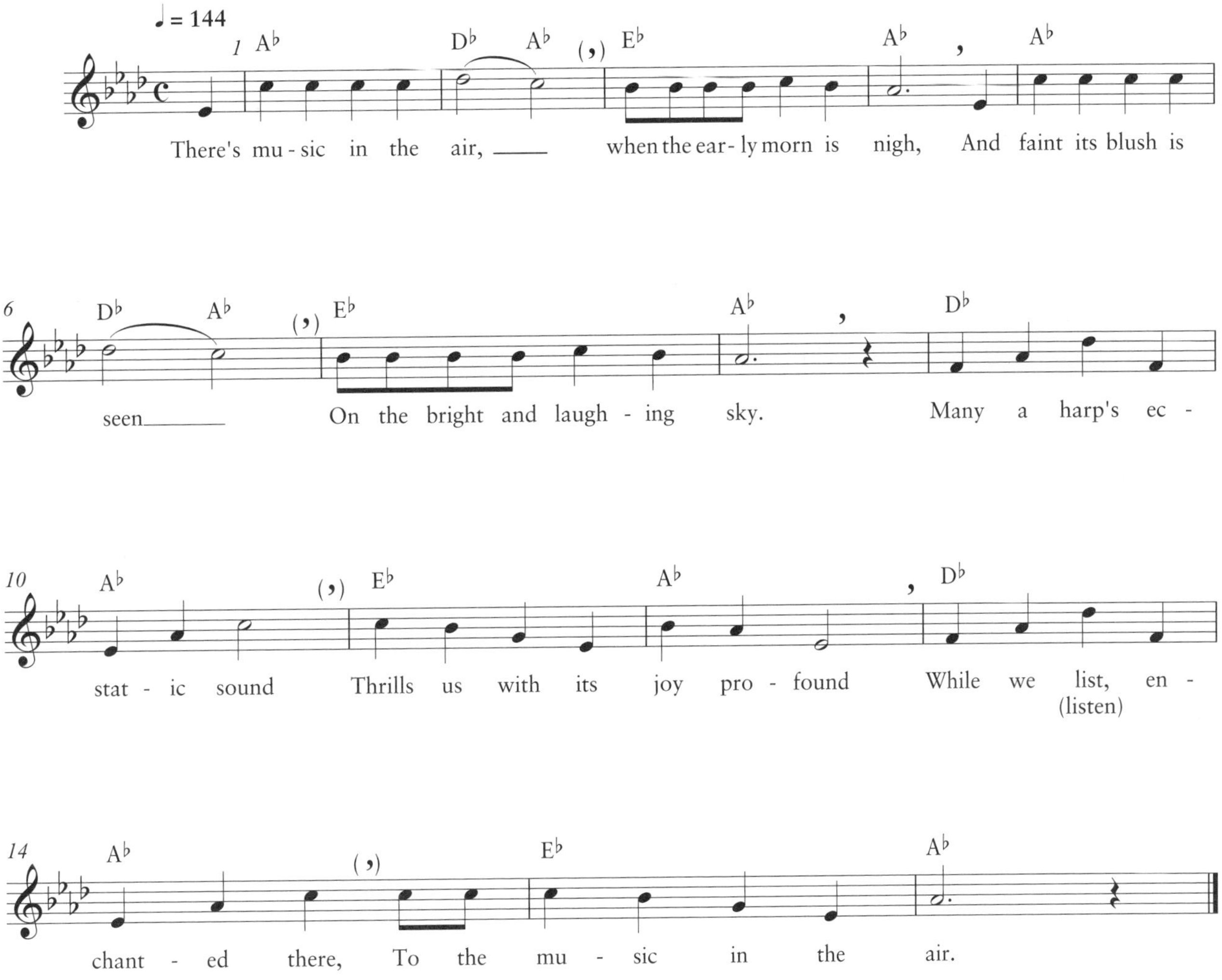
♩ = 144
1 A♭ D♭ A♭ (,) E♭ A♭ , A♭
There's mu - sic in the air, when the ear - ly morn is nigh, And faint its blush is
6 D♭ A♭ (,) E♭ A♭ , D♭
seen On the bright and laugh - ing sky. Many a harp's ec -
10 A♭ (,) E♭ A♭ , D♭
stat - ic sound Thrills us with its joy pro - found While we list, en -
(listen)
14 A♭ (,) E♭ A♭
chant - ed there, To the mu - sic in the air.

The Frog in the Bog

Words and Music by
H. Worthington Loomis
Canada

For background and performance notes, see page 34.

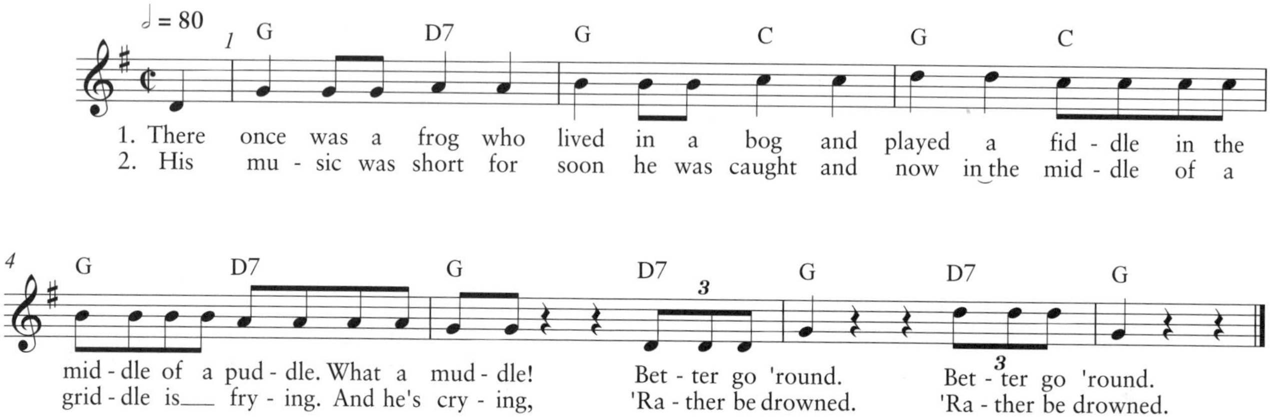
𝅗𝅥 = 80
1
G D7 G C G C
1. There once was a frog who lived in a bog and played a fid - dle in the
2. His mu - sic was short for soon he was caught and now in the mid - dle of a
4
G D7 G D7 G D7 G
3
mid - dle of a pud - dle. What a mud - dle! Bet - ter go 'round. Bet - ter go 'round.
grid - dle is fry - ing. And he's cry - ing, 'Ra - ther be drowned. 'Ra - ther be drowned.

Gaudeamus Igitur

Germany

For background and performance notes, see page 35.

♩ = 88
G C D G G
Gau - de - am - us ig - i - tur, Ju - ve - nes dum su - mus; Gau - de - a - mus
Let us now in youth re - joice, None can just - ly blame us. Let us now in
C D G D G D
ig - i - tur, Ju - ve - nes dum su - mus; Post ju - cun - dum ju - ven - tu - tem,
youth re - joice, None can just - ly blame us. For, when gold - en youth has fled
D G D D Em Am
Post mol - lest - am sen - ec - tu - tem, Nos ha - be - bit
And in age our joys are dead Then the dust does
G D G Em Am G D G
hu - mus, Nos ha - be - bit hu - mus.
Claim us, Then the dust does claim us.

Banana Boat Song (Day-O)
(Round)

Jamaica

For background and performance notes, see page 35.

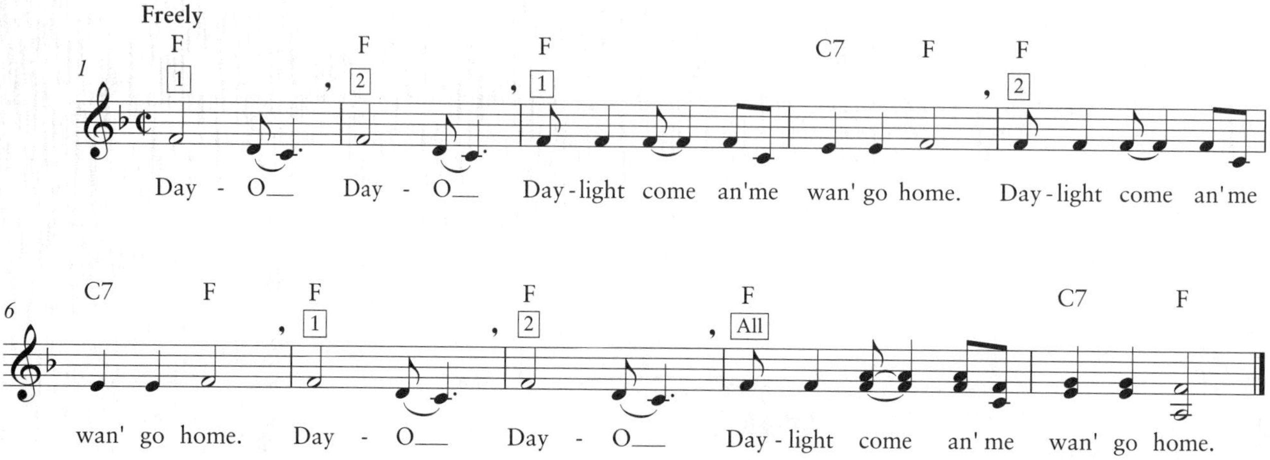
Freely
F F F C7 F F
Day - O— Day - O— Day-light come an'me wan' go home. Day-light come an'me
C7 F F F F C7 F
All
wan' go home. Day - O— Day - O— Day - light come an' me wan' go home.

Music Alone Shall Live
(Round)

Germany

For background and performance notes, see page 35.

♩=100
F Gm C F F Gm
All things shall per - ish from un - der the sky. Mu - sic a - lone shall live,
C7 F F Cm C F
mu - sic a - lone shall live, mu - sic a - lone shall live, ne - ver to die.

Oh, How Lovely Is the Evening
(Round)

Germany

For background and performance notes, see page 35.

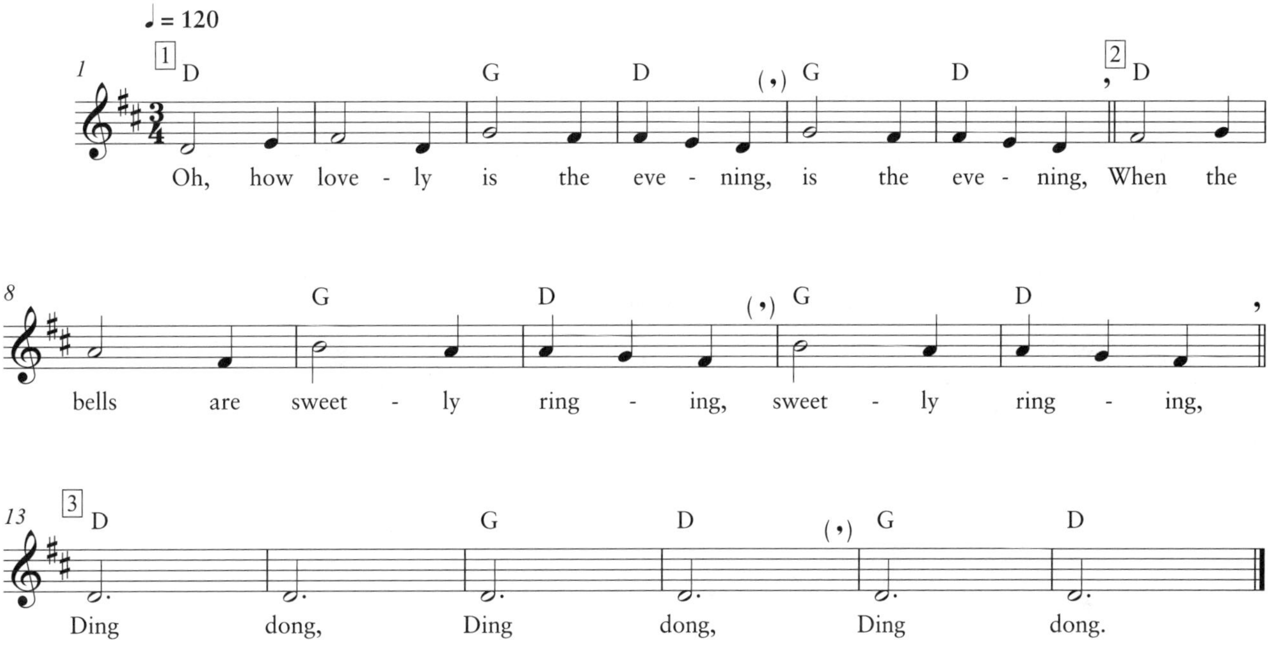
♩ = 120
1
D G D G D D
Oh, how love - ly is the eve - ning, is the eve - ning, When the
8
G D G D
bells are sweet - ly ring - ing, sweet - ly ring - ing,
13
D G D G D
Ding dong, Ding dong, Ding dong.

Babylon
(Round)

Music by William Billings
(1746–1800)

For background and performance notes, see page 35.

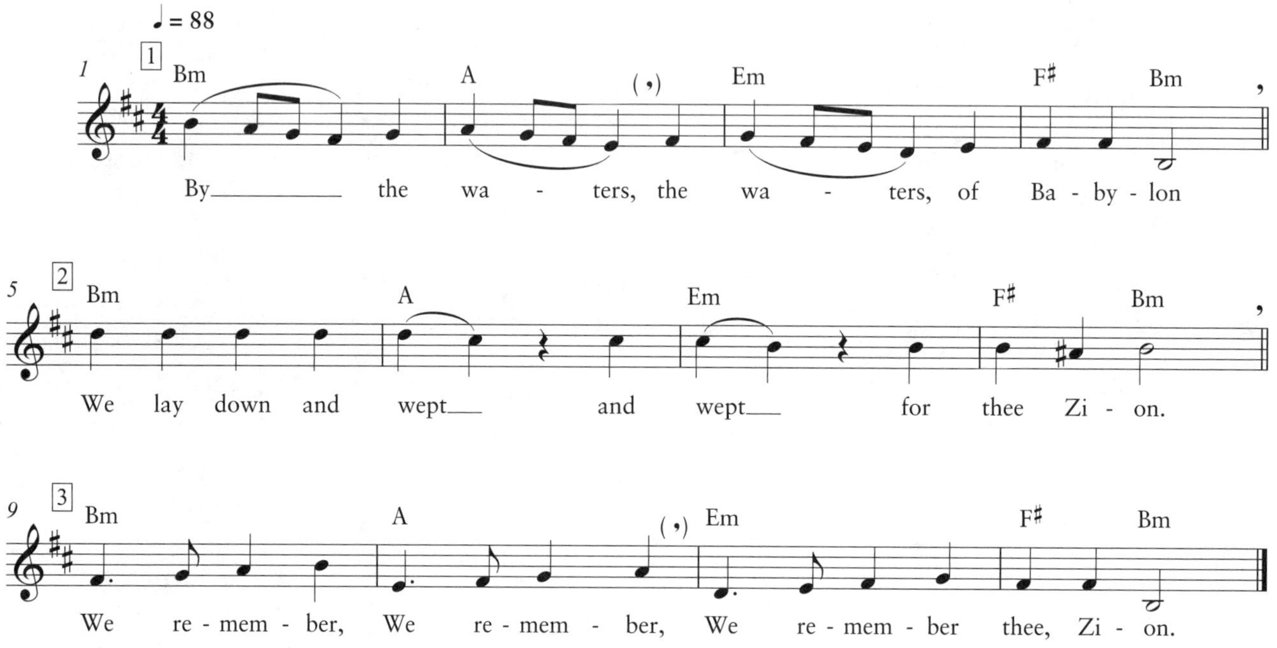
♩ = 88
1
Bm A Em F♯ Bm
By the wa - ters, the wa - ters, of Ba - by - lon
2
Bm A Em F♯ Bm
We lay down and wept and wept for thee Zi - on.
3
Bm A Em F♯ Bm
We re - mem - ber, We re - mem - ber, We re - mem - ber thee, Zi - on.

Dona Nobis Pacem

(Grant Us Peace)

(Round)

Latin

For background and performance notes, see page 35.

♩ = 100
1 [1] F C F F C Gm F
Do - na no - bis pa - cem, pa - cem, Do - na no - bis,
7 C F [2] F C F C Gm F
pa - cem. Do - na no - bis pa - cem, Do - na no - bis
15 C F [3] F C F
pa - - - cem. Do - na no - bis
20 F C Gm F C F
pa - cem, Do - na no - bis, pa - - cem.

Ego Sum Pauper

(Round)

Latin

For background and performance notes, see page 35.

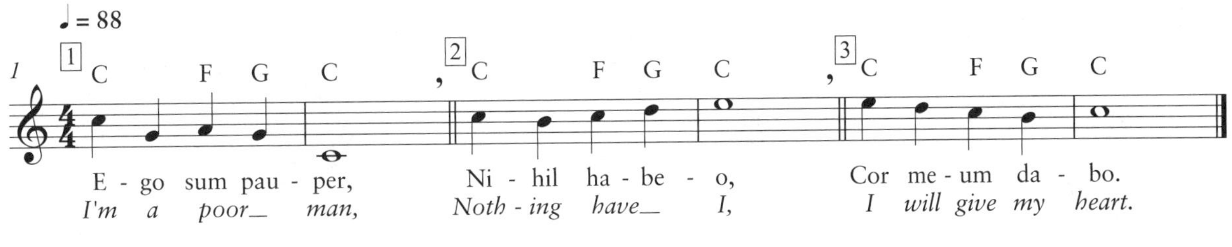
♩ = 88
1 [1] C F G C [2] C F G C [3] C F G C
E - go sum pau - per, Ni - hil ha - be - o, Cor me - um da - bo.
I'm a poor man, Noth - ing have I, I will give my heart.

Ah, Poor Bird
(Round)

America

For background and performance notes, see page 36.

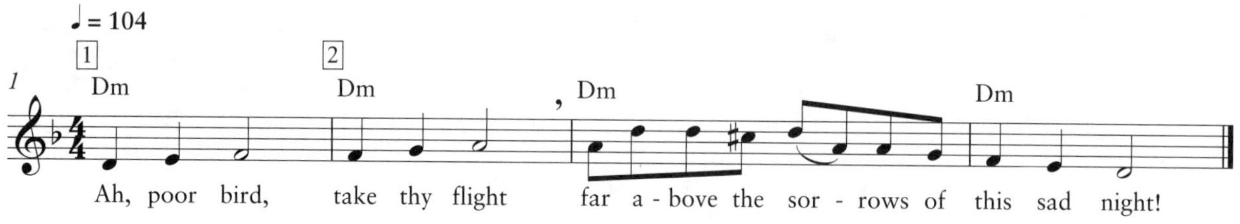
♩= 104
1
2
Dm
Dm
Dm
Dm
Ah, poor bird, take thy flight far a - bove the sor - rows of this sad night!

Shalom, Chaverim
(Round)

Israel

For background and performance notes, see page 36.

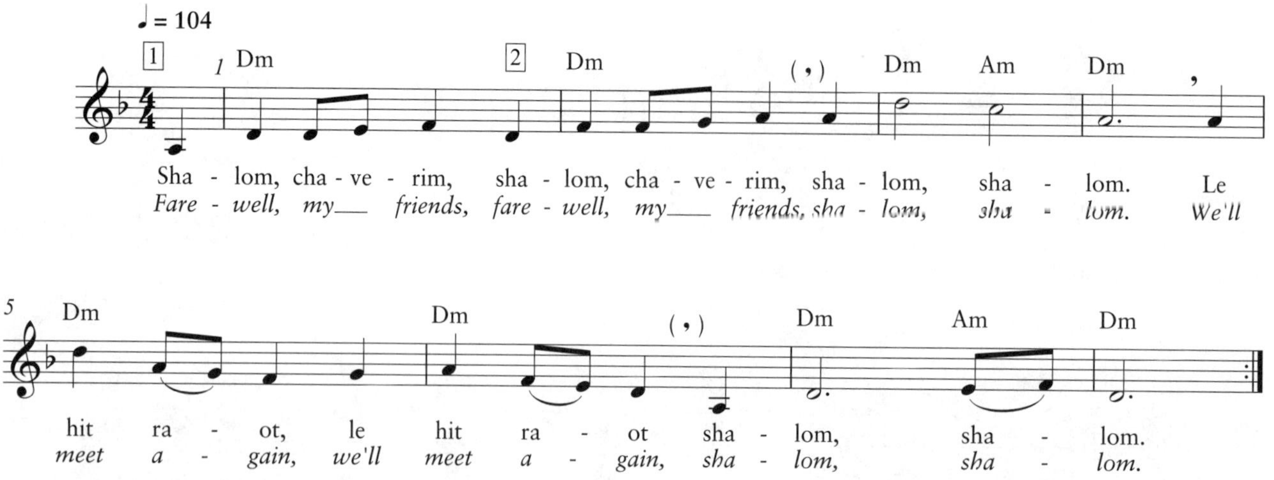
♩= 104
1
2
Dm Dm (,) Dm Am Dm
Sha - lom, cha - ve - rim, sha - lom, cha - ve - rim, sha - lom, sha - lom. Le
Fare - well, my friends, fare - well, my friends, sha - lom, sha - lom. We'll
Dm Dm (,) Dm Am Dm
hit ra - ot, le hit ra - ot sha - lom, sha - lom.
meet a - gain, we'll meet a - gain, sha - lom, sha - lom.

Optional text: Glad tidings we bring/ of peace on earth/ good will toward men. / Of peace on earth, / of peace on earth/ good will toward men.

Ah, Poor Bird/Shalom

(Duet)

Israel
America

For background and performance notes, see page 36.

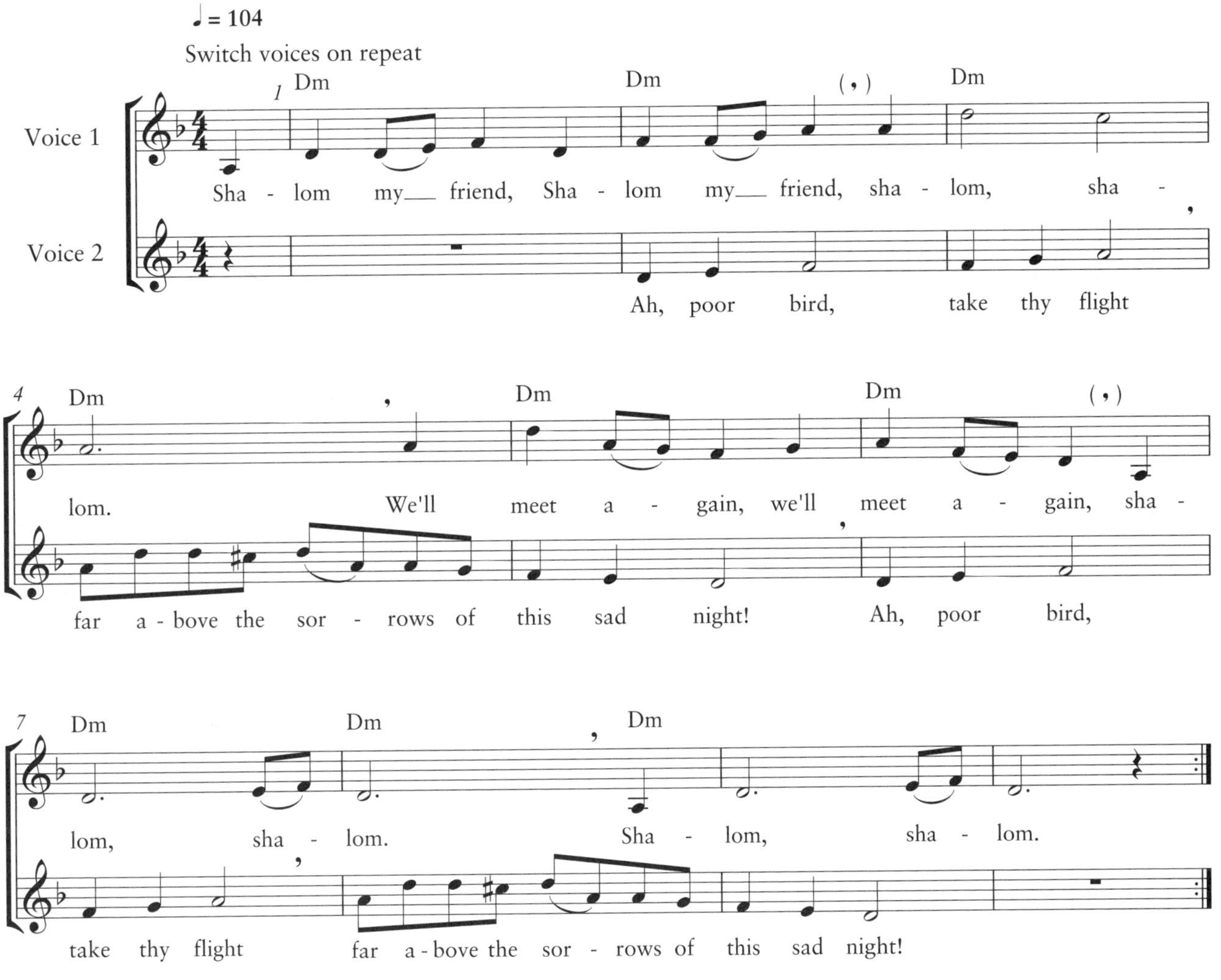
♩ = 104
Switch voices on repeat
Voice 1
Voice 2
Dm
Sha - lom my__ friend, Sha - lom my__ friend, sha - lom, sha - lom. We'll meet a - gain, we'll meet a - gain, sha - lom, sha - lom. Sha - lom, sha - lom.
Ah, poor bird, take thy flight far a - bove the sor - rows of this sad night! Ah, poor bird, take thy flight far a - bove the sor - rows of this sad night!

Three Alleluia Rounds

Music by
W. A. Mozart
(1756–1791)

For background and performance notes, see page 36.

I

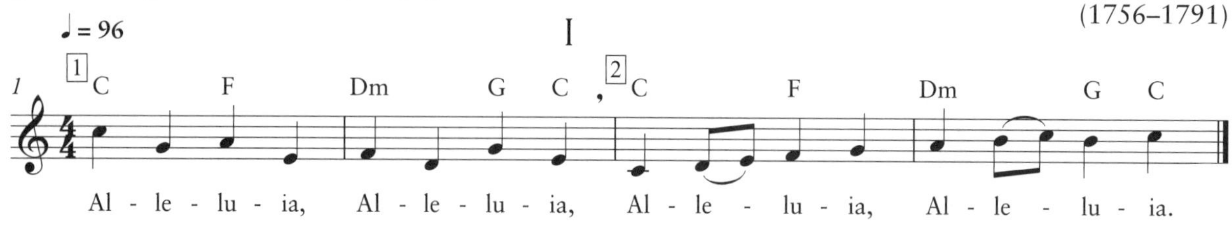
♩ = 96
1 C F Dm G C , 2 C F Dm G C
Al - le - lu - ia, Al - le - lu - ia, Al - le - lu - ia, Al - le - lu - ia.

Music by
W. A. Mozart

II

♩ = 100
1 F B♭ F F♯dim , C7 F C7 F ,
Al - le - lu - ia, Al - le - lu - ia, Al - le - lu - ia, Al - le - lu - ia.
2 F B♭ F F♯dim , F F C7 F ,
Al - le - lu - ia, Al - le - lu - ia, Al - le - lu - ia, Al - le - lu - ia.
3 F B♭ F F♯dim , C7 F C7 F
Al - le - lu - ia, Al - le - lu - ia.

Music by
William Boyce
(1711–1799)

III

♩ = 120
1 C G D G , F C
Al - le - lu - ia, Al - le - lu - - -
Dm G7 C 2 C G D G
- - ia. Al - le - lu - ia, Al - le - lu - ia, Al - le - lu - ia, Al -
F C Dm G7 C , 3 C G
- le - lu - ia, Al - le - lu - ia, Al - - le - lu - ia,
D G , F C , Dm G7 C
Al - le - lu - ia, Al - le - lu - ia, Al - le - lu - ia.

Folk Songs, Spirituals, and Hymns

Folk songs

Folk songs are myths and legends handed down in song. They were sung from generation to generation in every culture and form an important part of the oral tradition. Some tunes cross cultural boundaries and are found in a number of countries at once. The melodies were rarely written down and were sung either *a capella* (without accompaniment) or accompanied by folk instruments like guitars or dulcimers. Fortunately for us, in the eighteenth to twentieth centuries, men like James Childs, Cecil Sharpe, Bela Bartok, and John Jacob Niles traveled to rural areas to collect and preserve the traditional songs. These first "songcatchers," as they were sometimes called, listened carefully to the songs and wrote down the various versions of the words and music. Later they used recording equipment to collect the actual raw singing of songs that were fast disappearing. Composers like Joseph Haydn, Benjamin Britten, and Aaron Copland wrote their own arrangements of folk songs for solo voice with piano accompaniment; other composers used folk tunes in classical instrumental music.

Spirituals

"Negro spirituals" are distinctly American songs. These unaccompanied religious folk songs with African rhythmic and modal influences sprang up from the mid 1700s to about 1900, first as work songs for slaves and later as escape and revival songs. In the country, slaves gathered, sometimes in secret, to sing for hours at "camp meetings." Before slavery was abolished in 1865, slaves were drawn to songs about the Israelites' trials under the bondage of Egypt. There was a double meaning for Christian slaves. While they longed for heaven, here on earth they were desperate to "cross the River Jordan" and to enter the "the promised land" of "Canaan"—meaning anywhere North of the Ohio River.

Spirituals about trains and chariots were metaphors for the Underground Railroad, a network of abolitionists who helped slaves escape to the North. In the cities, as the religious Revival movement grew, blacks and whites gathered in stadiums and large tents for revival meetings.

For a while after the Civil War, few people wanted to sing the old spirituals that reminded them of the horrors of slavery. Before the end of the century, however, trained musicians began to arrange them in a European classical way for choruses and solo artists. European audiences were enchanted by American spirituals. Even now, touring American choruses and opera singers regularly include spirituals in their European concerts. From the cotton fields to symphony halls, the songs endure.

Hymns

Many traditional church hymns of the Christian-based religions also have a long history of inspiring hope and stirring passion in believers. From the very earliest biblical times the words "hymn" and "psalm" were used interchangeably to mean a religious song.

The first Catholic hymns were sung in Latin, and by the eleventh century there were nearly 300 Latin hymns in the liturgy. During the Reformation in Germany, Protestant hymns were written in the vernacular (or common) language. Martin Luther, and later J. S. Bach, wrote many hymns and "chorales" that are still an important part of the Lutheran and other Protestant churches.

Meanwhile, in England, John and Charles Wesley took hymns in a new direction in the early Methodist church. They felt that the old-fashioned psalm tunes were too rigid to express personal emotion, so the Wesleys followed a more secular musical style. The well-known hymn "Love Divine, All Loves Excelling" is actually an adaptation of a purely secular poem, Dryden's "Fairest Isle, all isles excelling." A turning point came in 1819 when the English legal court released state churches from "authorized" old-version hymns and decreed that churches could freely write their own versions of hymns and psalms.

By 1861, churches of many denominations in England and America were openly writing their own hymnals—whatever suited their theology and parishioners. The task of writing these new hymns usually fell to clergy of the individual churches, who were kept busy writing not only the Sunday sermon but also the weekly prayer meeting hymn. It is no wonder that the first published edition of *Olney Hymns* in 1779 (see "Amazing Grace") contained nearly 300 songs by the Reverend John Newton.

Shenandoah (p. 55)

Many traditional songs made their way to America from England, Scotland, and Ireland, but "Shenandoah" is a truly American folk song. It most likely began as a land ballad about a trader who fell in love with the daughter of an Indian chief named Shenandoah. As early as 1820, Missouri river boatmen carried the song to the deep-sea sailors, where it was particularly popular as a capstan chantey. As they sang, sailors pushed the massive capstan bars around to lift the ship's anchor. The song is still popular today and strikes a chord with anyone who is homesick for a distant place or far away lover.

Scarborough Fair (p. 58)

The earliest printed version of this popular English riddle song, "The Elphin King," dates back to 1670 and is derived from an ancient Viking epic. Riddle songs involved seeming contradictions, such as "I gave my love a cherry without a stone." At first glance, the story seems to be about the impossible demands of a jilted lover ("Tell her to make me a cambric shirt . . . with no seam or needlework"). But folklorists claim the song is a conversation between a maiden and a demon, the Elphin King. In plant mythology certain herbs were said to have supernatural powers. Parsley warded off the "evil eye" while sage assured wedded bliss, long life, and health. In 1579's *The Garden of Health,* William Lengham recommended bathing in rosemary "to make thee lusty, lively, joyfull, likeing and youngly" and a woman wearing thyme in her bosom was said to be irresistible. Modern audiences are most familiar with Simon and Garfunkle's hit recording of "Scarborough Fair" in the 1970s, which climbed pop charts with magical charm.

Danny Boy (p. 62)

"Danny Boy" was first published in 1855 in *Ancient Tunes of Ireland,* though it is unlikely that the poet, Fred E. Weatherly, an English lawyer and prolific songwriter, ever set foot in Ireland. Weatherly wrote "Danny Boy" in 1910. However, it did not become popular until two years later when his sister Margaret sent Weatherly the tune "Londonderry Air" that she heard played by an Irish immigrant fiddler in a Colorado gold rush camp. The tune was a perfect match to Weatherly's old lyrics and became a hit soon after Boosey published it in 1913. Even today, grown men weep when "Danny Boy" is sweetly sung by an Irish tenor. It is also appropriate for a woman to sing "Danny Boy." Weatherly was a smart businessman who usually kept the gender neutral in his popular songs so that he could sell more copies to amateur singers.

Civil War Medley (p. 64)

Wartime has always inspired songs of bravery on the battlefield and the heartache of loved ones left behind. This medley pairs two Civil War era songs, "When Johnny Comes Marching Home Again" and "The Cruel War Is Raging." Though the first song is credited to the Union Army bandmaster Patrick Gilmore, it was sung by Union and Confederate soldiers. In the full version of the second song, the young woman is so desperate to be with her lover that she dresses like a man and goes to war disguised as his comrade and is killed along with her lover.

The Water Is Wide (p. 68)

Cecil Sharp (1859–1924) was the most famous of the "songcatchers." Without his efforts, much British and American folk song and dance music from the sixteenth to nineteenth centuries would have been lost. In 1902 he visited English countryside villages to collect and record authentic specimens of English folk music. When the oral tradition of folk songs began to die out in Britain, Sharp found it to be flourishing in America. During World War I, Sharp and his secretary traveled to America's Appalachian mountain region to collect songs, including "The Water Is Wide," or "O Waly, Waly," as it was known in seventeenth-century Britain. ("Waly, Waly" is a form of the Anglo-Saxon "wa la wa" meaning "Woe, alas, woe.") This nearly lost song inspired generations of recording artists including folk legends Bob Dylan, Pete Seeger, and Joan Baez, and modern artists like Sarah McLaughlin, Charlotte Church, Jewel, James Taylor, Barbra Streisand, and Wendy Matthews. The tune is timeless and the text is universal. As Pete Seeger wrote, "We have to cross the oceans of misunderstanding between the peoples of this world."

The Lark in the Clear Air (p. 73)

The recent movie *Iris* introduced this old song to a new generation. Early in the film about the English novelist Iris Murdoch, actress Kate Winslett, as young Iris, holds a roomful of people spellbound with her tender rendition of an old Irish folk song. A poignant moment occurs late in the film, as age and illness have robbed the once-brilliant author of memory and speech. Dame Judi Dench, as the elderly Iris, unexpectedly recalls the sweet song, "I shall tell him all my love, all my soul's adoration . . . it is this that gives my soul all its joyous elation, As I hear the sweet lark sing in the clear air of the day."

Salley Gardens (p. 76)

The melody is the traditional Irish tune "The Maids of Mourne Shore." However, this is not a folk song in the true sense because the text was not written by an unknown, long-forgotten poet but was penned by Ireland's greatest poet, William Butler Yeats (1865–1939). Yeats was an Irish nationalist who rebelled against English rule and culture. He was a founder of the National Literacy Society in Dublin, and in 1923 he was the first Irishman to win the Nobel Prize in literature. His poetry remains very popular today, especially in Ireland where musicians like Van Morrison and the Cranberries recently recorded *Now and in Time to Be,* a CD of settings of Yeats's poetry.

Yeats's writings were influenced by ancient Celtic myths, mysticism, and unrequited love, and his poetry has been called musical and magical. When a beautiful woman, Maud Gonne, spurned Yeats's obsessive attention, the poet created some of the world's best love poetry, including "Down by the Salley Gardens." Interestingly, the girl in the poem isn't named "Sally." In this song "Salley" means a willow garden or a bog field that is useless for growing or grazing—just the ideal place for clandestine lovers to meet! A "weir" is a fence or dam set in a stream to catch fish.

Westryn Wynde (Western Wind) (p. 79)

This song was well known in England in the 1500s, yet the lyrics are probably a few hundred years older. Historians believe the words are a fragment of medieval poetry, possibly sung by a troubadour.

Troubadours were poets and composers of dramatic ballads and courtly love songs. Ancient artwork and modern movies portray them as men in tights wearing plumed hats. They often accompanied themselves on a lute, an early version of our modern acoustic guitar. Try singing *Westryn Wynde* with guitar accompaniment. The closing *melismas* (several notes set to one word) imitate the blowing wind.

Santa Lucia (p. 81)

There has been some confusion about whether "Santa Lucia" is a place or a person. The original Italian sailing song was inspired by the beautiful Bay of Naples outside the city of Santa Lucia near Mt. Vesuvius. In Scandinavia, Sankta Lucia (Saint Lucia) is a holiday tradition in which a young girl wearing a wreath of candles guides children bearing cakes and gifts. The Sankta Lucia Festival version of the song uses the same Italian melody with completely different Swedish words. The Italian version of "Santa Lucia," like other popular Neapolitan songs such as "O Solo Mio" and "Sorrento," has been recorded by opera singers Luciano Pavarotti and Placido Domingo and by popular singers Perry Como and Tony Bennett. Neapolitan songs are now being rediscovered by the new generation of classically trained pop singers: Josh Groban, Andrea Bocelli, and Charlotte Church. (For word-for-word translations and IPA symbols, see page 312.)

Paun I Kolo (p. 84)

"Paun I Kolo" tells of an ailing peacock that remains silent because it is grieving for its homeland. This song is featured, along with other ancient songs from Croatia, on the album *Dawn Maiden* by singer Lidija Bajuk. It is no surprise that the folk music of wartorn Bosnia and Herzegovina like this song is full of metaphors for freedom and love of country. Lidija Bajuk and other contemporary artists are passionate about keeping the old songs alive.

The lead singer of the Sarajevan pop group *Merlin* recently won a competition to write words for a new Bosnian National Anthem set to a traditional folk song. The winning lyrics include "You are the only homeland I have, Bosnia and Herzegovina. May God save you for the generations to come, the land of my forefathers." The music of a land reflects the people of a land giving them hope in difficult times. (For word-for-word translations and IPA symbols, see page 312.)

Ah! si mon moine voulait danser! (p. 86)

The title translates to "Ah! If My Monk Wanted to Dance" and is well known throughout French-speaking Canada, especially in Quebec. The title, a play on words, is deceptive, however, because it is not about a human monk but rather about a game. "Monk" is the name that French children used for a small spinning "toupee d'Allemagne"—a German spinning top. A child pulls the string to make the top spin, and then lightly whips the string in time to the music to make the top dance. The longer the top spins, the more verses the child can sing about giving the toy "monk" a hood, and a cloak, a belt, a psalm book and so on. Ah! If only the monk hadn't taken a vow of poverty! (For word-for-word translations and IPA symbols, see page 304.)

Niño precioso (p. 88)

Babies are known to respond best to their mothers' voices. The lullaby with its gentle swinging rhythm, accompanied by the comforting sounds of a mother's voice, has lulled babies throughout the world to sleep. This lullaby comes from Nicaragua and is also sung as a Christmas carol. The limited vocal range and rocking 3/4 rhythm are typical of lullabies in many cultures. The sudden change of tempo and rhythm at the refrain (chorus) may have occurred naturally as the child stirred from sleep. Luckily, the rocking rhythm returns at the end of the song so that baby and mother (or father) can get some rest. Shhhhhhh . . . sing the ending softly. (For word-for-word translations and IPA symbols, see page 311.)

Mi caballo blanco (p. 91)

The folk music of Chile is rich in tradition and has many distinct styles, from the "cueca," a quick dance in 6/8 rhythm accompanied by guitar, piano, or accordion, to the waltz and Chilean polka. "Mi caballo blanco" is a popular "tonada" about a man and his very best friend, his horse! A tonada is freer rhythmically than a cuesca and is usually accompanied by guitar, piano, or both. The music and lyrics to "Mi caballo blanco" were written by Francesco Flores del Campo; however, many tonadas are passed down anonymously from generation to generation. Like many South American songs, the rhythm changes at the refrain. As you sing this, imagine staying in the saddle as the horse picks up speed from a trot to a gallop! (For word-for-word translations and IPA symbols, see page 310.)

Dubinushka (Hammer Song) (p. 95)

"Dubinushka" was originally a barge hauler's work song set to a poem by B. Bogdanof in 1865. After the "Bloody Sunday" massacre in Russia the song became a powerful revolutionary song to protest the oppression of the people. The verses that were added later urge the laborers to wake up and use their work hammers to smash the oppressors who crush their strength and spill their blood.

Bloody Sunday took place on January 9, 1905. Troops fired on peaceful demonstrators who were seeking help from the Czar and were walking to the Winter Palace in St. Petersburg. Nearly 1,000 people were killed, and among those outraged at the senseless shootings were many prominent Russian musicians, including Rachmaninoff, Rimsky-Korsakov, and the famous operatic bass, Fyodor Chaliapin. Protests and workers' strikes sprang up everywhere and included underpaid chorus singers and orchestra members. Chaliapin shocked the audience and angered the government by singing "Dubinushka" during an opera performance at the Bolshoi Theater, and Nicholas the Second demanded his immediate dismissal. However, the theater owners feared such action would spark a full-blown revolution. Protected by his immense popularity, Chaliapin continued to lead the singing of "Dubinushka" for crowds of as many as 5,000 Russian workers. (For word-for-word translations and IPA symbols, see page 308.)

Dance of Youth (Xing Chun Wu Chu) (p. 97)

This popular Chinese folksong is known by many titles, including "Little Bird." It comes from the Xin Jiang province of northwest China, near the Russian border, and has been passed from generation to generation of Chinese and Chinese American singers. "Dance of Youth" is among the folksongs that were collected by one of the best-known Chinese songcatchers, Wang Lou Bin (1913–1996). Some scholars believe that Wang Lou Bin may have gathered the melody and added his own poem. During Chinese festivals, young people dance ("wu") together and sing this song. It is often accompanied by gymnasts. The moral of the song is "This is our youth, so enjoy the moment and be merry! Enjoy life."

My Lord, What a Mornin'! (p. 101)

This is a good example of a pre-abolition spiritual that slaves sang in the plantation fields. The steady rhythm and strong *downbeat* (the first beat of each measure) ensured that all of the slaves worked at the same pace, leaving no one to lag behind and be whipped by the overseers. On the surface, the song is about Resurrection Day, when the trumpet of God shall sound. Like most spiritual texts, the song allowed slaves to sing what they were forbidden to say: their desire for that great morning that would herald the fall of slavery. The "nations underground" may refer to the Underground Railroad.

Ev'ry Time I Feel the Spirit (p. 104)

This fiery revivalist song from 1874 was sung by both blacks and whites after the abolition of slavery. No composer is credited, and the song was possibly written by a former slave. During slavery, most slaves were allowed to sing but were strictly forbidden to play instruments or dance in public. In the 1890s, however, the African traditions returned with much shouting, stomping, dancing, and clapping. There was a lot of repetition of text, and a song could go on and on—as long as the spirit moved. The songs often depicted colorful stories of the Old Testament, such as God speaking to Moses through a burning bush: "Out of His mouth came fire and smoke."

Amazing Grace (p. 107)

By now, many Americans know the story of how the slave trader John Newton came to write this hugely popular hymn. It is probably true that the tune to "Amazing Grace" was originally a slave song that Newton had heard. It is also true that on May 10, 1748, in a deadly storm, Newton's fervent prayers for mercy were answered. His ship did not sink and

Newton vowed to God that he would be a changed man.

It is not as commonly known that after Newton's conversion he continued to sail slave ships until illness forced a career change. It was only then that Newton devoted himself to religious studies in Greek and Hebrew, and eventually became a beloved minister in the Church of England at Olney. Newton's job demanded that he write a new song for each weekly prayer meeting. It was here, along with the famous English poet William Cowper, that Newton wrote several editions of *Olney Hymns*, which included the song that came to be known as "Amazing Grace." The song has an incredible universal appeal and has been recorded by rock groups, country singers, pop singers, classical singers, choirs, and orchestras; it has also been used as background music for Olympic gymnasts and television commercials.

How Can I Keep from Singing? (p. 111)

This is a hymn from the Revival period in America, written by the Reverend R. Lowry in about 1865. (It is not an old Quaker or Shaker hymn, as some sources suggest.) This beautiful hymn isn't all that well known in churches, yet it frequently rises to the surface in times of national crisis as a song of the indomitable American spirit.

Doris Plenn added a verse during the McCarthy era: "In prison cell and dungeon vile our thoughts to them are winging, when friends by shame are undefiled, how can I keep from singing?" The song appeared during the Vietnam era and, more recently, after the terrorist attacks on September 11, 2001. Numerous print and TV journalists wrote and recited the words, "Through all the tumult and the strife I hear the music ringing. It sounds an echo in my soul, how can I keep from singing?"

Shenandoah

Arranged by Frank Ponzio

America

For background and performance notes, see page 50.

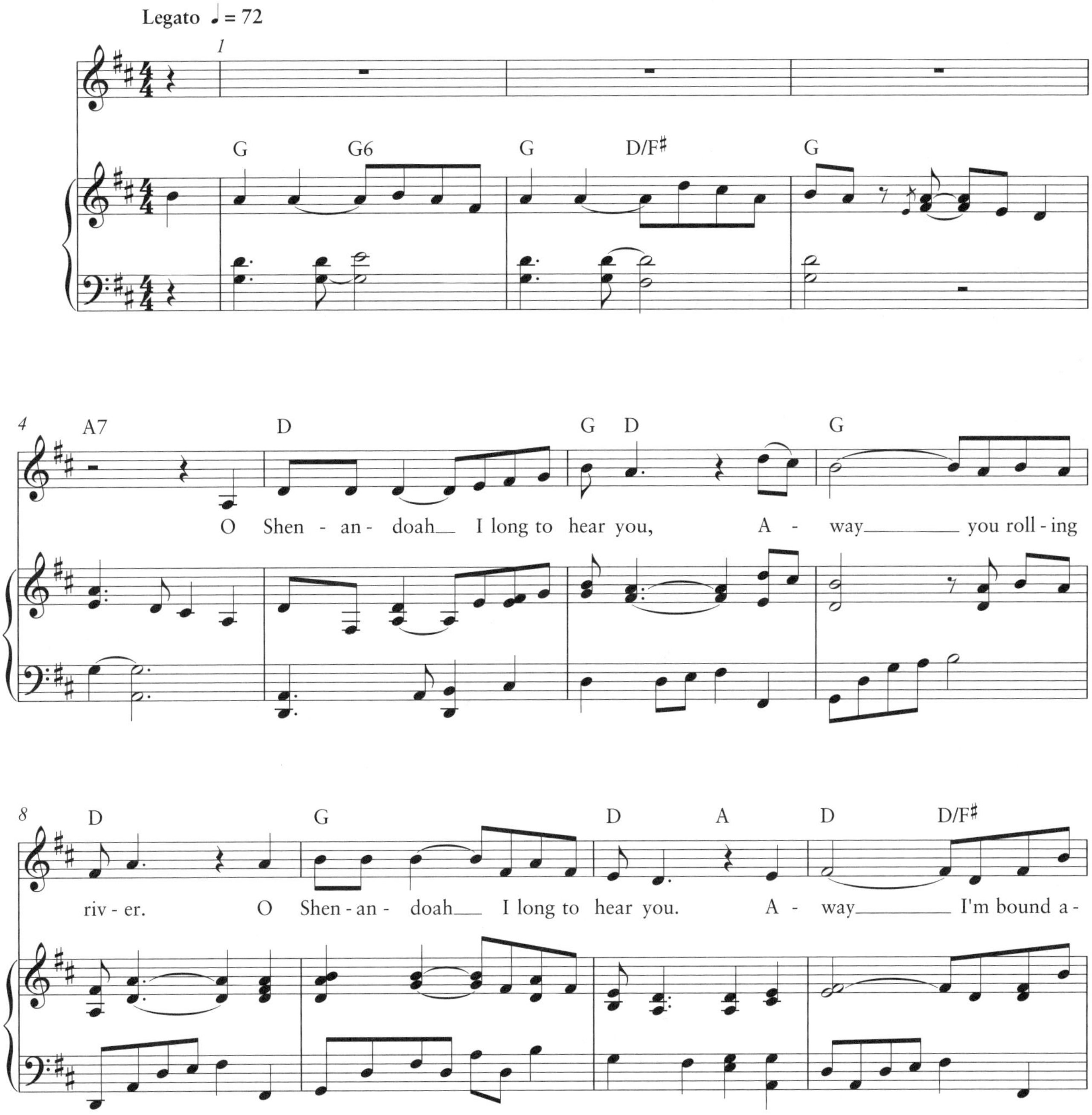
Legato ♩ = 72
G G6 G D/F♯ G
A7 D G D G
O Shen - an - doah I long to hear you, A - way you roll - ing
D G D A D D/F♯
riv - er. O Shen - an - doah I long to hear you. A - way I'm bound a -

12
G Gmaj7 A D G A
way cross the wide Mis - sour - i. O
16
D G D/F♯ G D
Shen - an - doah I'm bound to leave you. A - way you roll - ing riv - er. O
20
G Em Em/D D A D A D/F♯
Shen - an - doah I'll not de - ceive you. A - way I'm bound a - way, 'Cross the
24
G A7 Bm A D
wide Mis - sour - i. For

28 D G G
sev - en years I've been a rov - er A - way you roll - ing
31 D G D A7 D D/F♯
riv - er. But I'll re - turn to be your lov - er A - way I'm bound a -
35 G Freely Asus G G6
way, 'Cross the wide Mis - sour - i.
rit.
39 G D/F♯ G A7 D

Scarborough Fair

Arranged by Scarlett Antaloczy

England

For background and performance notes, see page 50.

Moderato ♩ = 92
Em D/Em Em D/Em
mp
Em Gmaj7 D Em
1. Are you go - ing to Scar - bor - ough fair?
2. Tell her (him) to make me a cam - bric shirt
D/Em G Em G6 A
Pars - ley, sage, rose - mar - y, and

13
Em D/Em Em D/Em
thyme.
Re - member me to one who lives there.
With - out a seam or fine need - le work.
17
Em Gmaj9 Em/G D/A G/B D
21
Em Dmaj9
rit.
Cmaj7(♯11) D6
She once was a true love of
(He)
1.
25
Em D/Em Em D/Em
mine.
p

2.
29
Em
D/Em
Em
Em
C/E
mine.
mf
33
E7sus4
E7sus4/G
E7sus4/D
Em
Tell her to wash it in yon - der dry well.
(him)
37
D/Em
G
Em
Bm
Em
D/G
G
A7sus4
Pars - ley, sage, rose - ma - ry, and
41
D/Em
D/Em
Cmaj7
D
Cmaj7
thyme.
Where

45 B7sus4 Cmaj7 A/C♯ G D9
wa - ter ne'er sprang nor drop of rain fell.
49 D Em Dmaj9 Cmaj7(♯11) D6
mf
For she (he) once was a true love of
53 Em D/E Em Gmaj7 D6 Cmaj7(♯11) D6
mine. She (He) once was a true love of
mp rit.
58 Em7/A Em D/Em Em
mine.
rit.
p
pp

Danny Boy

Londonderry Air

Fred C. Weatherly
(1848–1929)
England

Arranged by Frank Ponzio

For background and performance notes, see page 50.

♩ = 60
C F6 C/G Am D7 C/G F6 G7
Freely
C C C7 F6 Dm
1. O Dan - ny Boy, the pipes, the pipes are call - ing. From glen to
(2.) come, and all the flow'rs are dy - ing, And I am
C/E Fmaj7 Gsus4 G7 C C7
glen, and down the moun - tain side. The sum - mer's gone and all the ro - ses
dead, as dead I well may be, Ye'll come and find the place where I am

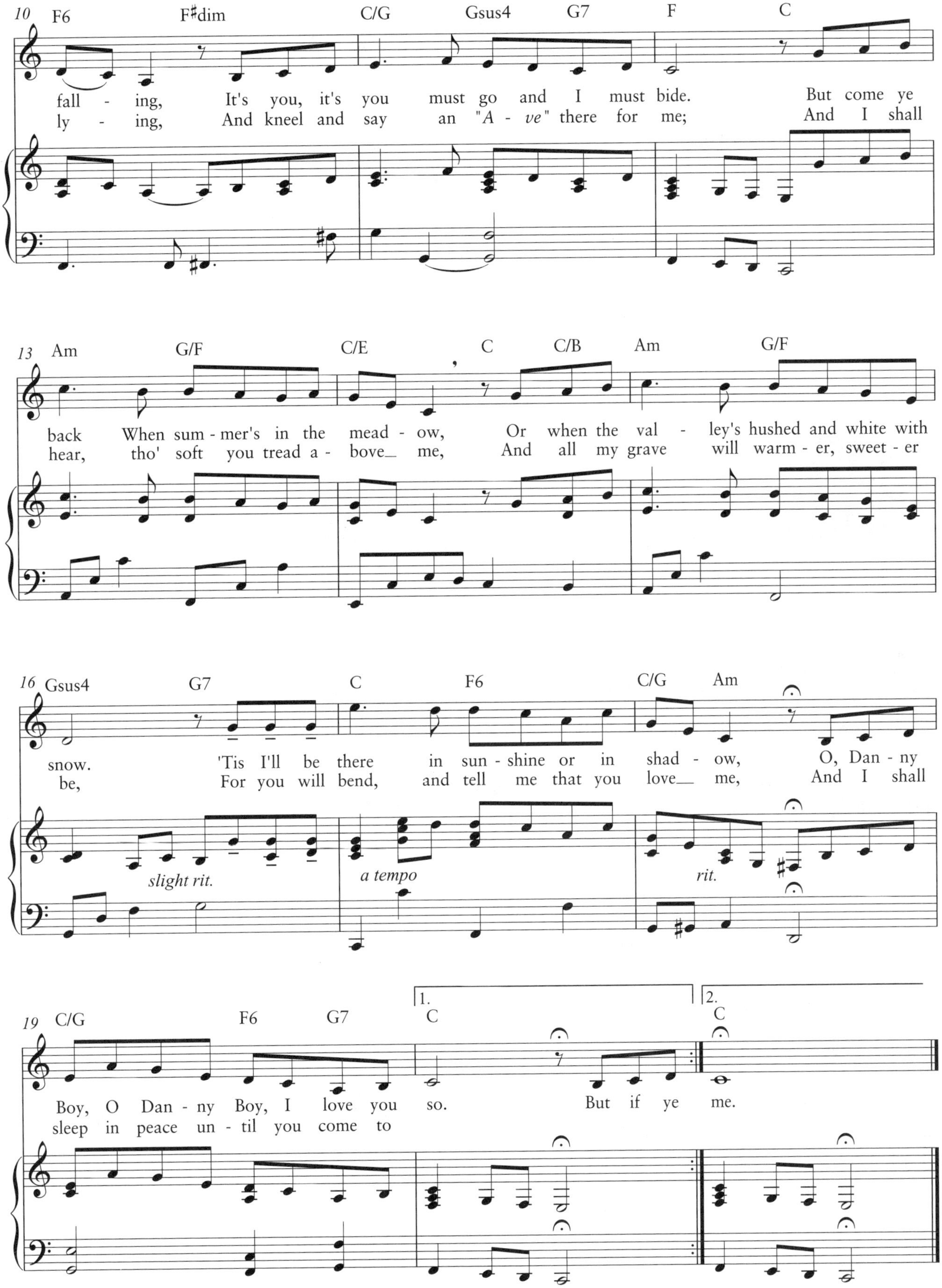
10 F6 F♯dim C/G Gsus4 G7 F C
fall - ing, It's you, it's you must go and I must bide. But come ye
ly - ing, And kneel and say an "A - ve" there for me; And I shall
13 Am G/F C/E C C/B Am G/F
back When sum - mer's in the mead - ow, Or when the val - ley's hushed and white with
hear, tho' soft you tread a - bove me, And all my grave will warm - er, sweet - er
16 Gsus4 G7 C F6 C/G Am
snow. 'Tis I'll be there in sun - shine or in shad - ow, O, Dan - ny
be, For you will bend, and tell me that you love me, And I shall
slight rit.
a tempo
rit.
19 C/G F6 G7
1. C
2. C
Boy, O Dan - ny Boy, I love you so. But if ye me.
sleep in peace un - til you come to

Civil War Medley

When Johnny Comes Marching Home/ The Cruel War Is Raging

Arranged by Frank Ponzio

America

For background and performance notes, see page 50.

1
Martial ♩. = 88
When

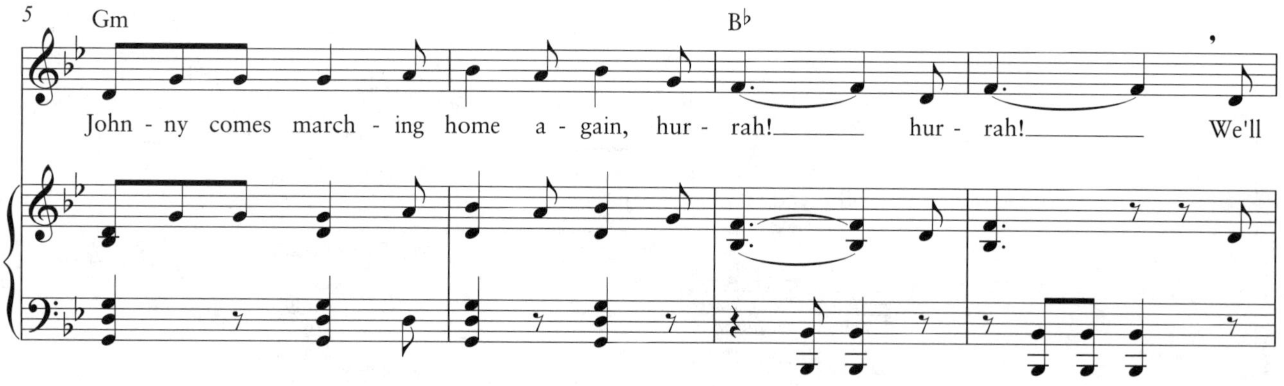
5
Gm
B♭
John - ny comes march - ing home a - gain, hur - rah! hur - rah! We'll

9
Gm G/F E♭ B♭/D B♭
give him a heart - y wel - come then, hur - rah! hur - rah!

rit.
𝅗𝅥 = 66
13
B♭ D/A G C
The cruel war is rag - ing,
rit.
17
D7 D♯dim Em C G/B B7 C
John - ny has to fight. I want to be with him from
21
G/D C G G Em7
morn - ing till night. I want to be with him. It
25
Am7 D7 Am7 G/B C
grieves my heart__ so, Won't you let me go with you?

29 G/D D7 Gsus G Dsus G C
No, my love, No. I'll go to your Cap - tain,
33 F♯ø7 B7 Em7 Em/D C C
get down on my knees, ten thou - sand gold gui - neas I'd
37 G/D C G G Em7
give for your re - lease. I want to be with you. It
41 Am7 D7 Am7 C
grieves my heart so, Won't you let me go with you.

♩. = 66
45 G/D D7 Gm B♭ F/A
No, my love, no. Oh, the men will cheer and the boys will shout. The
49 Gm Dm B♭ F/A
la - dies they will all turn out.
rit.
rall.
52 Gm F Gm F
Please, John - ny come march - ing home.
drums
56
dim.

The Water Is Wide

Waly, Waly

Arranged by Scarlett Antaloczy

England

For background and performance notes, see page 51.

♩ = 84
G/B Am/C G/D F/E♭ F G/B Gm/B♭
A7sus4 D7sus4 G Am/G G
1. The wa-ter is wide I can-not cross o'er
2. A ship_there is And she sails the seas.
G G/F♯ Em Em/D D7sus4
And neith-er have_ I wings to fly.
She's la-den deep_ as deep can be.

13 D D/C Bm7 Cmaj9 (add13)
Build me a boat that can car - ry two,
But not so deep as the love I'm in,
17 G/D D7sus4 G
And both shall row my love and I.
I know not if I sink or swim.
21 D7sus4 rit. G C/G D/G
I leaned my back a - gainst an old oak.
rit.
25 G G/F♯ Em D
I thought it was a trust - y tree.

29
D D/C Bm7 Cmaj9 (add13)
But first it bend - - - ed and then it broke,
33
G/D D7sus4
Interlude
G/B Am/C G/D
Thus did my love prove false to— me.
p
37
F/E♭ F G/B♭ Am/C G/D Bm G/B Am/C G/D
41
F/E♭ F G/B Am/C G/D
Broader
♩ = 80
E9/B A
O love is hand - -

45
D/A A A A/G♯ F♯m9
- some and love is fine. Pure as a jew - el
49
E E E/D A/C♯ E7/B C♯ø7
when first it is new. But love grows old
ff
53
F♯7 Bm9 G7
And wax - eth cold and fades a -
57
C♯m Dmaj7/E D Em/D A/C♯ Bm/D A/E G/F G
rit. rit.
way Like the morn - ing dew.
rit. rit. mf

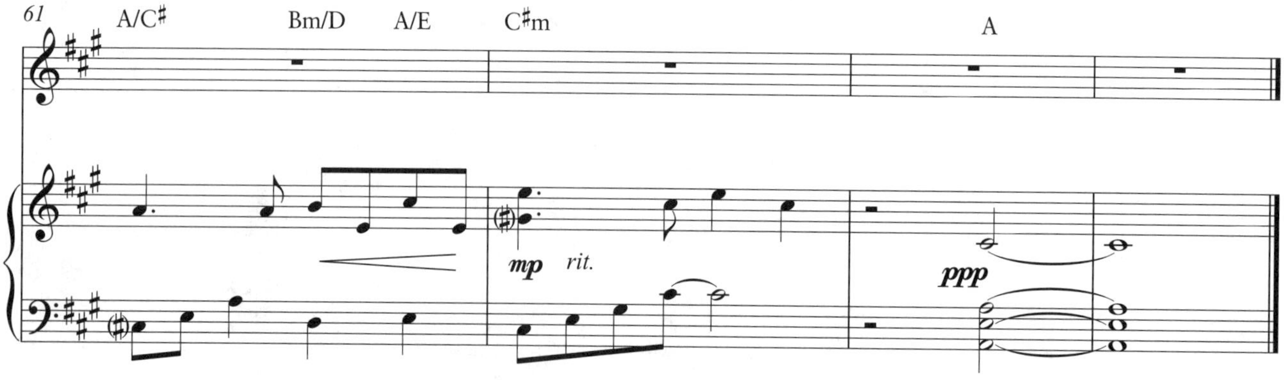
61
A/C♯
Bm/D
A/E
C♯m
A
mp
rit.
ppp

The Lark in the Clear Air

Sir Samuel Ferguson
Ireland

Arranged by Frank Ponzio

For background and performance notes, see page 51.

Moderato
♩ = 88
G C D7 G
Dear
G C D7 G C
thoughts are in my mind. And my soul soars en - chant - ed, As I hear the sweet lark
G C D7 G C D7 G/B C
sing in the clear air of the day. For a ten - der beam - ing smile to my

15
G C D7 G C G
hope has been grant - ed. And to - mor - row she shall hear all my
(he)
19
G/B C D7 G G C G
fond heart would say. I shall tell her all my love, all my
(him)
23
C G/B Am7 Am7 D7 G C G
soul's a - dor - a - tion, And I think she will hear me, And
(he)
27
C D7 G D/F# Em D/F# G
will not say me nay. It is this that give my soul all its

31
G/B C Am7 D7 G C G
joy - ous e - la - tion, As I hear the sweet lark sing in the
3
rall.
35
C D7 G C G C D7 G
clear air of the day.
rall.

Salley Gardens

Arranged by Frank Ponzio

Traditional Irish tune
"The Maids of Mourne Shore"
Words by W. B. Yeats
(1865–1939)

For background and performance notes, see page 51.

♩ = 80
D Dsus G D G A
D D A G D/F♯ G A7
Down by the Sal - ley Gar - dens my love and I did
(his) (he)
D D A/C♯ G D G A
meet. She passed the Sal - ley Gar - dens with lit - tle snow white

13 D Bm G F♯m (,) G A
feet. She bid me take life ea - sy, as the leaves grow on the
(him)
17 D D Dsus G D/F♯ (,) G A7
tree, But I be - ing young and fool - ish with her did not a -
(he)
21 D Em D D A7 G D/F♯ (,)
gree. In a field by the riv - er my
(his)
25 G Dsus D D A G D/F♯ (,)
love and I did stand and on my lean - ing shoul - der she
(he) (his)

29
G A7 D Bm G F♯m D (,)
placed her_ snow white hand. She bid me_ take life eas - y as the
(him)
33
G A Dsus D D G6
grass grows_ on_ the_ weirs, But_ I was_ young and_
(he)
36
G F♯m D/F♯ Em7 Asus D
(,)
rit.
fool - ish and_ now am_ full of tears.
(is)
rit.

Westryn Wynde

Arranged by Scarlett Antaloczy

England

For background and performance notes, see page 51.

♩ = 80
Em D/E Cmaj7 B7sus4 Em C/E D/E B7sus4
mf
Em Cmaj7 D Bm Em C D
West - ryn Wynde when wilt thou blow? The small rain down doth rain
Em Cmaj7 D Bm (,) D/C Am9 (,) Bm
Ah, that my love were in my arms and I were at home a - gain.

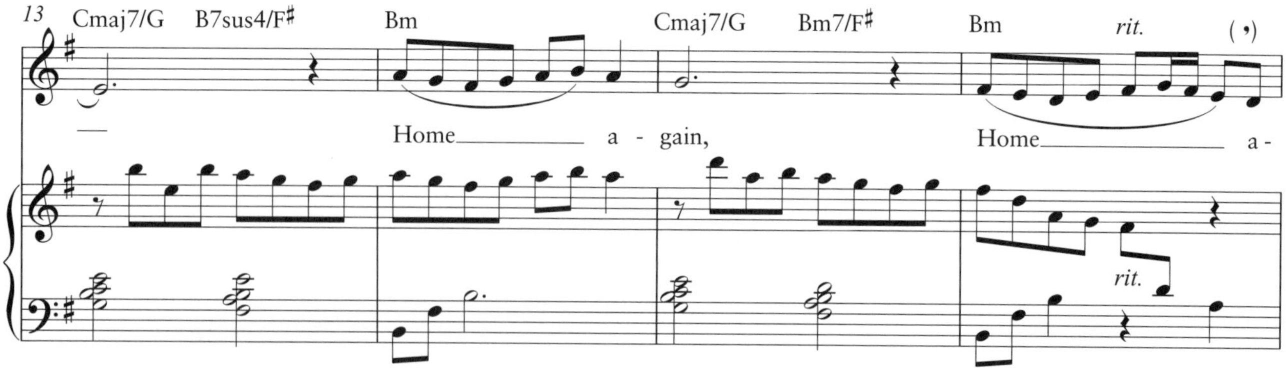
13
Cmaj7/G B7sus4/F♯
Bm
Cmaj7/G Bm7/F♯
Bm
rit.
(,)
Home a - gain,
Home a -
rit.

1.
(a tempo)
17
Em D/Em
Cmaj7/G B7sus4/F♯
Em C/E
B7sus4/E
2.
E
gain.
gain.
(a tempo)

Santa Lucia

Music by Teodoro Cottrau
Italy

Arranged by Scarlett Antaloczy

For background and performance notes, see page 51.

♩ = 100
C Dm G7 C
mf
rit.
C G7 Dm G7 C
1. Sul ma - re luc - ci - ca, l'as stro d'ar - gen - to,
Now 'neath the sil - ver moon, o - cean is glow - ing,
2. Con que - sto zef - fi - ro, Co - sì so - a - ve,
When o'er the wa - ters, Light winds are play - ing,
A A7 Dm G7 C
pla - ci - da è l'on da, pros - pe - ro è il ven - to.
O'er the calm bil - lows, soft winds are blow - ing.
Oh! co - m'è bel - lo, Star sul - la na - ve!
Thy spell can soothe us, All cares al - lay - ing.

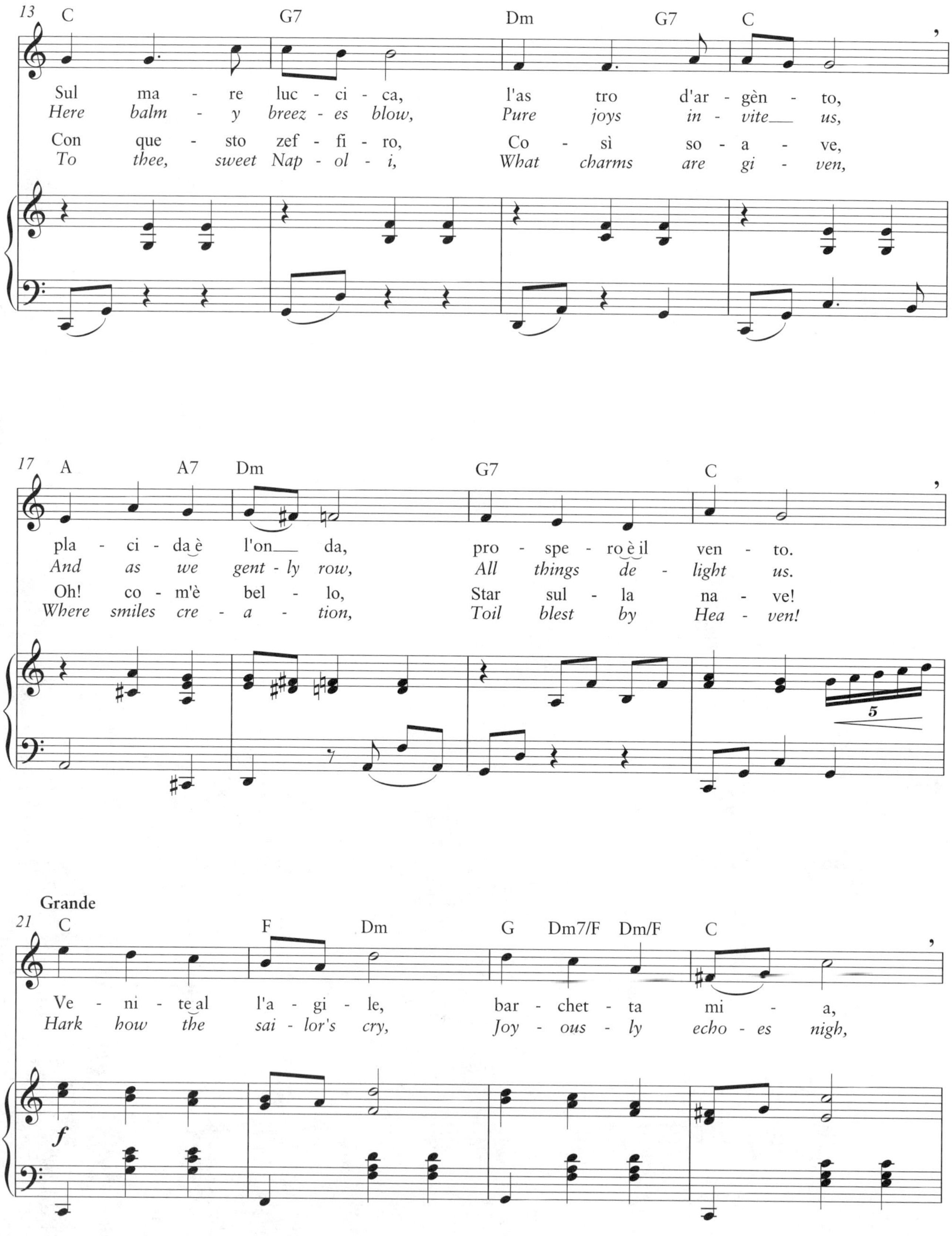
13
C G7 Dm G7 C
Sul ma - re luc - ci - ca, l'as tro d'ar - gèn - to,
Here balm - y breez - es blow, Pure joys in - vite us,
Con que - sto zef - fi - ro, Co - sì so - a - ve,
To thee, sweet Nap - ol - i, What charms are gi - ven,
5
17
A A7 Dm G7 C
pla - ci - da è l'on da, pro - spe - ro è il ven - to.
And as we gent - ly row, All things de - light us.
Oh! co - m'è bel - lo, Star sul - la na - ve!
Where smiles cre - a - tion, Toil blest by Hea - ven!
Grande
21
C F Dm G Dm7/F Dm/F C
Ve - ni - te al l'a - gi - le, bar - chet - ta mi - a,
Hark how the sai - lor's cry, Joy - ous - ly echo - es nigh,
f

25
C Dm F G7 C
San - ta Lu - ci - a, San - ta Lu - ci - a.
3
3
Molto Grande
29
C F Dm G Dm7/F Dm/F C
Ve - ni te al l'a - gi - le, bar - chet - ta mi - a,
Hark how the sai - lor's cry, Joy - ous - ly echo - es nigh,
tr tr tr
tr tr tr
33
C Dm F G7 C
rit.
San - ta Lu - ci - a, San - ta Lu - ci - a.
3
rit.

Verse 1: On the sea the silver star sparkles.
The waves are placid and the wind is prosperous.
Chorus: Come to my agile little boat! Santa Lucia!
Verse 2: With this breeze so sweet
Oh, how beautiful it is to be on a ship!

Paun I Kolo

(Peacock and Dance)

Arranged by Scarlett Antaloczy
English verson by Cynthia Vaughn

Bosnia

For background and performance notes, see page 52.

♩ = 48
G C/E Dsus4 G G/F♯ Em Am7 D
G C/E Dsus4 G G/F♯ Em Am7 D D9 D7/F♯ G
Pa - un pa - se, tra - va_ ra - ste pa - u - ne moj! pa - u - ne___
Proud bird gra - zes, grass is__ grow - ing. Why are you so sad? Proud___ bird_of_
Slightly faster
D D9 D7/F♯ G D D/C Gsus4 G/D Dsus4 C Am7
moj! pa - u - ne___ moj! Pa - u - na__ nam no - ge bo - le, pa-
mine! Proud___ bird_of_ mine. Are you griev - ing for your home - land, oh

15
D G G C
un moj, pa - un moj! Pa - u - na___ nam o - ci bo - le, pa -
proud bird, oh proud bird! Does your heart_ long for___ free - dom? Oh
19
1. ♩ = 48
D G C/E Dsus4 G Em Am7
un moj pa - un moj!
proud bird of___ mine!
23
2. ♩ = 48
D G C/E Dsus4 G
moj!
mine!
rit.
8va
pp
ppp

Peacock grazes, grass is growing, peacock mine!
Peacock's legs ail, peacock mine!
Peacock's eyes ail, peacock mine!—*Translation by Nenja Hasanic*

Ah! si mon moine voulait danser!

(Oh! If You Wanted to Dance with Me!)

Arranged by Frank Ponzio
English verson by Cynthia Vaughn

Canada

For background and performance notes, see page 52.

Lively ♩ = 80
G C6 D7 G C
D7 G G C6 D7 G C
Ah! si mon moi - ne vou - lait dan - ser! Ah! si mon moi - ne vou -
Oh! If you want - ed to dance with me! Oh! If you want - ed to
D7 G G Em C6 D7 G C C♯dim
lait dan - ser! Un ca - pu - chon je lui don - ne - rais, Un ca - pu - chon je lui
dance with me! A fine new hat I would give to thee, A fine new hat I would

12
D7 G D7 G D7 G D7 Em7
don - ne rais. Dan - se, mon moin', dan - se! Tu n'en - tends pas la
give to thee. Dance, my friend, come dance now! Oh! do you hear the
16
Am7 D7 G C D7 G Em
dan - se. Tu n'en - tends pas mon mou - lin, lon la, Tu n'en - tends pas mon mou -
mu - sic? Oh, if you want - ed to dance with me, We'd join the dance and be
20
D7 G G C D7 G
lin mar - cher.
fan - cy free.

Ah! If my monk wanted to dance!
A hood I would give to him.
Dance, my monk, dance!
You don't hear the dance,
you don't hear my music, la-la.

Niño precioso

(Precious Child)

Arranged by Scarlett Antaloczy
English version by Cynthia Vaughn

Nicaragua

For background and performance notes, see page 52.

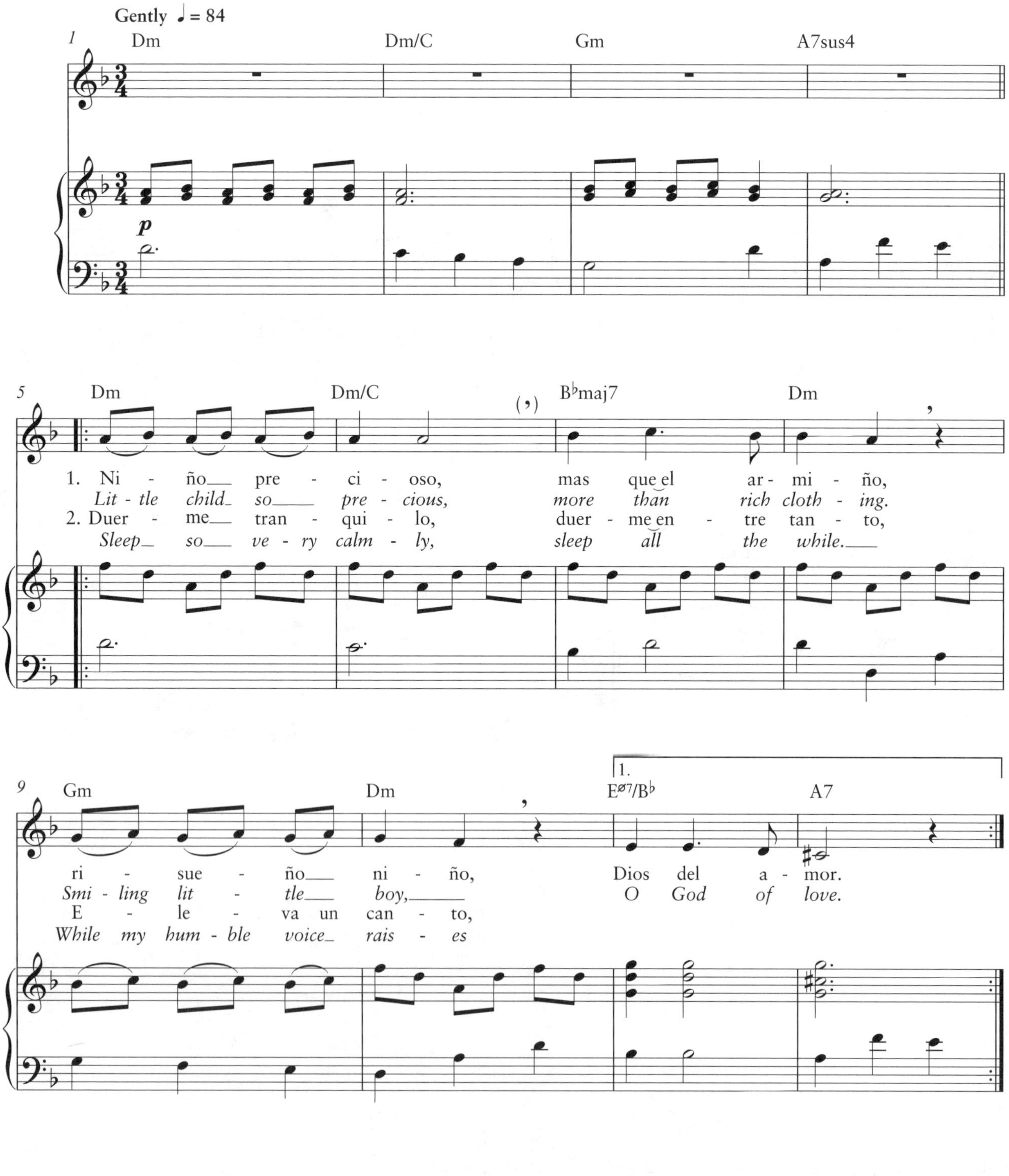
Gently ♩ = 84
Dm Dm/C Gm A7sus4
p
Dm Dm/C B♭maj7 Dm
1. Ni - ño pre - ci - oso, mas que el ar - mi - ño,
Lit - tle child so pre - cious, more than rich cloth - ing.
2. Duer - me tran - qui - lo, duer - me en - tre tan - to,
Sleep so ve - ry calm - ly, sleep all the while.
Gm Dm 1. Eø7/B♭ A7
ri - sue - ño ni - ño, Dios del a - mor.
Smi - ling lit - tle boy, O God of love.
E - le - va un can - to,
While my hum - ble voice rais - es

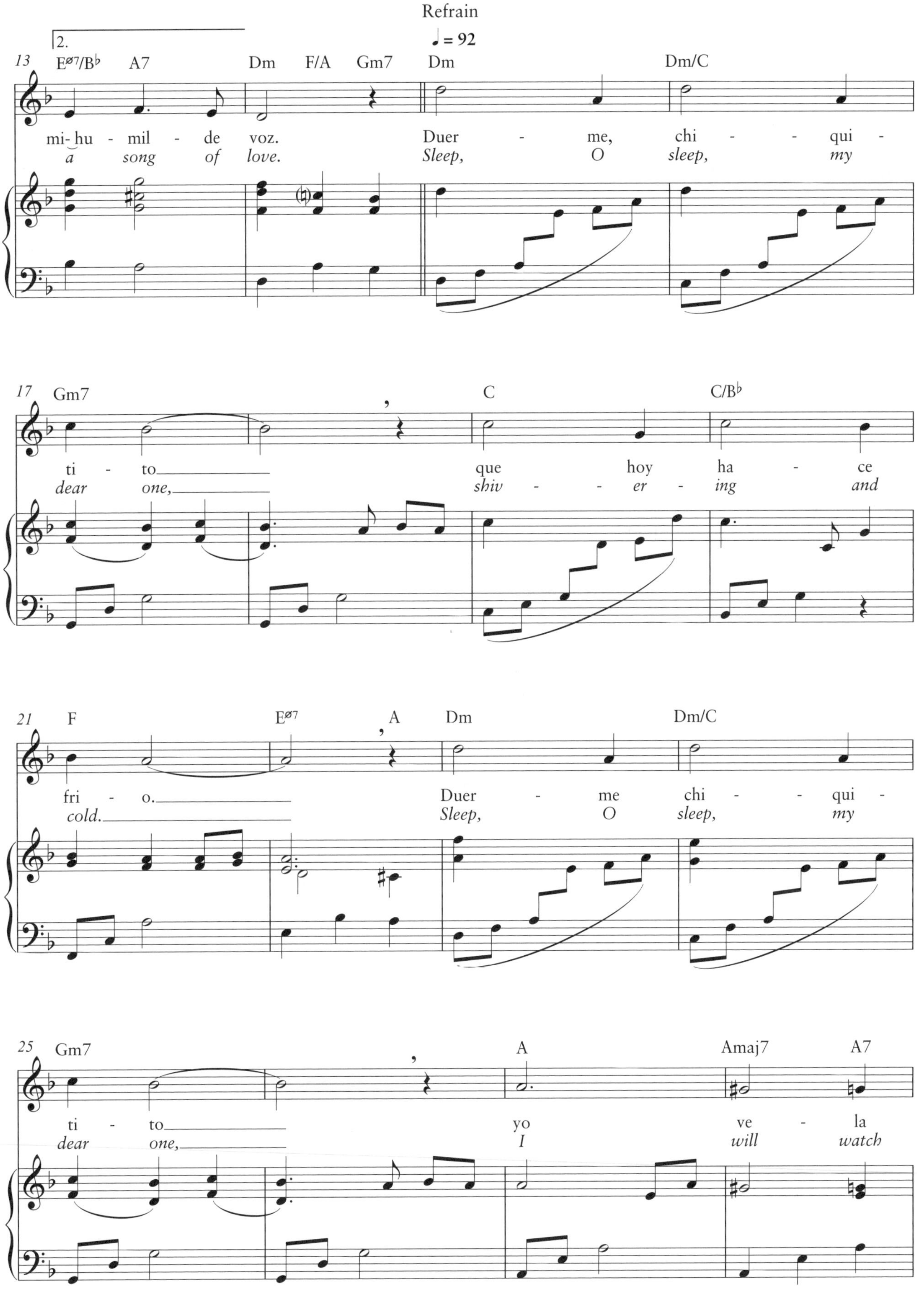
Refrain
2.
♩ = 92
13
Eø7/B♭ A7 Dm F/A Gm7 Dm Dm/C
mi-hu - mil - de voz. Duer - me, chi - - qui -
a song of love. Sleep, O sleep, my
17
Gm7 C C/B♭
ti - to que hoy ha - ce
dear one, shiv - - er - ing and
21
F Eø7 A Dm Dm/C
fri - o. Duer - me chi - - qui -
cold. Sleep, O sleep, my
25
Gm7 A Amaj7 A7
ti - to yo ve - la
dear one, I will watch

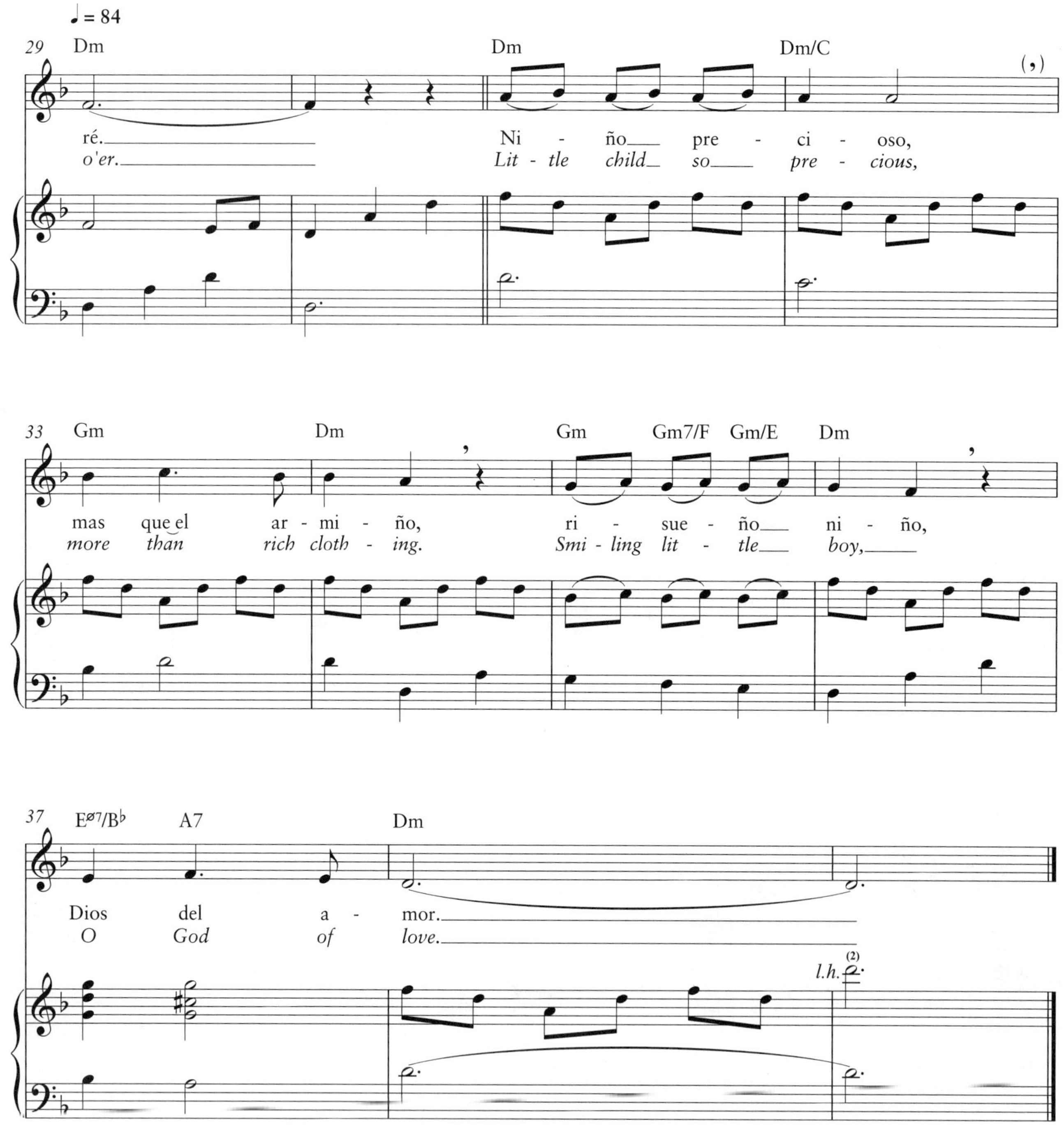
♩ = 84
29 Dm Dm Dm/C
ré.
o'er.
Ni - ño pre - ci - oso,
Lit - tle child so pre - cious,
33 Gm Dm Gm Gm7/F Gm/E Dm
mas que el ar - mi - ño, ri - sue - ño ni - ño,
more than rich cloth - ing. Smi - ling lit - tle boy,
37 Eø7/B♭ A7 Dm
Dios del a - mor.
O God of love.
l.h.

Verses 1, 3: Child more precious than the finest cloth,
Smiling boy, God of love.
Verse 2: Sleep calmly,
sleep while my humble voice raises a song.
Refrain: Sleep little boy who is cold.
Sleep little boy.
I will keep vigil.—*Translation by Noemi Lugo*

Mi caballo blanco

(My White Horse)

Arranged by Frank Ponzio
English version by Cynthia Vaughn

Frances Flores del Campo
Chile

For background and performance notes, see page 52.

♩ = 120
1 Em D C B
5 Em Am B Em
1. Es mi ca - bal - lo blan - co, Co - mo un a - man - e - cer,
My white horse is so hand - some, Shin - ing as bright as dawn.
2. En a - las de u - na di - cha Mi ca - bal - lo co - mo,
On wings of joy he gal - lops Though my arms feel the pain
simile
9 Am6 Em B Em
Siem - pre jun - ti - tos va - mos, Es mi a - mi - go mas fiel.
Al - ways we ride to - geth - er. Faith - ful, we tra - vel on.
Y en bra - zos de u - na pe - na Tam - bien el me lle - vo.
We bare - ly stop to rest On, on we go a - gain.

13
Am Em B Em
Mi ca - bal - lo, mi ca - bal - lo, ga - lo - pan - do va.
17
Am Em B Em
Mi ca - bal - lo, mi ca - bal - lo, se va y se va.
21
Em D C B
Ah Oo
25
Em Am6 Bsus B

29 Em7 Am (,) B Em
3. Has - ta que a Dios le pi - do Que lo ten - ga muy bien,
3. I pray God will pro - tect us As the years gal - lop so,
33 Am6 Em (,) B Em
Si a su la - do me lla - ma En mi blan - qui - to i ré.
And when I'm called to Hea - ven On my white horse I'll go.
37 Am Em B Em
Mi ca - bal - lo, mi ca - bal - lo, ga - lo - pan - do va.
41 Am Em B7 Em Em
Mi ca - bal - lo, mi ca - bal - lo, se va y se va. Ah

46
D
C
B
Em
Am
Em
Oo

Verse 1: My white horse is like dawn. Always we go together. He is my most faithful friend.
Refrain: My horse, my horse galloping goes. My horse, my horse runs and runs.
Verse 2: My horse ran after happiness and in arms of sorrow he took me.
Verse 3: I will ask God to keep him well, but I will go on my white horse if He calls me to its side.—*Translation by Noemi Lugo*

Dubinushka

(Hammer Song)

Arranged by Scarlett Antaloczy
English version by Cynthia Vaughn

Russia

For background and performance notes, see page 53.

♩ = 120
Dm A Dm
Dm
I have heard man - y songs in the land that I love, They have
mf
Gm
Dm A Dm
Gm
told me of sad - ness and sor - row. Yet there's one song that I will
A Dm A
Dm A Dm
rall.
sing all my life, It's the song that brings hope for to - mor - row.

1st time ♩ = 60
2nd time, faster and faster
10
Dm
Gm
Dm
Ex, du - bi - nush - ka, uh - nem!
13
Dm
Gm
Dm
Ex, zel - yo - na - ya sa - ma poj - dyot! Po - dyor - nem! Po -
17
Dm
A
1.
Dm
2.
Dm
dyor - nem, Da uh - nem! nem.
3
3
ff
8vb

Oh! Dubinushka,* heave-ho!
Oh! Green stick, it will yield if you push it hard!
Push and heave-ho!—*Translation by Alex Pudov*

*Dubinushka is a large wooden club.

Dance of Youth

(Xing Chun Wu Chu)

Arranged by Scarlett Antaloczy
English version by Jeson Yan

China

For background and performance notes, see page 53.

♩ = 66
Dm Am/C B♭ Am Gm Am B♭ Asus4
The
mf
Dm Dm/C B♭ A7sus4 A7 Dm Dm/C
sun_ sets be - hind the moun - tain 'til to - mor - row. Fad - ed flow'rs will bloom next year in
mf
f
B♭ Asus4 Dm Am B♭ Asus4
joy and sor - row. Pret - ty lit - tle bird flew a - way with no trace. My
p

11
Dm Dm/C B♭ A7sus4 Dm Dm/C B♭ Asus4
youth will not re - turn like pret - ty bird flown a - way. Youth will not re - turn like pret - ty bird flown a - way.
mf
f
15
Dm Dm/C B♭ Asus4 Gm Asus4 Dm
mf Pret - ty lit - tle bird flew__ far a - way. My youth will not re - turn like pret - ty bird flown a - way.
p La la la la la la la la la la la la la la la la la la la la la la la.
1.
19
Dm Am/C B♭ Am Gm Asus4 Dm Gm7
2.
23
E7sus4 Bm7/D Cmaj7 Bm7 Am Bm C B7sus4
The
f

27
Em Em/D C B7sus4 B7 Em Em/D
sun__ sets be-hind the moun-tain 'til to- mor-row. Fad-ed flow'rs will bloom next year in
mf
f
30
C B7sus4 Em Bm C B7sus4
joy and sor-row. Pret-ty lit-tle bird flew a-way with no trace. My
p
33
Em Em/D C B7sus4 B Em Em/D C B7sus4
youth will not re-turn like pret-ty bird flown a-way. Youth will not re-turn like pret-ty bird flown a-way.
mf
f
37
Em Em/D C B7sus4 B7 Am B7sus4
1.
Em
mf Pret-ty lit-tle bird flew__ far a-way. My youth will not re-turn like pret-ty bird flown a-way.
p La la la la la la la la la la la la la la la la la la la la la la la.

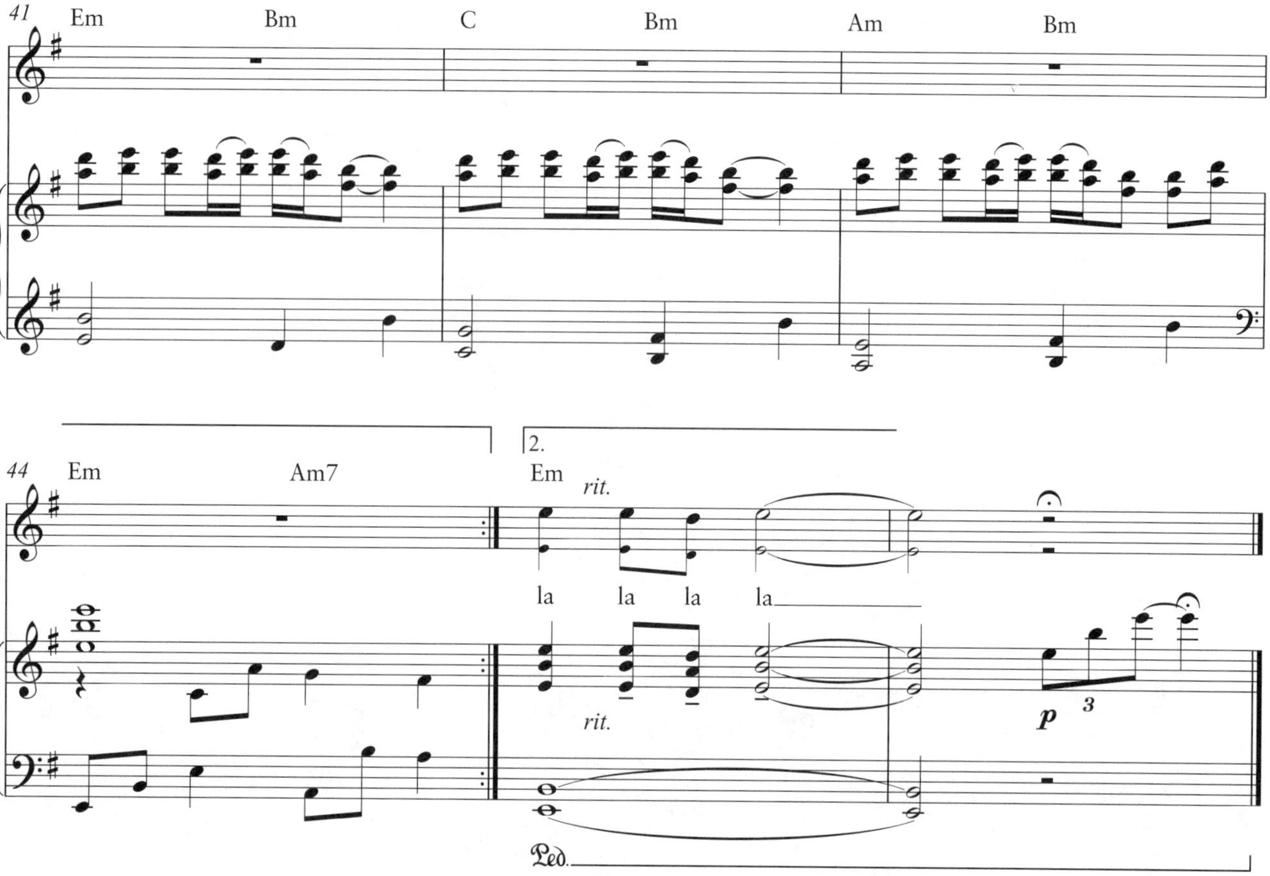
41
Em
Bm
C
Bm
Am
Bm
44
Em
Am7
2.
Em
rit.
la
la
la
la
rit.
p
3
Ped.

青春嘆

太陽下山明朝依舊爬上来，

花儿謝了明年還是一樣地開。

美麗小鳥飛去無影蹤，

我的青春和小鳥一樣不回来。

啦……，啦……，

我的青春和小鳥一樣不回来！

My Lord, What a Mornin'!

Arranged by Frank Ponzio

American Spiritual

For background and performance notes, see page 53.

Freely ♩ = 80
F F7 B♭ B♭dim F/C C F
F C7 F B♭ Am7 Dm7 C7
My Lord, What a morn - in', My Lord, What a morn - in', O
mp mf f
F F7 B♭ B♭m7 F/C C F
My Lord, What a morn - in', when the stars be - gin to fall. You'll
f

13
F F/A B♭ Gm Bdim Csus C7
hear the trum - pets sound to wake the na - tions un - der ground.
17
F Em7 A7 Dm7 B♭ B♭dim Am7 D7 Gm7 C7 F
Look - in' to my God's right hand When the stars be - gin to fall.
21
B⌀7 B♭dim F Gm Am7 Dm7 B♭ Csus B♭/D Edim
My Lord, What a morn - in', My Lord, What a morn - in', O
mp
mf
25
F F7/A B♭ B♭dim F/C Gm/C C♯dim
My Lord, What a morn - in' when the stars be - gin to
f

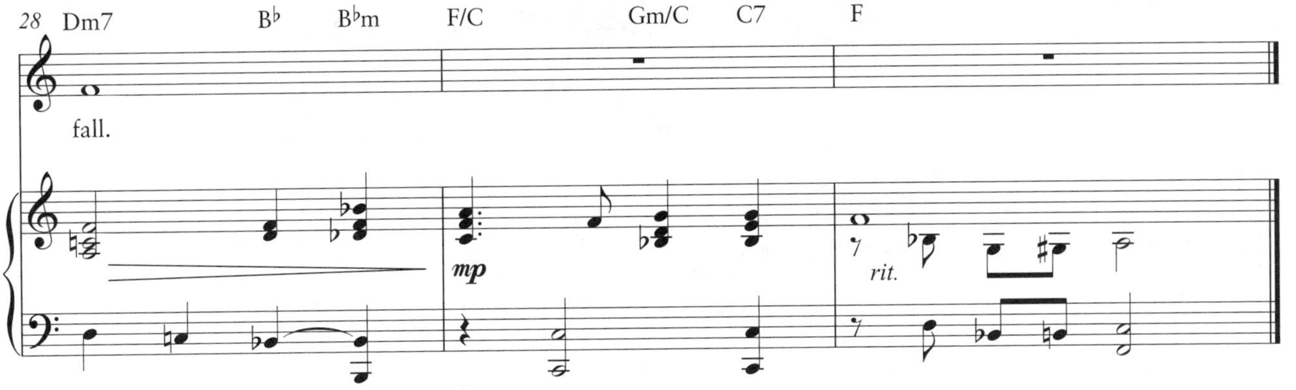
28
Dm7
B♭
B♭m
F/C
Gm/C
C7
F
fall.
mp
rit.

Ev'ry Time I Feel the Spirit

Arrangement by Scarlett Antaloczy

American Spiritual
c. 1874

For background and performance notes, see page 53.

Joyfully ♩ = 100
G D/F♯ D Em7 Em7sus4 D G D
Ev' - ry
f
G D/F♯ D Em D D7
time I feel the spir - it mov - ing in my heart I will pray Ev' - ry
G D/F♯ D Em D G D
time I feel the spir - it mov - ing in my heart I will pray. Up on the

13
D G D D Em D D G D Em D
moun - tain when my lord spoke Out of His mouth came fire and smoke. Looks all a-
sor - rows and I have woe And I have heart - ache here be - low. But while God
17
D G D D Em D F♯m Em7 A7sus4 D G D
round me it looked so fine till I asked my Lord if all were mine. Ev' - ry
leads me I'll ne - ver fear for I am shel - tered by His care.
21
G D/F♯ D Em D D7
time I feel the spir - it mov - ing in my heart I will pray. Ev' - ry
25
G D/F♯ 1. D Em D G D
time I feel the spir - it mov - ing in my soul I will pray. Oh I have

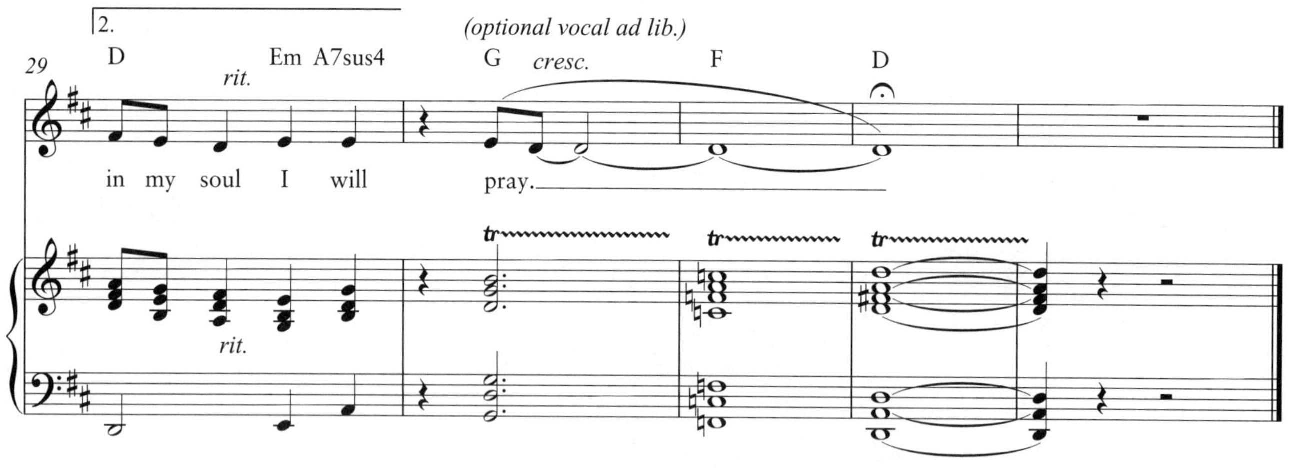
2.
(optional vocal ad lib.)
29
D
rit.
Em A7sus4
G
cresc.
F
D
in my soul I will pray.
tr
tr
tr
rit.

Amazing Grace

Music by John Newton
(1725–1807)
America

Arranged by Scarlett Antaloczy

For background and performance notes, see page 53.

Moderately with feeling ♩ = 80
Am7 Bm Cmaj7(add 13) D7sus4 G C/G G D7sus4/E
A -
mf
G G C/G G D/F♯
maz - ing grace, How sweet the sound, that
Em G/D D7sus4 D Em7 D/F♯
saved a wretch like me. I

13
G G7 C G D/F♯
once was lost but now am found, Was
17
Am7 Bm Cmaj7(add13) D7sus4 G D7sus4/E
blind but now I see. 'Twas
21
G G C/G D/G
grace that taught my heart to fear and
25
Em G/D D7sus4 D Em7 D/F♯
grace my fears re - lieved. How

29
G
G7
C
G
D/F♯
pre - cious did that grace ap - pear the
33
Am7
Bm
Cmaj7(add 13)
D7sus4
G
C/G
G
D7sus4/E
hour I first be - lieved. Through
37
G
G7/F
C/E
Cm/E♭
ma - ny dan - gers, toils, and snares I
41
G/D
C♯ø7
A7sus4
D
Em7
D/F♯
have al - read - y come. 'Tis

45
Dm/G F/G G G7 Dm/G C G D/F♯
grace hath brought me safe thus far, And
49
Am7 Bm Cmaj7(add 13) D7sus4 G C/G G
(,) rit.
grace will lead me home.
rit.

How Can I Keep from Singing?

Reverend L. Lowry
America c. 1865

Arrangement by Frank Ponzio

For background and performance notes, see page 54.

Dolce, legato ♩ = 72
F F7/A B♭ Bdim F/C
Gm/F F F F7/A B♭ Bdim F Dm7
My life flows on in end - less praise a - bove earth's lam - en -
Gm7 C7 F7 F7/A B♭ Bdim F/C Gm7 C7
ta - tion. I hear the sweet though far off hymn that hails a new cre -

12 B♭/F F/C Am D7 Gm7 Csus C♯dim Dm G/B
a - tion. Though all the tu - mult and the strife I hear the mu - sic
16 C7 F F7 B♭ Am Gm7 C7
ring - ing. It finds an ech - o___ in my soul; How can I keep from
Broadly
20 Gm/F F Csus F F7/A B♭ Bdim
sing - ing? I lift my eyes, the cloud grows thin, I
24 F C/E Dm7 Gm7 C7 F F7/A B♭ Bdim
see the blue a - bove_ it. And day by day this path - way clears since

rall.
28 F/C Gm/F F mp Am7 D7 Gm7 Csus C♯dim
first I learned to love__ it. The peace of God re - stores my soul, A
mp
a tempo
32 Dm7 G7/B Gm/C C7 f F F7/A B♭ F/A Am/F♯
foun-tain e - ver spring - ing. All things are mine since__ I am loved. How
f
rit.
36 Gm7 C7 Gm/F B♭ Am Gm7 C7 B♭/F F/C
can I keep from sing - ing? How can I keep from sing - ing?
mf

Theater, Film, and Television Songs

Theater Songs

Americans love musical theater. From Broadway blockbusters to off-Broadway sleepers, community theater to bus-and-truck touring productions, dinner theater to the local high school drama clubs—musicals are here to stay.

In the late 1800s America's theaters and music halls were filled with imported operettas (Gilbert and Sullivan, Franz Lehar) and bawdy British musical comedies. After the turn of the century George M. Cohan captured the audience's attention with uniquely American musicals like *Little Johnny Jones* in 1904.

Musical theater grew in popularity after World War I when theater audiences were humming the tunes of Jerome Kern, George Gershwin, and Cole Porter. The golden period of American musical theater is considered to be the twenty-year period from Rodgers and Hammerstein's *Oklahoma!* of 1943 to Harnick and Bock's *Fiddler on the Roof* in 1964. Other classic musicals from this era include Rodgers and Hammerstein's *The Sound of Music,* Irving Berlin's *Annie Get Your Gun,* Cole Porter's *Kiss Me, Kate,* Frank Loesser's *Guys and Dolls,* Lerner and Loewe's *My Fair Lady,* Meredith Willson's *The Music Man,* and Leonard Bernstein's *West Side Story.* All of these successful stage musicals were later turned into successful movie musicals.

The popularity of stage and movie musicals waned during the Vietnam war, but musicals by Stephen Sondheim (*Sweeney Todd, Into the Woods*) and England's Andrew Lloyd Webber (*Cats, Phantom of the Opera*) filled Broadway theaters in the 1980s.

Today's musical theater cannot be so easily defined. More than ever, Broadway performers must be "triple-threats," equally competent in singing, dancing, and acting. Recent Broadway shows range from revivals of classic musicals (*Showboat*) to rock musicals (*Rent*), to pop-style musicals by Frank Wildhorne (*Jekyll and Hyde*).

One very recent development is to turn successful movies into stage musicals like *The Wizard of Oz, The Producers, Singin' in the Rain, Hairspray, The Full Monty, Urban Cowboy,* and Disney's *The Lion King* and *Beauty and the Beast.* No stylistic musical stone has been left unturned. One of the biggest hits of 2002 was *MAMMA MIA!* which featured middle-aged women dressed in spandex belting out tunes by the 1970s Swedish pop group, ABBA. Maybe we haven't come so far from vaudeville, after all.

Film and Television Songs

The newest types of songs are those written for film and TV. They appear in live and animated children's shows like *Sesame Street,* in film scores like *Titanic,* and in movie musicals like *Moulin Rouge.* Movie musicals include songs borrowed from the stage version as well as new pieces. Some movies and television shows, like *That 70's Show,* recycle music from the time period. Original songs for film and TV usually fall into one of three categories:

1. Broadway-style songs (Disney's *Prince of Egypt, Lion King*)
2. Pop-style songs (*Titanic,* James Bond theme songs, songs from TV's *Ally MacBeal,* Disney's *Little Mermaid, Toy Story*)
3. Period-style songs that invoke the historical time period (film version of Jane Austen's *Pride and Prejudice,* Shakespeare films)

Some movies use more than one version of the same song. For example, in Disney's *Pocahontas,* Broadway actress Judy Kuhn sings "Colors of the Wind," and pop star Vanessa Williams sings the same song under the closing credits. Regardless of the style, movie and TV songs have great appeal and can reach a wide audience through video/DVD rentals and soundtrack sales.

I Move On, from the film *Chicago* (p. 118)

Catherine Zeta-Jones and Renée Zellweger sing this Academy Award-nominated song under the closing credits of *Chicago,* the 2002 Oscar-winning movie based on the 1975 Broadway musical. Songwriter John Kander and lyricist Fred Ebb intended to insert the new song after "Nowadays" but finally decided that "I Move On" was too strong to be anything but an epilogue to the tale of Roxie Hart and Velma Kelly. Both the movie and the stage musical are set in the Roaring '20s, where murderess showgirls Roxie and Velma try to win fame and avoid the death penalty.

Kander and Ebb also wrote the hit Broadway musicals *Cabaret* and *Kiss of the Spider Woman.* In a radical departure from the sunny musicals of Rodgers and Hammerstein and Lerner and Leowe in the 1950s and 1960s, Kander and Ebb embraced sexuality and explored the darker side of human nature. Whether in Nazi Germany (*Cabaret*) or a Chicago jailhouse, survival under difficult or surreal situations is a common Kander and Ebb theme. "I'm out of dreams and life has got me down, I don't despair. . . . I just move on."

Wand'rin' Star, from *Paint Your Wagon* (p. 123)

Disillusioned fortune hunter Ben Rumson sings this song when the gold runs out in a mining town during the California gold rush of 1853. However, "Wandr'in' Star" can be sung by any restless soul who longs to see what better things life has to offer down the road. Frederick Loewe and Alan Jay Lerner, creators of the 1953 musical *Paint Your Wagon,* followed their own wandering stars.

Loewe was trained in classical music like his father, a Viennese opera singer, and, no doubt, Lerner's family expected him to stay in the family business (Lerner's department stores). They struck their own musical gold with hit Broadway musicals *Brigadoon, My Fair Lady, Gigi,* and *Paint Your Wagon.* Lerner and Loewe's stage musicals were later made into movies, and the 1969 movie version of *Paint Your Wagon* starred Lee Marvin as Ben Rumson.

Goodnight, My Someone, from *The Music Man* (p. 127)

The song "Goodnight, My Someone" introduces us to the straight-laced character of Marian the Librarian. Marian is giving a piano lesson to young Amaryllis. While the girl plays her simple piano tune, we see a tender side of the teacher as Marian dreamily sings to the evening star.

Did you know that "Goodnight, My Someone" uses the same melody as "Seventy Six Trombones"? By altering the tempo and the meter, Willson transformed a sweet waltz into a stirring march.

The Music Man was Meredith Willson's first and most enduring musical. Willson grew up in Mason City, Iowa, and later built his musical career in New York City where he was principal flutist with the New York Philharmonic and wrote music for radio shows. Willson told many stories of his childhood, and the Broadway composer Frank Loesser convinced him that Iowa would make a great setting for a musical. Willson's characters were based on composites of real "stubborn" Iowans he knew. The character of Marian, however, is based on Willson's mother.

No Other Love, from *Me and Juliet* (p. 131)

The characters in *Me and Juliet* are all actors and stage crew in a Broadway show. The chorus girl, Jeanie, sings of her love for the assistant stage manager, whom she has secretly married. It is a show within a show, with all the backstage drama of a real Broadway show. Other show-within-a-show musicals include *Forty-Second Street* and Cole Porter's *Kiss Me, Kate. Me and Juliet* is one of the lesser known musicals by Rodgers and Hammerstein, whose hit shows include *Oklahoma!, The Sound of Music,* and *Carousel.*

I Got the Sun in the Morning, from *Annie Get Your Gun* (p. 134)

The sharpshooter Annie Oakley sings of the virtues of being happy without many material possessions. *Annie Get Your Gun* is based loosely on the true story of Oakley and her romantic and business relationship with Wild West star Buffalo Bill.

This is a good example of a show that enjoyed a successful revival. Fifty-three years after Ethel Merman played Annie Oakley on Broadway, Bernadette Peters starred in the 1995 Broadway revival. The show's many memorable tunes by Irving Berlin include "There's No Business Like Show Business," "The Girl That I Marry," and "You Can't Get a Man with a Gun."

Where Is Love?, from *Oliver!* (p. 139)

The young orphan Oliver sings this hauntingly beautiful song to the mother he never knew. However, the song works very well as a love ballad for either a man or a woman when performed outside the context of the show's story. Many hit songs in musicals were designed to stand alone. In fact, some composers, like Gershwin, would write songs for one show and then insert them in a completely different musical.

The 1963 stage musical *Oliver!* was based on Charles Dickens's Victorian novel *Oliver Twist.* Five years later it was made into a movie, and when the musical was revived in London in 1994, it was revised and re-orchestrated to make it more like the movie version.

Over the Rainbow, from the movie *The Wizard of Oz* (p. 141)

This universally appealing song was written for the 1939 Hollywood musical, *The Wizard of Oz.* In 2000 it was named the number one "Song of the Century." Oddly enough, this beautiful, inspirational ballad was actually cut from the film three times. In the story, young Dorothy Gale is scolded by her aunt, "Find a place where you won't get into any trouble." Crestfallen, Dorothy asks her dog, Toto, "Do you suppose there is such a place? There must be. It's far, far away, behind the moon, behind the rain."

Some film executives thought the song should be cut because it slowed down the movie's action and they didn't understand why the girl was singing in a barnyard. The music publisher complained that the middle of the song was too simple and the octave leap on "some-where" was unsingable. Fortunately, composer Harold Arlen and the film's producer Arthur Freed convinced the powers-that-be to leave the song in. It became Judy Garland's personal theme song and has been recorded by artists like country star Willie Nelson, jazz greats Sarah Vaughan, Jimmy Scott, and Eva Cassidy, and rhythm-and-blues singer Patti LaBelle.

Sing! from the TV show *Sesame Street* (p. 149)

This catchy tune by Joe Raposo is a popular song from the famous children's television show. The deeper message, however, may be intended more for self-conscious adults. Raposo urges everyone to simply "Sing!" and not to worry about what anyone else thinks. That is also the point of this book: to inspire a lifelong love for singing.

Somewhere Out There, from the film *An American Tail* (p. 152)

This tender duet is from the Don Bluth animated film *An American Tail* that was nominated for an

Academy Award in 1986. It is the story of a family of Russian mice who immigrate to the United States. When young Fieval Mousekewitz is accidentally separated from his family at Ellis Island, he sings "Somewhere Out There." In another part of the city, "underneath the same big sky" little sister Tanya Mouskewitz joins in the song.

The song is often performed as a love duet and appears in several wedding song anthologies. The James Ingram/Linda Ronstadt version that played under the film's closing credits climbed to the top of the pop charts.

James Horner is an award-winning composer of film scores and movie songs. He also wrote "All Love Can Be" from *A Beautiful Mind,* and "My Heart Will Go On" from *Titanic.*

A Time for Us, love theme from the film *Romeo and Juliet* (p. 156)

Nino Rota's genius was his ability to write new music that captured the style, mood, and pageantry of the time period of the film setting. His musical score for Zefirelli's *Romeo and Juliet* evoked Shakespeare's Italy and "A Time for Us" is in the style of a courtly Baroque lute song. You can compare it to an original lute song, John Dowland's "Come Again, Sweet Love" on p. 185.

Nino Rota (1911–1979) was Italy's finest composer of film music. He is best remembered as the creator of the score for the film *The Godfather,* but Rota was a classically trained composer who wrote symphonies, chamber works, and an opera, *The Straw Hat.* His first film music collaborations were with the famed director Federico Fellini.

I Move On

FROM *Chicago*

Lyrics by Fred Ebb

Music by John Kander

For background and performance notes, see page 115.

Bluesy vamp
= 60
A6/9
mf
easy
While
Amaj9
G♯7
A9/G
truck - in' down the road of life
When ev - 'ry hope seems gone,

12
F♯7sus(♭9)
F♯7
F(♯5)
F(♭5)
E7(13)
I just move on.
15
A6/9
When
19
Amaj9
G♯7
A9/G
I can't find a single star That I can wish up - on
22
F♯7sus(♭9)
F♯7
F(♯5)
F(♭5)
E9
I just move on.
I move on.

25
A6/9
I run so fast,
29
D9(#11)
C#m7
F#m7
Bm7
E7sus
a shot - gun blast Can't hurt me not one bit.
I'm out of dreams And life has got me down.
(D.S.)
32
A(9)
D9(#11)
C#m7
F#m7
I'm on my toes 'cause hea - ven knows. A
I don't des - pair. I don't go there. I
35
B9
Bm7
E7
C(#9)/E♭
E9sus
mov - ing tar - get's hard to hit.
hang my bon - net out of town.
8va

38
C(♯9)/E♭ E9sus C(♯9)/E♭ E9sus
(8)
So,
So,
41
Amaj9 G♯7 A9/G
as I play in life's bal - let, I'm not the dy - in' swan,
there's no doubt I'm well cut out, To run life's mar - a - thon
to CODA
44
F♯7sus(♭9) F♯7 F(♯5) F(♭5) E9 A6/9
I just move on, I move on.
D.S. al CODA
48
Just when it seems

CODA
51
Bm9(♭5)
E7sus(♭9) E9sus
C♯m7
F♯9sus F♯9
I move on.
I just move on.
So
55
Bm7
E9sus
fleet of foot. I can't stay put, I just move on, Yeah. I move on.
ff
59
A6/9
mf
dim. poco a poco
63
p

Wand'rin' Star

FROM *Paint Your Wagon*

Lyrics by
Alan Jay Lerner

Music by
Frederick Loewe

For background and performance notes, see page 115.

Moderato ♩ = 88
C G7
I was
p
C G7 C
born un - der a wand' - - rin' star.
C Am
I was born un - der a wand' - - rin'

10
F
G7
F
star.
Wheels are made for roll - in',
Mules are made to pack.
I
mf
13
C
Em
C♯dim
Am7
D7
Dm7
G7
C
G7
nev - er seen a sight that didn't look bet - ter look - in' back.
I
was
16
C
G7
C
born
un - der a wand' - - rin'
star.
19
Em
Bm
Em
Mud can make you pris' - ner and the plains can make you dry.
Snow can burn your eyes but on - ly

22 Bm Dm Am
peo - ple make you cry. Home is made for com - in' from, for dreams of go - in' to
f
25 Dm Dm7 G7 C G7
Which, with an - y luck will never come true. I was
28 C G7 C
born un - der a wand' - - rin' star.
31 C Am
I was born un - der a wand' - - rin'

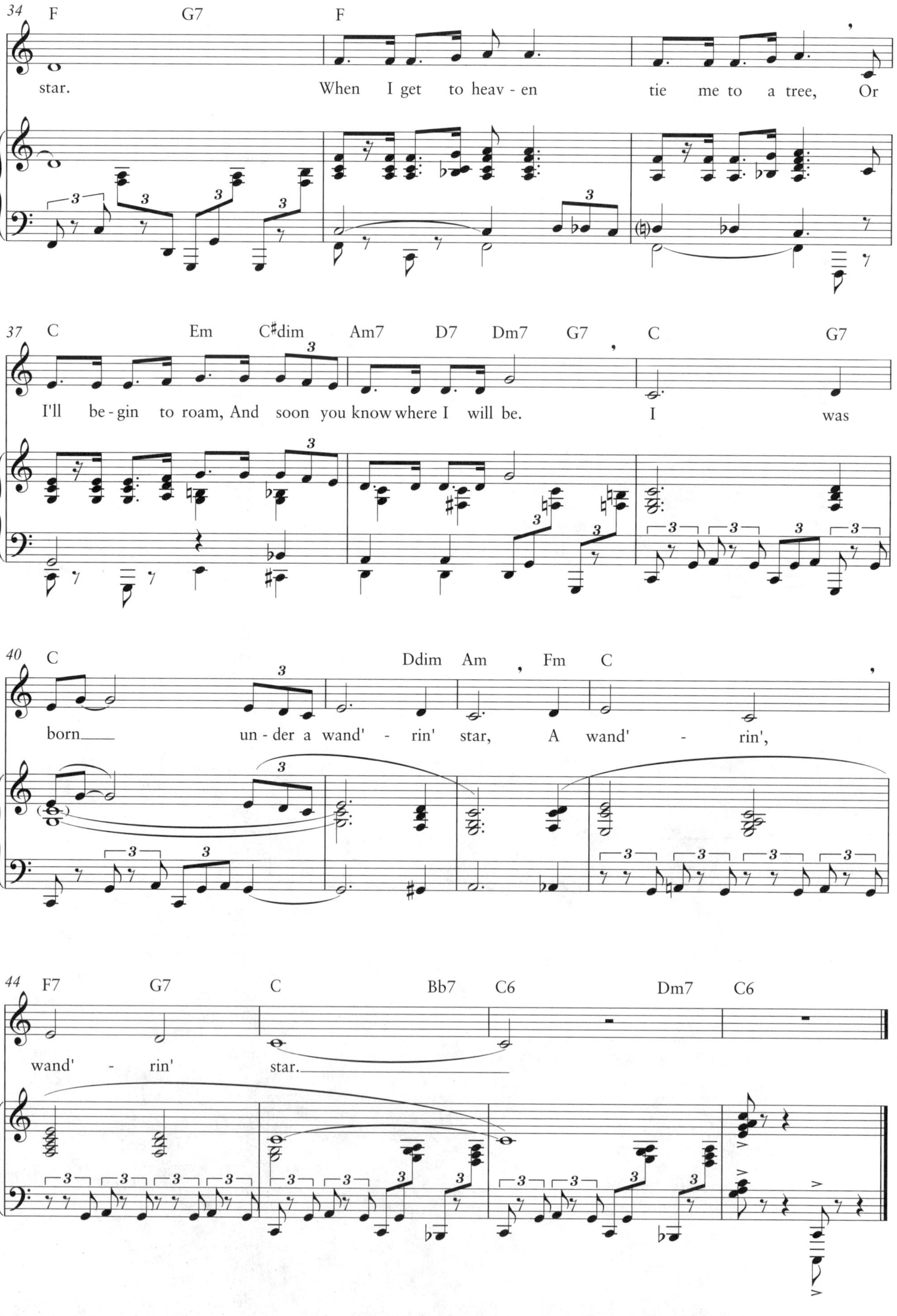
34
F G7 F
star. When I get to heav - en tie me to a tree, Or
37
C Em C♯dim Am7 D7 Dm7 G7 C G7
I'll be - gin to roam, And soon you know where I will be. I was
40
C Ddim Am Fm C
born un - der a wand' - rin' star, A wand' - rin',
44
F7 G7 C Bb7 C6 Dm7 C6
wand' - rin' star.

Goodnight, My Someone

from *The Music Man*

Lyrics and Music by
Meredith Willson

For background and performance notes, see page 115.

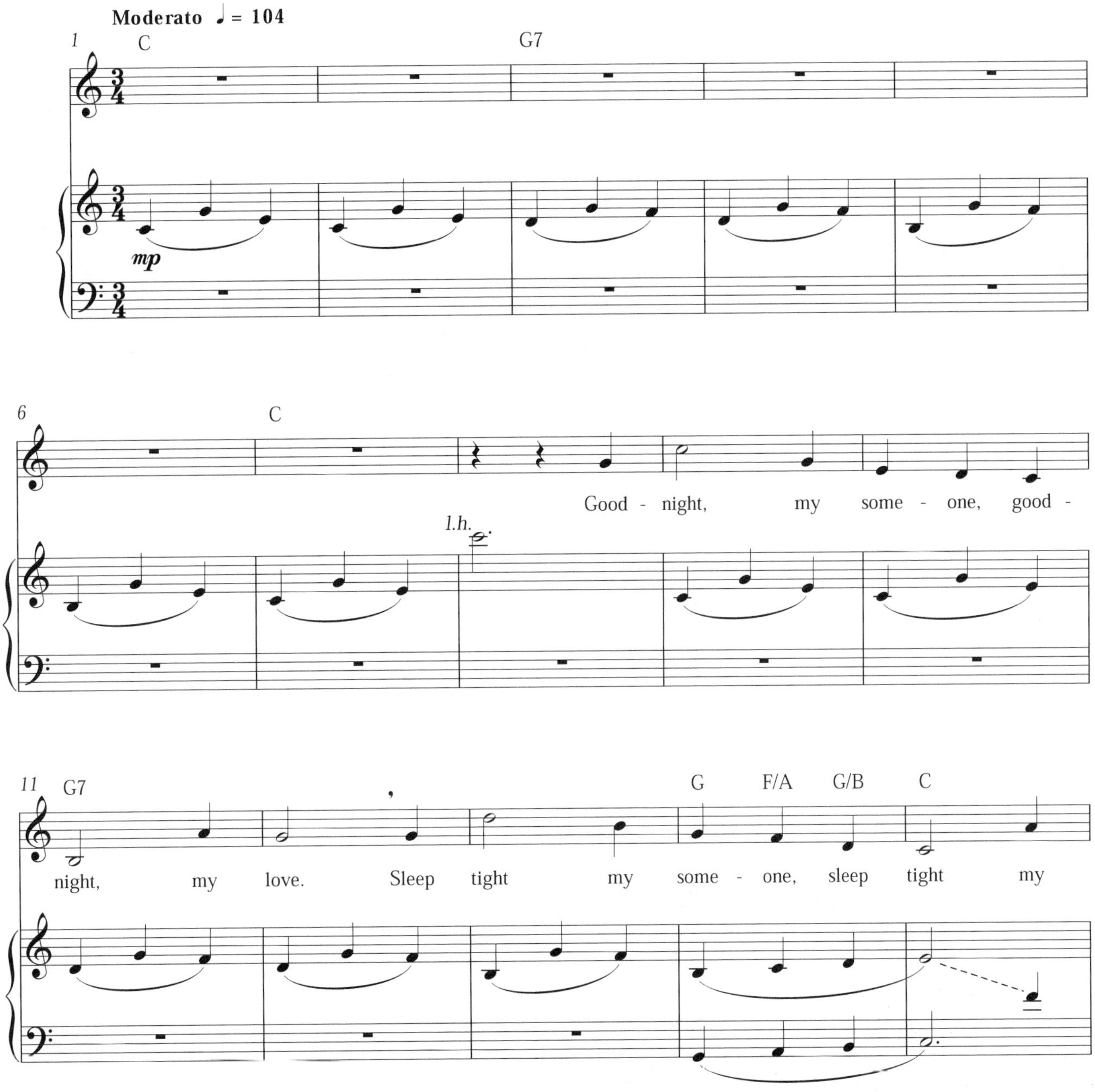
Moderato ♩ = 104
C
G7
mp
C
l.h.
Good - night, my some - one, good -
G7
night, my love. Sleep tight my some - one, sleep tight my
G
F/A
G/B
C

Freely
16 Am7/E F/D G Am/C Gm7/C C7 B♭/F F E♭7(♯11) D7
love. Our star is shin - ing its bright - est light for good-
p
21 Gdim G D7 Gsus4 G G7 C
night, my love, for good - night. Sweet dreams be
26 C6 G7/F Adim/E♭ G/D G7/D A7/C♯ G7/D G F/G G7
yours, dear, if dreams there be; Sweet dreams to car - ry you
l.h.
31 C Am/C C G6 G6/B Am7 C7 C7(♯11) C7/G F F6
close to me. I wish they may, and I wish they

36 D7/F♯ Em/G F/G G7(♭9) C Dmaj/C Ddim/C C7
might. Now good - night, my some - one, good - night. True
8va
l.h.
41 F E/F F F♯aug F♯dim Gm7 D♯dim/G C7 Cdim C7 D/C C7
love can be whis - pered from heart to heart, when lov - ers are
46 C7aug F F E/F F F6 F F♯dim
part - ed they say. But I must de - pend on a
8va
l.h.
51 C/G poco rit. Am/G C G/D D G/D G D7/F♯ G F/G G7
wish and a star, as long as my heart does - n't know who you are. Sweet
poco rit.

Tempo I
57
C G7/F E♭dim G7/D A7/C♯ G7/D G7
dreams be yours, dear, if dreams there be. Sweet dreams to
pp
62
G F/A G/B Cdim C G Dm7 G7 Cmaj7 C7
car - ry you close to me. I wish they may, and I
67
F F♯dim G G7(♭9) C
ten.
wish they might. Now good-night, my some - one, good - night
ten.
ten.
colla parte
ten.
72
Cdim C/G G7 C
Good - night. Good - night.
l.h.
pp

No Other Love

from *Me and Juliet*

Lyrics by Oscar Hammerstein II

Music by Richard Rodgers

For background and performance notes, see page 116.

Tempo di Tango 𝅗𝅥 = 54
G C/G G C/G G C/D G/D G
No oth - er love have I
p espress.
G C/D G/D F♯ Am/C Em7 Am A/C♯
On - ly my love for you, On - ly the dream we knew
A♭7(♯11) D7 Gmaj7 G C/D G/D G C/D G/D
No oth - er love. Watch - ing the night go by,
pp

13
G C/D G/D F♯ Am/C Em7 Am
Wish - ing that you could be Watch - ing the night with me,
16
A/C♯ A♭7(♯11) D7 G
In - to the night I cry: Hur - ry home, come
19
F/A F/C F C7/G C7 D/F♯ D/A D
home to me! Set me
22
A/E A7 B/D♯ B/F♯ B E E/G♯
free, Free from doubt And

25
A7
D7
G
C/D
G/D
free from long - ing. In - to your arms I'll fly.
mf
28
G
G
C/D
G/D
F♯
Locked in your arms I'll stay,
31
Am/C
Em7
Am
A/C♯
A♭7(♯11)
D7
Wait - ing to hear you say: No oth - er love have
34
G
rit.
C
C/A
G
I, No oth - er love.
rit.
cresc.
sf

I Got the Sun in the Morning

from *Annie Get Your Gun*

Lyrics and Music by
Irving Berlin

For background and performance notes, see page 116.

Light bounce ♩ = 130
Swing
C9/B♭ C9 C6/9 Gm7
mf
C9 F6 E♭6
Tak - ing stock of what I have and what I
F6 C9 C9(♯5) F Dm7
have - n't, what do I find? The things I've got will

10
G7 C7 F6 Gm7 F6
keep me sat - is - fied.
13
A♭6 G♭6 A♭6
Check - ing up on what I have and what I have - n't,
16
Adim C/G A7 Dm7 G7 C7
what do I find? A health - y bal - ance on the cred - it side.
19
C7
Medium jump tempo
C7(♭5)/G♭ F6
Got no dia - mond,

22
C7(♭5)/G♭ F6 C7(♭5)/G♭ F6 F7
got no pearl, still I think I'm a luck - y girl. I got the
25
B♭ F/A Gm7 F6 B♭ F
sun in the morn - ing and the moon at night.
28
Gm7 F6 C7(♭5)/G♭ F6 C7(♭5)/G♭ F6
Got no man - sion, got no yacht,
31
C7(♭5)/G♭ F6 F7 B♭ F/A
still I'm hap - py with what I've got. I got the sun in the morn - ing and the

34
Gm7 F6 B♭ F Gm7 F6
moon at night.
37
A7 D7sus
Sun - shine gives me a love - ly day.
40
D9 G7 B♭maj7/C
Moon - light gives me the milk-
43
C9 C7(♭5)/G♭ F6
- y way.
Got no check - books,

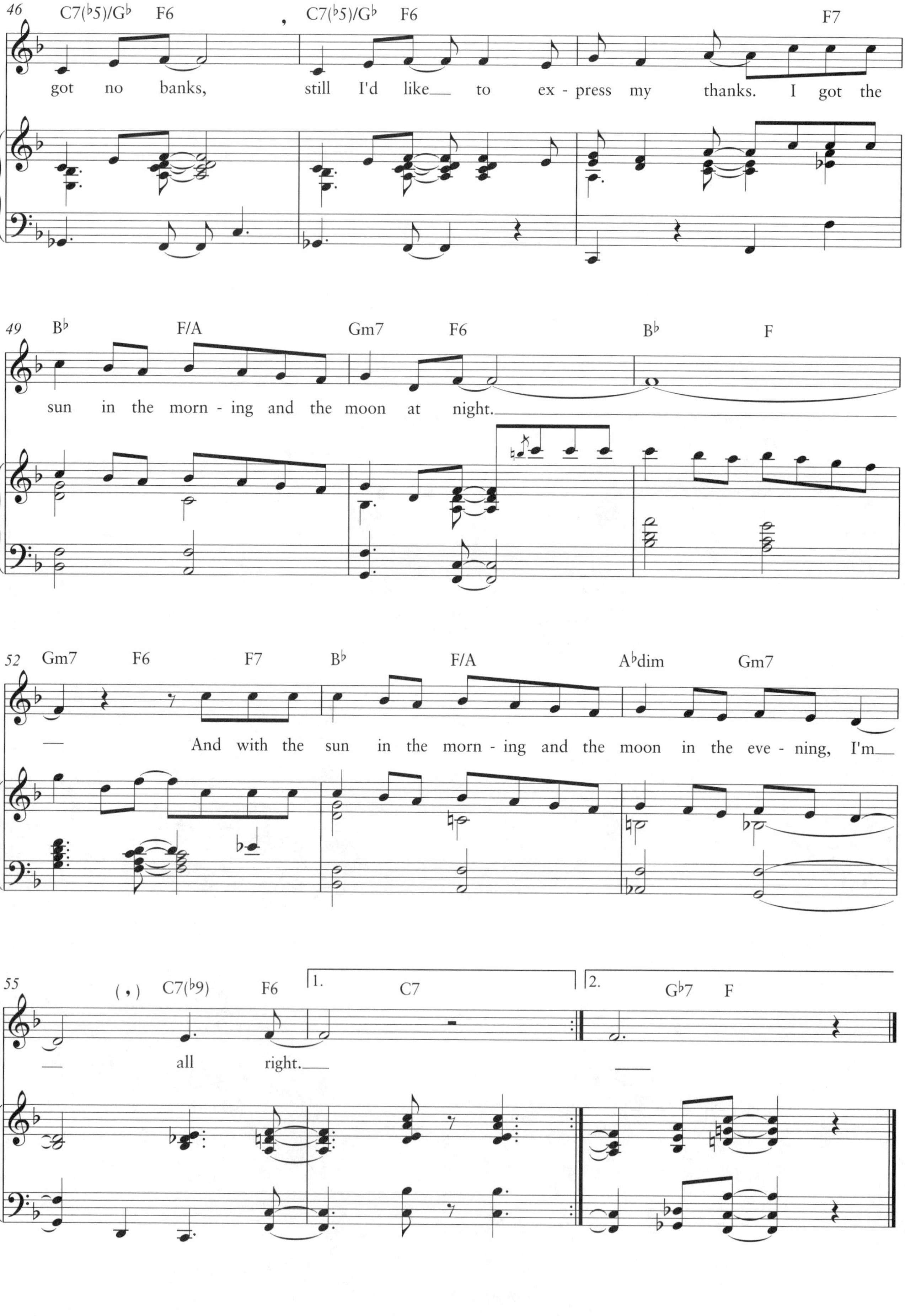
46
C7(♭5)/G♭ F6 C7(♭5)/G♭ F6 F7
got no banks, still I'd like to ex - press my thanks. I got the
49
B♭ F/A Gm7 F6 B♭ F
sun in the morn - ing and the moon at night.
52
Gm7 F6 F7 B♭ F/A A♭dim Gm7
And with the sun in the morn - ing and the moon in the eve - ning, I'm
55
C7(♭9) F6 1. C7 2. G♭7 F
all right.

Where Is Love?

FROM *Oliver!*

Lyrics and Music by
Lionel Bart

For background and performance notes, see page 116.

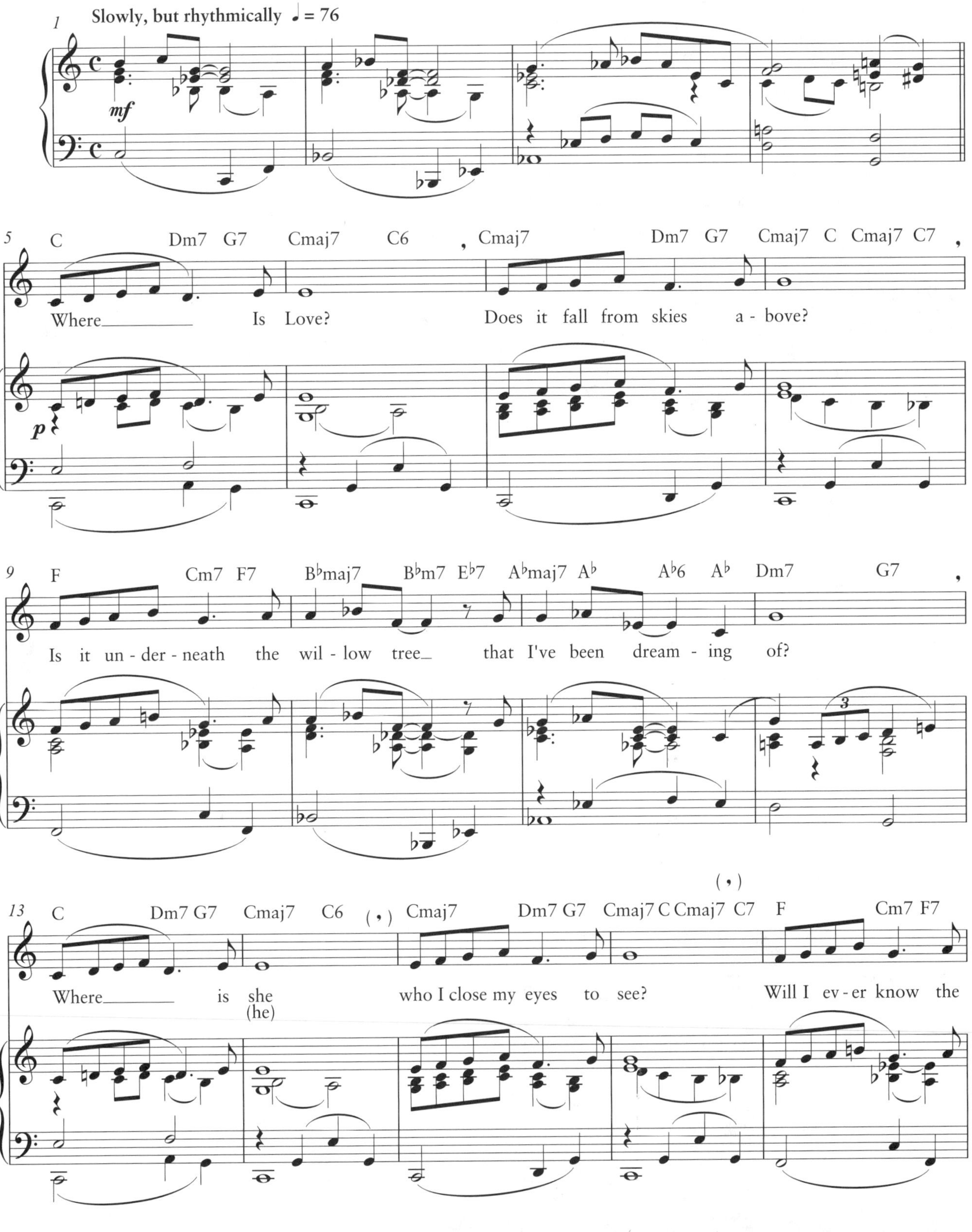
Slowly, but rhythmically ♩ = 76
mf
C Dm7 G7 Cmaj7 C6 Cmaj7 Dm7 G7 Cmaj7 C Cmaj7 C7
Where Is Love? Does it fall from skies a - bove?
p
F Cm7 F7 B♭maj7 B♭m7 E♭7 A♭maj7 A♭ A♭6 A♭ Dm7 G7
Is it un - der - neath the wil - low tree that I've been dream - ing of?
C Dm7 G7 Cmaj7 C6 Cmaj7 Dm7 G7 Cmaj7 C Cmaj7 C7 F Cm7 F7
Where is she (he) who I close my eyes to see? Will I ev - er know the

18 B♭maj7 B♭m7 E♭7 A♭maj7 A♭ A♭6 A♭ Dm7 G7 C Dm7 G7
sweet "hel - lo"_ that's meant for on - ly me? Who can say where she may
(he)
Ev - 'ry night I kneel and
22 Cmaj7 C Cmaj7 C7 F G7 C C♯dim Dm7 G7
hide? Must I trav - el far and wide Till I am be - side the
pray, Let to - mor - row be the day When I see the face of
26 Cmaj7 Cm7 F9 B♭maj7 B♭6 Amaj7 A7(♭9) Dm7 Am
some - one who_ I can mean some - thing to?_ Where,
30 Dm7 G7(♭9) 1. C Am Dm7 G7 2. C F6 Fdim Cmaj7 C6
Where Is Love? Love?
rit.

Over the Rainbow

from *The Wizard of Oz*

(High Key)

Lyrics by
E. Y. Harburg

Music by
Harold Arlen

For background and performance notes, see page 116.

Moderately (not fast)
E♭ Fm7/E♭ E♭6 B♭/E♭ A♭/E♭ B♭7/E♭ A♭ E♭
ten.
mf
E♭ A♭/E♭ E♭maj7 Fm7 B♭7
When all the world is a hope - less jum - ble and the rain - drops tum - ble all a - round,
E♭ Edim7 Fm7 B♭7(♭9) E♭
heav - en o - pens a mag - ic lane.
l.h.
E♭ A♭/E♭ E♭maj7 Dm7 G7
When all the clouds dark - en up the sky - way, there's a rain - bow high - way to be found.

17
Cm A♭7 F9 Fm7/B♭ E♭/B♭
lead - ing from your win - dow - pane to a place be - hind the
cresc.
21
Fm7/B♭ E♭/B♭ Fm7/B♭ B♭7
sun. just a step be - yond the rain.
Chorus
♩ = 84
25
E♭ Gm E♭7 A♭ Gm7
Some - where o - ver the rain - bow way up high,
p - mf
29
A♭6 A♭m6 E♭/B♭ C7(♭9) F7 Eb
there's a land that I heard of once in a lull - a - by.

33
E♭ Gm E♭7 A♭ Gm7
Some - where o - ver the rain - bow skies are blue,
37
A♭6 A♭m6 E♭/B♭ C7(♭9) F7 E♭
and the dreams that you dare to dream real - ly do come true. Some
41
E♭ Fm7/B♭ B♭7/E♭ E♭6
day I'll wish up - on a star and wake - up where the clouds are far be - hind me, where
45
E♭ E♭6 E♭ F♯dim7 Fm6 B♭9(♯5)
trou - bles melt like lem - on drops, a - way, a - bove the chim - ney tops that's where you'll find me,

49
E♭ Gm E♭7 A♭ A♭maj7 A♭7 Gm7 Edim7 A♭6 A♭m6
Some - where o - ver the rain - bow blue - birds fly. Birds fly
54
E♭/B♭ C7(♭9) F7 Fm7/B♭ B♭7 E♭ B♭9 B♭7(♭9) E♭ B♭7(♭9)
1. 2.
o - ver the rain - bow, why then, oh why can't I? I?
rall.
58
A♭/E♭ E♭6 Fm7 B♭7/F
If
62
rit.
E♭ Fm7 B♭7 E♭6
hap - py lit - tle blue - birds fly be - yond the rain - bow, why oh why can't I?
dim.
pp
l.h.
ten.

Over the Rainbow

FROM *The Wizard of Oz*

(LOW KEY)

Lyrics by
E. Y. Harburg

Music by
Harold Arlen

For background and performance notes, see page 116.

Moderately (not fast)
1 C Dm7/C C6 G/C F F/C C G7/C ten.
mf
5 C F/C (,) Cmaj7 Dm7 G7 ,
When all the world is a hope - less jum - ble and the rain - drops tum - ble all a - round,
9 C C♯dim7 Dm7 G7(♭9) C
3
heav - en o - pens a mag - ic lane.
l.h.
13 C F/C (,) Cmaj7 Bm7 E7 ,
When all the clouds dark - en up the sky - way, there's a rain - bow high - way to be found.

17 Am F7 D9 Dm7/G C/G
lead - ing from your win - dow - pane to a place be - hind the
cresc.
21 Dm7/G C/G Dm7/G G7
sun. just a step be - yond the rain.
Chorus
♩ = 84
25 C Em C7 F Em7
Some - where o - ver the rain - bow way up high,
p - mf
29 F6 Fm6 C/G A7(♭9) D7 C
there's a land that I heard of once in a lull - a - by.

33
C Em C7 (,) F Em7
Some - where o - ver the rain - bow skies are blue,
37
F6 Fm6 C/G A7(♭9) D7 C
and the dreams that you dare to dream real - ly do come true. Some
41
C Dm7/G G7/C C6
day I'll wish up - on a star and wake - up where the clouds are far be - hind me, where
45
C C6 C D♯dim7 Dm6 G9(♯5)
trou - bles melt like lem - on drops, a - way, a - bove the chim - ney tops that's where you'll find me,

49
C Em C7 (•) F Fmaj7 F7 Em7 C♯dim7 F6 Fm6
Some - where o - ver the rain - bow blue - birds fly. Birds fly
54
C/G A7(♭9) D7 Dm7/G G7 C G9 G7(♭9) C G7(♭9)
1. 2.
o - ver the rain - bow, why then, oh why can't I? I?
rall.
58
F/C C6 Dm7 G7/D
If
rit.
62
C Dm7 G7 C6
hap - py lit - tle blue - birds fly be - yond the rain - bow, why oh why can't I?
dim.
pp
l.h.
ten.

Sing!

from *Sesame Street*

Lyrics and Music
Joe Raposo

For background and performance notes, see page 116.

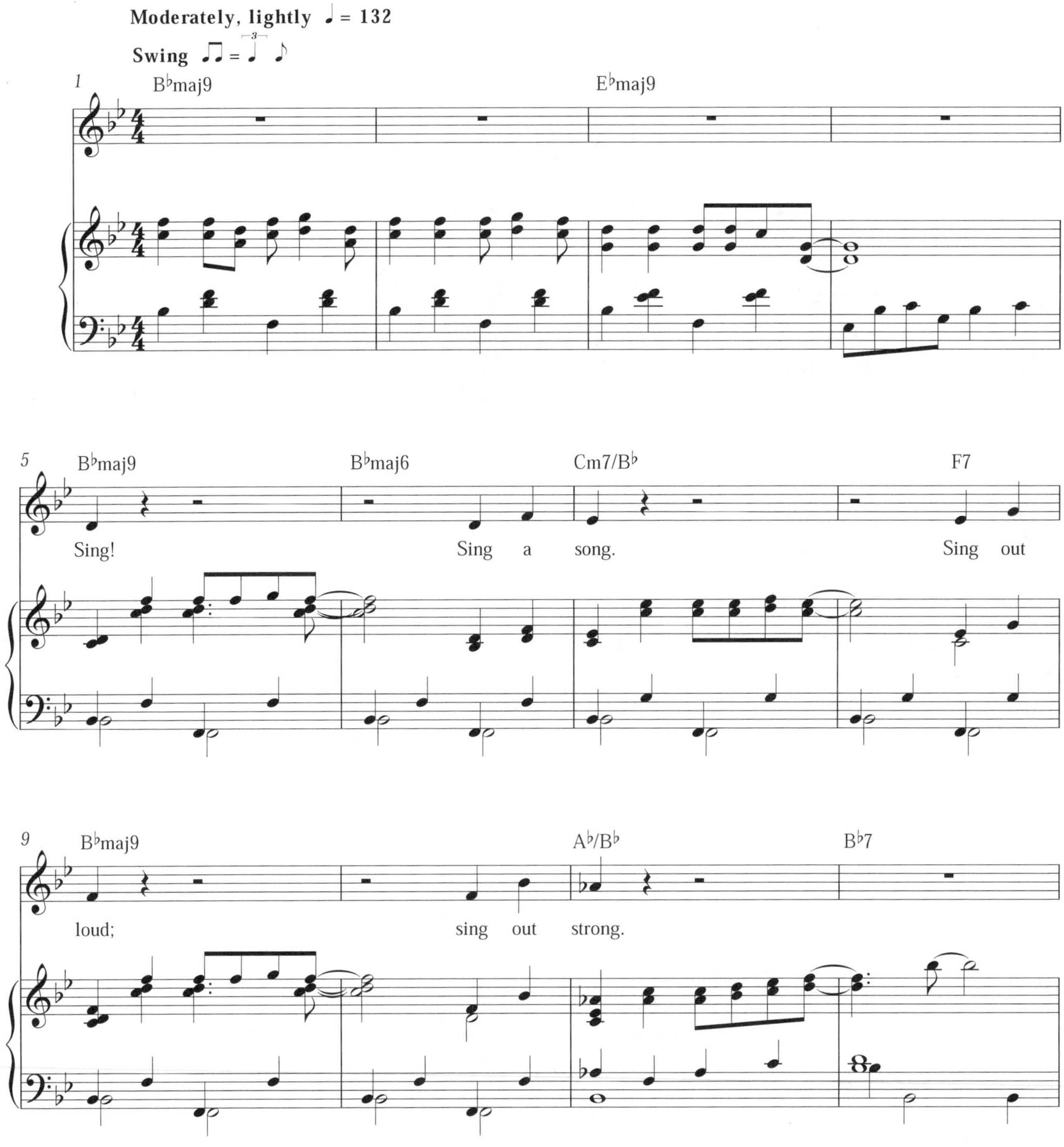
Moderately, lightly ♩ = 132
Swing
B♭maj9
E♭maj9
B♭maj9
B♭maj6
Cm7/B♭
F7
Sing! Sing a song. Sing out
B♭maj9
A♭/B♭
B♭7
loud; sing out strong.

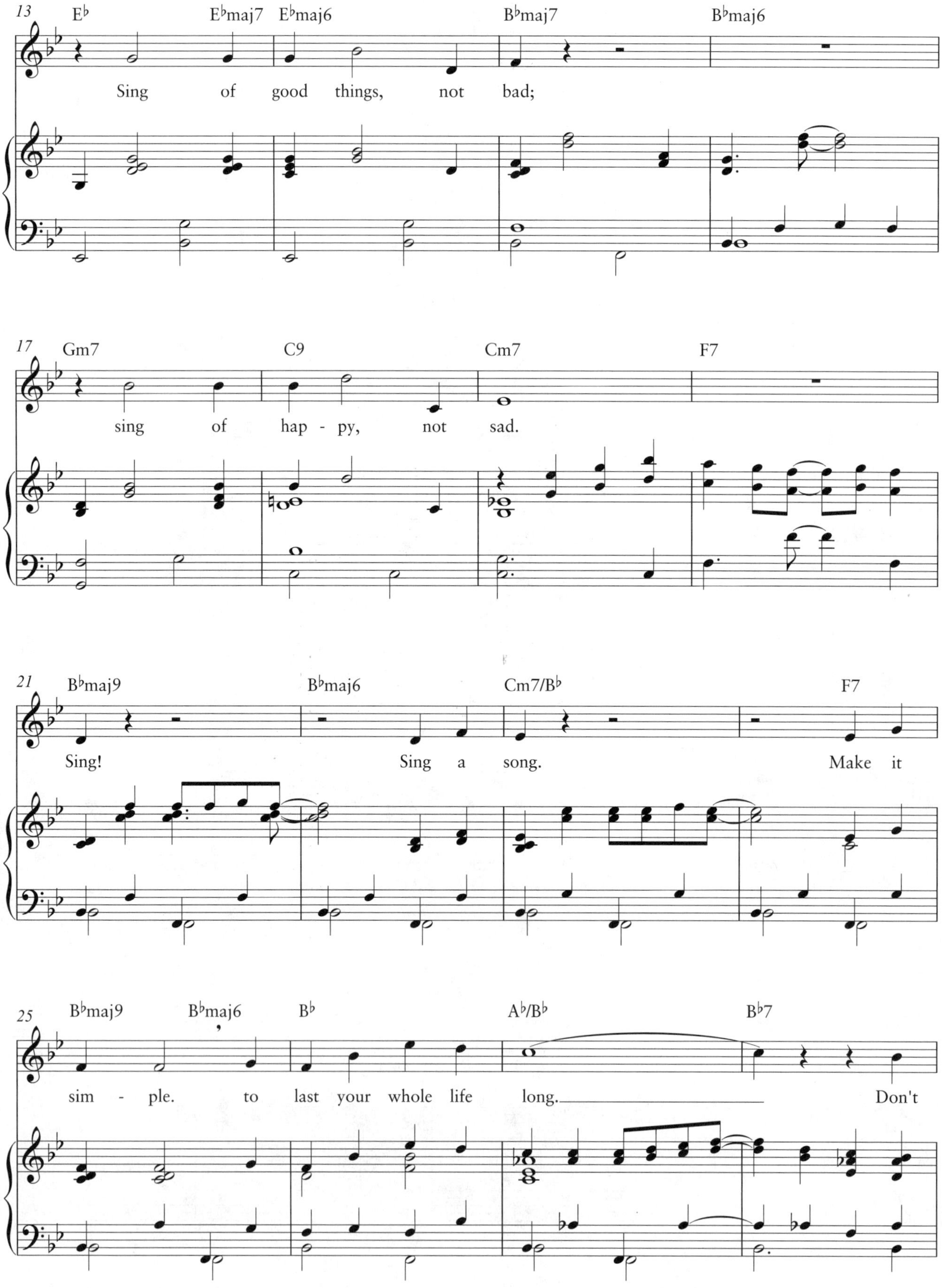
13
E♭ E♭maj7 E♭maj6 B♭maj7 B♭maj6
Sing of good things, not bad;
17
Gm7 C9 Cm7 F7
sing of hap - py, not sad.
21
B♭maj9 B♭maj6 Cm7/B♭ F7
Sing! Sing a song. Make it
25
B♭maj9 B♭maj6 B♭ A♭/B♭ B♭7
sim - ple. to last your whole life long.
Don't

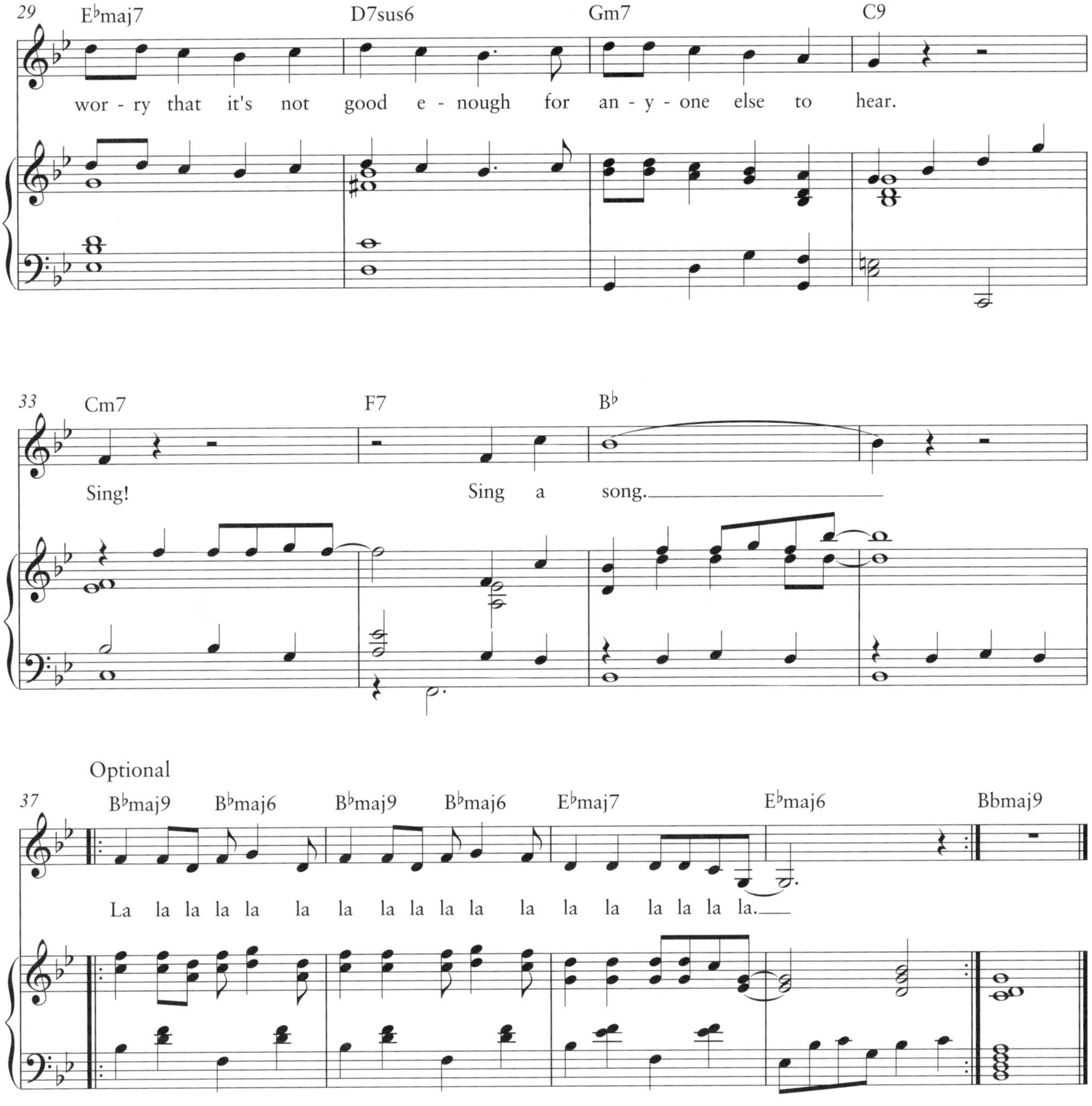
29
E♭maj7
D7sus6
Gm7
C9
wor - ry that it's not good e - nough for an - y - one else to hear.
33
Cm7
F7
B♭
Sing! Sing a song.
Optional
37
B♭maj9
B♭maj6
B♭maj9
B♭maj6
E♭maj7
E♭maj6
Bbmaj9
La la la la la la la la la la la la la la la la la.

Somewhere Out There

FROM *An American Tail*

(Optional Duet)

Lyrics by
James Ingram

Music by
James Horner, Barry Mann,
and Cynthia Weil

For background and performance notes, see page 116.

Moderately, with expression ♩ = 84
C Cmaj7/E C/F G7sus C C/E F(add9)
mp
Ped.
Dm G/F Em7 Am7 F G
C(add9) Cmaj7/E C/F F/G C(add9) C/E
Voice 1
Some - where out there be - neath the pale moon -
mf

12 F Dm7 G/F Em Am Dm7
light some - one's think - in' of me and
15 Dm7 C/E F Gsus G C(add9) Cma7/E
Voice 2
lov - ing me to - night. Some - where out
18 C/F F/G C(add9) C/E F
there some - one's say - ing a prayer that
21 Dm7 G/F Cm7 Am Dm7 C/E F/G
we'll find one a - noth - er in that big some - where out

24
C
Both
F
G/F
F
G/F
there. And e - ven though I know how ve - ry far a - part we are it
27
Fmaj7
G/F
F
G/F
Voice 2
helps to think we might be wish - in' on the same bright star. And
29
A♭
B♭/A♭
A♭
B♭/A♭
Voice 1
when the night - wind starts to sing a lone - some lul - la - by it
31
A♭
B♭/A♭
poco rit.
G
a tempo
helps to think we're sleep - ing un - der - neath the same big sky.
poco rit.
a tempo

34
C Cmaj7/E Fmaj9 F/G C C/E F
Both
(Melody)
Some - where out there if love can see us through,
Dm
38 through)
G/F Em7 Am F G
3
poco rit.
then we'll be to - geth - er some - where out there, out where dreams come
Ped.
42 C Cmaj7/E C/F G7sus C(add9)
true.
a tempo

A Time for Us

from *Romeo and Juliet*

Lyrics by
Larry Kusik and Eddie Snyder

Music by
Nino Rota

For background and performance notes, see page 117.

Slowly and very expressively ♩ = 80
1
Dm
A time for us some day there'll
mf dim.
p mp
6
E♭ Cm Dm B♭ Cm Gm Dm
be when chains are torn by cour - age born of a love that's free. A time when dreams so long de -
11
E♭ Cm Dm Gm Dm Gm
nied can flour - ish as we un - veil the love we now must hide. A
dim.
mf

17 B♭ F Cm Gm A♭
time for us at last to see a life worth
f dim. poco
22 E♭ Dm Gm Dm E♭
while for you and me. And with our love through tears and thorns we will en-
mp
27 Dm B♭ Cm Gm Dm E♭
dure as we pass sure - ly through ev' - ry storm. A time for us some day there'll be a
1. 2.
32 Cm Dm Gm Dm Gm Gm
new world. a world of shin - ing hope for you and me. A time for me.
dim.
rall.
p

Popular and Jazz Standards

Jazz, blues, pop, and standards are all variations of popular or nonclassical styles of music. They are not so easily differentiated because there is a lot of crossover between the genres. However, here is a nutshell summary of each.

Jazz, according to the late great Louis Armstrong, "is music that's never played the same way once." While there is no strict definition of jazz, this homegrown twentieth-century American music form has two key elements: improvisation and swing rhythm. Swing can be loosely defined as anything that propels the music forward: accents, free rhythm, and especially uneven short notes instead of "straight" eighth notes.

Jazz originated in New Orleans in 1917 and quickly spread to Chicago, New York, Memphis, and Kansas City. Its popularity transcends race, region, country, gender, and generations. Some important jazz musicians include Louis Armstrong, Duke Ellington, the Dorsey brothers, Benny Goodman, Billie Holiday, Charlie Parker, Miles Davis, Count Basie, John Coltrane, Ornette Coleman, and Wynton Marsalis.

Blues refers generally to music in a melancholy state. Originally, blues was a black American folk song tradition that influenced jazz and twentieth-century music. "Blues notes" (flatted 3rd, 5th, 7th notes in a major scale that give it a melancholy mood), pitch bending, and improvisation are all part of the style. A contemporary offshoot of the blues is rhythm and blues, or R&B.

Famous blues singers include Charley Patton, Lightnin' Hopkins, Mamie Smith, Ma Rainey, B. B. King, and, more recently Nina Simone. Jazz great Duke Ellington wrote many instrumental and vocal blues.

Pop songs are usually contemporary favorites, are commercially successful, climb the Top 40 pop charts, and dominate the radio airwaves. The global interest in pop music has never been greater, as evidenced by the popularity of television shows like "American Idol." Today's pop stars and vocal groups typically have a very short shelf life. Does anyone remember Milli Vanilli, Hanson, and The Spice Girls?

Popular singers and pop groups occasionally transcend their time. Songs by Elvis Presley and the Beatles are among the best examples of timeless pop standards. The Beatles were the most popular and successful rock group in history ever, selling more recordings than any other band. Their original songs, written by Paul McCartney and John Lennon in the 1960s, ranged from sweet love ballads to edgy songs of rebellion.

Standards, or jazz standards as they are often called, can be loosely defined as songs that were popular from 1920 to about 1955. These include songs made famous by singers like Frank Sinatra, Rosemary Clooney, Bing Crosby, Tony Bennett, Sarah Vaughan, Ella Fitzgerald, and Mel Torme. Composers include Cole Porter, Hoagy Carmichael, Irving Berlin, and George Gershwin.

Music of this bygone era is surprisingly popular on today's college campuses. Part of the popular appeal is freedom of personal expression—the songs don't have to be sung exactly the same each time. Use the standards in the *The Singing Book* collection to experiment with your own improvisation. Keep the lyrics and tune relatively intact while making changes with rhythm, dynamics, and tempo. This is a more conservative type of improvisation than jazz. If you have any recordings of this music, compare the sung version to the actual written music and you will find many small differences. The tune and rhythm are only guidelines for some artists.

Blue Skies, from *Betsy* (p. 161)

When the stock market crashed in 1929, the most popular song in America was Irving Berlin's optimistic "Blue Skies." Countless singers have covered this song—or recorded it after its introduction—including Lyle Lovett, the Chanticleer vocal ensemble, and the android Data in the 2002 film, *Star Trek: Nemesis.*

Irving Berlin (born Israel Baline in Russia) immigrated to United States with his family in 1893 and became one of America's great composers. Many of his 1,500 songs, including some written for film and stage, have become standards. Though "Blue Skies" stands on it own, it was interpolated first into a little-known Rogers and Hart musical, *Betsy,* in 1926. In 1946 Berlin borrowed his own song and title for the movie musical *Blue Skies* with Bing Crosby and Fred Astaire.

When I Fall in Love (p. 163)

This song was used in the sound track of the 1993 romantic film *Sleepless in Seattle.* Critics and audiences loved the original and cover versions of the lush ballads and swing standards in this film. It is worth renting the video for the sound track alone. Celine Dion and Clive Griffin's duet version of Victor Young's "When I Fall in Love" rivals earlier recordings by Nat King Cole, Doris Day, and Lena Horne.

Composer Victor Young was a conservatory-trained musician who began his career as a classical composer and concert violinist. In the 1920s, however, he turned to popular and film music. Young wrote hundreds of award-winning film scores and songs as chief composer and arranger for Hollywood's Paramount Pictures Studios, until his untimely death at age 56.

They Can't Take That Away from Me, from *Shall We Dance?* (p. 165)

It is hard to pin down a character for this popular song since it appeared in two movies and a stage show, and resides in the collective consciousness of the country. It serves as a "break-up" song for anyone who has ever been dumped in a romantic relationship and chooses to dwell on the good memories.

The song first appeared in the 1937 Fred Astaire/Ginger Rodgers movie classic *Shall We Dance?* and later in the 1949 MGM film *The Barkleys of Broadway.* It was also featured in the 1994 "new" Gershwin Broadway hit *Crazy for You* that Ken Ludwig loosely adapted from Gershwin's 1920s stage musical *Girl Crazy.* This enduring standard by George and Ira Gershwin has been performed by Frank Sinatra, Ella Fitzgerald, Peggy Lee, Fred Astaire, Rosemary Clooney, Bobby Short, and more recently, Michael Feinstein and Diana Krall. You can't take this song away from America!

Skylark (p. 169)

Many nostalgic and love songs use bird imagery. Larks, bluebirds, whippoorwills, doves, and skylarks carry love's message on their wings (see Mendelssohn, p. 201). "Skylark" was a very lucky bird for songwriter Hoagy Carmichael. It was one of his many popular songs that topped the Hit Parade in the 1940s.

When Carmichael was still relatively unknown, his earlier songs like "Lazy River" and "Georgia on My Mind" were already being recorded by Duke Ellington, Louis Armstrong, and others. In 1936 Carmichael headed for Hollywood, where he teamed with lyricists like Johnny Mercer and Frank Loesser to write and sing songs like "Skylark," "Stardust," and "Heart and Soul." He quickly became a star on stage, screen, and recordings. Audiences liked the Indiana-born composer's folksy "down-home" charm, much the way modern audiences are drawn to Garrison Keillor and *Prairie Home Companion.*

Night and Day, from *Anything Goes* (p. 172)

"Night and Day" is a torch song about steamy love and longing. Picture yourself leaning seductively against a candle-lit grand piano, microphone (or martini) in hand, and you've got the idea. "Night and Day" is one of the nearly 1,000 popular songs that Cole Porter wrote.

Originally composed for the 1932 stage musical *The Gay Divorcee,* it is also the title of a fictionalized 1964 movie biography with Cary Grant portraying the famous composer.

Porter was influenced by the years he spent writing songs and complete musicals to his own lyrics at Yale University and during the years he spent in wartorn Paris. He credited some of his musical success to his teacher Dr. Abercrombie of Worcester Academy, who advised the young Cole Porter, "Words and music must be so inseparably wedded to each other that they are like one."

God Bless' the Child (p. 175)

You might call this a blues song, a swing spiritual, or even a torch song. Depending on the mood of the singer at a given moment, any of these descriptions could apply. Jazz singer and composer Billie Holiday claimed that she couldn't stand to sing the same song the same way two nights in succession. "If you copy, it means you're working without any real feeling." Billie freely changed the beat, the melody, and the tempo when she performed. She "bent" the pitch (sang between notes), added harmonies, and often sang the text purposely late, a little behind the beat. She is credited with changing popular music by creating a song style that was highly personal, deeply emotional, and constantly changing.

Billie Holiday (born Eleonore Fagan) sang about what she knew—a life marked by abuse, poverty, and depression. She died in 1959 at the age of 44 of alcohol and drug abuse. However, at the height of her singing career in the 1930s and 1940s she sang with all the great American bands: Count Basie, Artie Shaw, Benny Goodman, and Louis Armstrong. She appeared on the stages of the finest nightclubs and even sang at Carnegie Hall. One of her best-known songs, "God Bless' the Child," is taken from a biblical proverb "God blesses the child who has his own." It is a song of longing for financial freedom and individual strength. "God Bless' the Child" has been covered by many singers, including Whitney Houston, Stevie Wonder, Blood Sweat & Tears, Diane Schuur, and Rosemary Clooney.

Blue Skies

FROM *Betsy*

Lyrics and Music by
Irving Berlin

For background and performance notes, see page 159.

Moderate swing ♩ = 80
Swing
F Csus C7 F Dm
Blue skies
mf
A(♯5) F Bm7(♭5) G E♭(♯5) F B♭9 C7 F
smil - ing at me, noth - ing but blue skies do I see.
F Dm A(♯5) A7 F
Blue - birds sing - ing a song.

16
Bm7(♭5) G Eb(♯5) F B♭9 C7 F
(even)
noth - ing but blue - birds all day long.
21
B♭m F B♭m F B♭m F
Nev - er saw the sun shin - ing so bright, nev - er saw things go - ing so right. No - tic - ing the days
26
B♭m F B♭m F C7 F A7 D A(♯5) A
Swing
hur - ry - ing by; when you're in love, my how they fly. Blue days, all of them
31
F Bm7(♭5) G Eb(♯5) F B♭9 C7 F
gone, noth - ing but blue skies from now on.

When I Fall in Love

Lyrics by
Edward Heyman

Music by
Victor Young

For background and performance notes, see page 159.

Slowly, with much feeling ♩ = 82
mf
E♭
When I fall in love it will be for - ev - er, or I'll nev - er fall in love.
B♭7 E♭ C7(♯5) C7 Fm7
A♭dim E♭/G A♭dim E♭/G B♭m/D♭ C7
In a rest - less world like this is, love is end - ed be - fore it's be - gun, and too

17
Fm7 C7(♭9) Fm Fm7 B♭/D B♭7 E♭
man - y moon - light kiss - es seem to cool in the warmth of the sun. When I give my
22
B♭7 E♭ C7(♯5) C7 Fm
heart it will be com - plete - ly, or I'll nev - er give my heart;
28
A♭dim E♭/G A♭ C7 Fm A♭m6 E♭/B♭
And the mo - ment I can feel that you feel that way too is when I fall in
34
Fm7 B♭7 E♭ G♭dim Fm7 B♭7(♭9) E♭ A♭9 C♭9 E♭
love with you. you.

They Can't Take That Away from Me

from *Shall We Dance?*

Lyrics and Music by
George Gershwin
and Ira Gershwin

For background and performance notes, see page 159.

Moderately ♩ = 84
p
rit.
E♭ C7 Fm7 B♭7 E♭6 B7 B♭7
Our ro - mance won't end on a sor - row - ful note, Though by to - mor - row you're
mp a tempo
E♭ A♭maj7 E♭ C7 Fm B♭7 E♭
gone; The song is end - ed, but as the song - writ - er wrote, The

13
Am7 D7 G6 Am7 D7 Gmaj7 G6 G
mel - o - dy ling - ers on. They may take you from me, I'll
17
Am7 D7 Gm A♭ A♭(♯5) Edim7 Fm B♭/D Edim7
miss your fond ca - ress. But though they take you from me, I'll still pos -
Refrain (non fast)
Swing
21
F7/C B7(♭5) B♭7 A♭ B♭11 E♭6 B♭6 E♭ G♭dim7
ess: The way you wear your hat, The way you sip your tea,
poco marcato
slowly with warmth
mp - mf
25
B♭7sus4 B♭7 Fm7 B♭11 B♭m E♭ B♭7(♯5) Gm7(♭5) Cm D7(♭5) Gm7(♭5)
The mem'-ry of all that No, no! They
mf

29 A♭ Fm C9 F7 A♭ B♭11 E♭6 B♭6 E♭ G♭dim7
can't take that a-way from me! The way your smile just beams, The way you sing off key,
mp
33 B♭7sus4 B♭7 Fm7 B♭11 B♭m E♭ B♭7(♯5) Gm7(♭5) D7(♭5) Cm Gm7(♭5)
The way you haunt my dreams, No, no! They
mf
37 A♭ Fm B♭7 sus4 B♭7 E♭6 E♭ Gm C7 D7(♭5) Gm C7 D7(♭5)
can't take that a-way from me! We may nev-er, nev-er meet a-gain On the
con calore
41 Gm Em7(♭5) A7(♯5) A7sus4 D7 Gm C7 D7(♭5) Gm Gm7(♭5) C7
bump-y road to love, Still I'll al-ways, al-ways keep the mem'-ry

45
F7 F7(♭5) B♭7 A♭ A♭maj7 Fm7 E♭6 B♭6 E♭ G♭dim7
of The way you hold your knife, The way we danced till three.
mf f
49
B♭7sus4 B♭7 Fm7 B♭11 E♭9 D7(♭5) Gm7(♭5) D♭(add E♭) Cm E♭/D♭
The way you've changed my life. No, no! They
53
A♭ Fm B♭7sus4 B♭7 Cm Fm7(♭5) E♭ B♭11 E♭/B♭ E♭maj7/B♭ B♭11 B♭7
can't take that a - way from me! No! They can't take that a - way from
mp
57
1.
E♭ E♭maj7 B♭ E♭ B♭7 B♭11 B♭ 9 7
me! The way you wear your hat
mf
2.
E♭ E♭maj7 Cm7(♭5) B♭9(♭5) E♭ E♭6
me!
p pp

Skylark

Lyrics by
Johnny Mercer

Music by
Hoagy Carmichael

For background and performance notes, see page 159.

1
Moderato ♩ = 88
E♭6 B♭7
SKY - LARK,
mp cresc.
3
4
E♭ A♭ E♭ Gm A♭ E♭
Have you an - y - thing to say to me?
Won't you tell me where my
7
A♭ E♭ F7 B♭7 E♭ Cm Cm7
love can be?
Is there a mea - dow in the mist,
Where some - one's

10
A♭ Fm7 B♭7 E♭6 B♭7 E♭ A♭
wait - ing to be kissed? SKY - LARK, Have you seen a val - ley
13
E♭ Gm A♭ E♭ A♭ E♭
green with Spring, Where my heart can go on jour- ney - ing,
3
16
F7 B♭7 E♭ B♭7 E♭
3
O - ver the sha - dows and the rain, to a blos - som cov - ered lane? And in your
3
19
A♭ E♭6 Fm7 E7 E♭7 A♭(maj7) E♭dim A♭6 D♭7
3
lone - ly flight, Have - n't you heard the mu - sic in the night,
3

22
C7 Ddim C7 Fm Fm7 Fdim D♭ Fm E♭7 A♭7
— Won - der - ful mu - sic, Faint as a "will o' the wisp," Craz - y as a loon,
25
G A7 D7 G B♭7 E♭6 B♭7
Sad as a gyp - sy ser - e - nad - ing the moon. (Oh,) SKY - LARK,
28
E♭ A♭ E♭ Gm A♭ E♭ A♭ E♭
— I don't know if you can find these things, But my heart is rid - ing on your wings,
32
F7 B♭7 E♭ B♭7
1. E♭ B13 B♭13
2. E♭ E6 E♭6
— So, if you see them an - y where, Won't you lead me there? there?

Night and Day

from *Anything Goes*

Lyrics and Music by
Cole Porter

For background and performance notes, see page 160.

Moderately 𝅗𝅥 = 54
Swing
1
C D7 G7 A♭maj7 G7
Night and Day you are the
f mf p - mf
5
C A♭maj7 G7
one, On - ly you be - neath the moon and un - der the
9
C F♯dim Fm7
sun. Wheth - er near to me or far. It's no

13 Em7 E♭dim Dm11 G7
mat - ter, dar - ling, where you are I think of you Night and Day.
r.h.
17 C A♭maj7 G7 C
Day and night Why is it so,
22 A♭maj7 G7 C
That this long - ing for you fol - lows wher - ev - er I go? In the
27 F♯dim Fm7 Em7 E♭dim Dm11
roar - ing traf - fic's boom In the si - lence of my lone - ly room. I think of you.
r.h.

32 G7 C E♭ C
Night and Day. Night and Day under the hide of me
espr.
38 E♭ C
There's an Oh, such a hun-gry yearn-ing, burn-ing in-side of me. And its
43 F♯dim Fm7 Em7 D7 Dm7
tor-ment won't be through 'Til you let me spend my life mak-ing love to you, day and night.
48 G7 Dm7 C D7 G7 C
1. 2.
Night and Day. Night and Day
8vb

God Bless' the Child

Lyrics and Music by
Arthur Herzog, Jr.
and Billie Holiday

For background and performance notes, see page 160.

Slowly, with feeling, freely (♩ = 76)
Them that's
E♭maj7 E♭7 A♭6 (,) E♭maj7 E♭7 A♭6 , B♭m7 G♭7 E♭13 ,
got shall get, them that's not shall lose, So the Bi - ble said, and it
B♭m7 E9(♭5) E♭9 , A♭maj7 A♭6 , A♭m , Gm C7 C7(♭9)
still is news; Ma - ma may have, Pa - pa may have, but God Bless' the child that's

12
Fm9 B♭7 E♭6 Gm Cm Gm A♭6 Fm7 B♭7
got his own! That's got his own. Yes, the
p
15
E♭maj7 E♭7 A♭6 (,) E♭maj7 E♭7 A♭6 B♭m7 G♭7 E♭13
strong gets more, while the weak ones fade, Emp - ty pock - ets don't ev - er
mf - p
18
B♭m7 E9(♭5) E♭9 A♭maj7 A♭6 A♭m
make the grade; Ma - ma may have, Pa - pa may have, But
21
Gm C7 C7(♭9) Fm9 B♭7 E♭6
God Bless' the child that's got his own! That's got his own.
p
mp

24
A♭7 G7 Cm Cm(♯7) Cm7 Cm6 (,)
Mon - ey, you got lots o' friends,
27
Gm D7 G7 , Cm Cm(♯7)
crow - din' 'round the door, When you're gone and
mf
30
Cm7 Cm6 , Gm C7 B9(♭5) B♭9 Fm7 B♭
spend - in' ends, they don't come no more. Rich re -
p
33
E♭maj7 E♭7 A♭6 (,) E♭maj7 E♭7 A♭6 , B♭7 G♭7 E♭13 (,)
la - tions give, Crust of bread and such, You can help your - self, but don't

36
B♭m7 E9(♭5) E♭9 A♭maj7 A♭6 A♭m
take too much! Ma - ma may have, Pa - pa may have, But
39
Gm C7 C7(♭9) Fm7 B♭7 E♭6
1.
God Bless' the child that's got his own! That's got his own!
42
Cm7 F13 B7 Fm7 B♭ E♭6 B6 Eb6
2.
Them that's got his own.

Art Songs and Arias

Art Songs

When you look at how old some of these art songs are it is easy to think they belong in a museum. Great works of art are hung in museums so that everyone can enjoy them, and they are so expensive that most of us would never be able to own an original. We have to stick with reprints. However, unlike visual art, original "art" music can be sung and repeated forever. This is the great tradition we have in art music, especially the great songs of composers such as Schubert, Schumann, Brahms, Fauré, Debussy, and others. Museum-quality American art song writers include Copland, Barber, Ives, and Rorem. Their songs live today because of the universal appeal of the music and the message.

Art songs differ from folk song and popular music in several ways:

1. Art songs are written down by composers trained musically rather than being passed on by oral tradition like folk songs. Some popular composers do write their music; however, many pop and rock songwriters create the music "by ear" and rely on other musicians to faithfully write it out.

2. Art songs are usually performed as written, with little deviation except for historically appropriate ornaments. The duty of the singer of art song is to interpret the musical message of the poet and the composer. Folk songs, pop songs, and especially jazz and standards rely more on the singer's ability to improvise, "stylize," and personalize a song.

3. Art song recitals (concerts) are typically performed without amplification in small to medium-size recital halls. This is why trained singers learn to sing with energized voices that can fill large spaces. Microphones and electronically amplified instruments help pop and rock musicians play to huge crowds in clubs or outdoor arenas. While jazz and standards vocalists also use microphones, they typically play to smaller, more intimate venues.

4. Composers of art song and musical theater consider words and music to be of equal importance. However, art song composers often set famous poetry by such well-known poets as Shakespeare, Emily Dickinson, and the great German and French poets Goethe, Heine, and Verlaine. Ideally, art songs are sung in the original language of the poet. Classically trained singers study Italian, German, French, and sometimes other languages and usually provide English translations of the foreign texts in programs so that the audience can follow the story or mood. Folk music and popular music is usually sung in the vernacular, or local, language.

5. Art songs are usually compositions for solo voice and piano. When other instruments are added or used instead of a piano, the compositions are called *chamber music.* Folk singers may perform with just a guitar while popular singers may perform with piano or electronic keyboards, back-up singers, and an entire band.

These distinctions are not set in stone and there is increasing crossover (fusion) between art music and popular styles today. Many classically trained song composers (like David Baker and Davide Zannoni) also have jazz training and some of their art songs have a definite jazz flavor. Other contemporary art song composers (like Richard Pearson Thomas) infuse their art songs with Celtic and folk-like melodies. Libby Larson's *Cowboy Songs* and *Songs from Letters (Calamity Jane)* incorporate traditional elements of Americana. Still other composers like John Kander ("A Letter from Sullivan Ballou") write for both the concert hall and the Broadway stage.

Arias

Operatic arias are sung at points in an opera where the story line slows down to express emotion. Arias are designed to magnify the mood or the conflict the character is feeling. "I love you" sung on an extremely high note is far more dramatic than if it is simply spoken. This is why "opera buffs" are so passionate about opera—it gives them a real buzz. You can find many nonsingers who will gladly pay a fortune to see an opera anytime they have the chance.

Operas are big theatrical productions that demand big voices most of the time. Opera singers have to sing, usually with no microphone, over orchestras that may have 100 instrumentalists. This is why they spend years working on their voices.

Every opera has a story and each aria is part of that story. Therefore, singers need to know the context of the arias they sing. Oratorios, like Handel's *Messiah,* are similar to opera; however, they use biblical texts or tell a sacred story. Operas and oratorios also include recitatives (declamatory sections that move the story along), duets and other ensembles (see *Hansel and Gretel* duet, p. 221), and chorus numbers.

Come Again, Sweet Love (p. 185)

This song was published in John Dowland's *First Book of Songes or Ayres* in 1597. It was so popular that it was reprinted six times. He followed this success with a second and third book of airs. During Dowland's time "songs" and "airs" (or "songes" and "ayres") were used interchangeably to mean song. (*Note:* Though they are spelled similarly, an "air" is not the same thing as an "aria.")

Dowland lived in England during the time of Shakespeare and his songs were written for voice and lute, a stringed instrument that is a forerunner to today's guitar. Since the singer and the lutenist were often the same person, the texture of the accompaniment is kept light and unobtrusive so the singer can easily be heard. As Dowland wrote in the dedication for his First Book, "to the sweetness of instrument applies the lively voice of man, expressing some worthy sentence or excellent poem." The arrangement in this book is for piano and voice and if a guitarist is available the effect is even better.

The Angler's Song (duet) (p. 187)

This fishing song by Henry Lawes, the leading English composer during the reign of Charles I, was first published in Izaak Walton's classic guide, *The Compleat Angler* in 1653. Walton's best-selling book, which has been reprinted more than 300 times, tells the idyllic story of a fisherman, a hunter, and a fowler as they travel the river Lea in the spring. The story is sprinkled with illustrations, woodcuts, and practical fishing advice as well as writer's quotations and several songs. The singers in "The Angler's Song" rationalize that since life is just a "hodge-podge of bus'ness, and money, and care," you might as well go fishing! Interestingly, the music for Lawe's song was printed with the bass part upside down to allow the two singers to face each other while they sang.

Henry Lawes wrote more than 430 songs and set many texts by famous poets and playwrights, including Thomas Carew and John Milton. When Izaak Walton wasn't fishing or singing, he was writing notable biographies of historical British figures such as Sir Henry Wotton and Dr. John Donne.

Donzelle, fuggite (p. 189)

This aria or "canzone" (Italian for song) by Francesco Cavalli was probably inspired by Greek and Roman mythology. The maidens in "Donzelle, fugitte" are warned to run away from provocative beauty. If the look of love penetrates your heart, you will be wounded by its darts!

Like many outstanding song composers, Cavalli was himself a fine singer. He knew how to write expressive vocal lines to interweave with the instrumental lines. This is a "da capo" aria in ABA form, which means that the beginning and ending part are the same, with a contrasting, slower middle section. It is standard for the singer to add some *ornaments* (embellished notes) on the repeat of the A section. Cavalli wrote more than forty mostly forgotten Italian operas that contain arias in this style. (For word-for-word translations and IPA symbols, see page 307.)

He Shall Feed His Flock like a Shepherd (Aria and Recitative) from *Messiah* (p. 192)

The alto solo from Handel's oratorio *Messiah* "recites" or announces God's healing miracles, then sings tenderly of the good shepherd's care. This is an example of a "recitative" paired with an "aria." The first part is in a rather speech-like singing style. The second part is beautifully and lyrically sung, with a warm expressive tone.

Most people are familiar with the "Hallelujah Chorus" from *Messiah,* even if they haven't heard the entire work. *Messiah* is regularly performed in America, especially at Christmas time. In Handel's time, however, *Messiah* wasn't just a holiday offering. People flocked to the performances as if it were a modern-day Broadway hit. Handel, who was born in Germany, originally wrote *Messiah* in English. When he wrote it, he had been living in England for nearly thirty years—a German composer writing Italian opera and English oratorio in London.

Ombra mai fù, from *Serse* (p. 195)

In this famous aria from George Frideric Handel's opera *Serse* (*Xerxes*), the Prince of Persia, Xerxes, sings of his love for a tree. Though the opera's story is mostly fictional, it is based on Herodotus's account of the Greek-Persian Wars, around 450 B.C.E., that tells of Xerxes attempt to bridge the Hellespont and also refers to the king's fondness for a certain plane tree. Sinces *Serse* is considered Handel's only comic opera, historian Stanley Sadie suggests that this ode to a tree is presumably satirical, "but its perfectly shaped melody and grave beauty have made it the most famous of Handel's opera songs." In Handel's day, heroic leading roles such as Xerxes were played by "castrati" (sexually neutered male singers). When Handel's operas were revived in the twentieth century, due to a lack of available eunichs, the leading roles were played by mezzo-sopranos such as Marilyn Horne. The new trend is for countertenors (males with a strong falsetto voice) to sing the castrati roles. Countertenor Andreas Scholl has recently recorded "Ombra mai fù." It is also featured on tenor Andrea Bocelli's CD of *Sacred Arias,* and on *Handel for Dummies.* Several instrumental versions of the aria have been recorded under the title Handel's "Largo," but the original tempo (*larghetto*) makes it easier for singers to get through the long phrases. (For word-for-word translations and IPA symbols, see page 312.)

Auf Flügeln des Gesanges (p. 201)

This "lied" (German song), written in 1834, is one of Mendelssohn's most beautiful melodies set to one of the German poet Heinrich Heine's most sensual love poems. The singer can't be with his "dear little heart" physically, so he imagines that his love song will transport the lovers to the most beautiful place on earth, a bed of red flowers and lotus blossoms. The piano accompaniment has a harp-like effect that enhances the text and keeps the vocal line moving along, flying on the wings of song toward the lovers' rendezvous.

Heine's poems of love, loss, and war (the French Revolution) inspired some of the day's best song composers. During his lifetime, Heine was more respected outside his homeland than in Germany, and he spent much time in France. Heine was Jewish and in World War II the Nazis removed his name from poetry books, citing the author as "unknown." Heine's poems inspired Mendelssohn, Schubert, and Schumann, the great composers of the "Romantic" musical era that lasted from 1800 to about 1910.

The composer Felix Mendelssohn was a child prodigy who played several instruments, spoke a number of languages, composed and conducted his own works, and even painted well. He and his sister Fanny Hensel wrote many songs that are performed regularly in modern recitals. During Mendelssohn's time people listened mainly to music that was new. We owe him thanks for starting the trend of preserving the music of famous composers like J. S. Bach, Mozart, and Beethoven. (For word-for-word translations and IPA symbols, see page 304.)

Bitte (p. 206)

This plaintive love song is one of about 350 lieder (German songs) by Robert Franz. The poet, Nicolaus Lenau, pleads to be taken completely under the power of his loved one, whose magical dark eyes will take him away from this world and unite them forever. Lenau is best known for his poem *Don Juan* that Richard Strauss used as the inspiration for a famous, and controversial, orchestral work.

Franz uses the same melody to begin and end the song using the same form that is often seen in folk songs. Robert Franz's songs were greatly admired by his famous contemporary, Schumann. Today, well-known recitalists like operatic baritone Thomas Hampson are championing the songs of Robert Franz in concerts and recordings. (For word-for-word translations and IPA symbols, see page 306.)

Ici-bas (p. 208)

This is one of the best-loved "chanson" (French songs) by Gabriel Fauré, a master of the French Romantic art song. The singer laments the temporary nature of everything here below on earth—flowers die, bird songs are interrupted, seasons move on, and hearts are broken. The singer longs for love and kisses that will go on forever, perhaps after death. Fauré carefully chose poetry from France's finest literary figures including Victor Hugo, Gautier, Baudelaire, and Paul Verlaine. (For word-for-word translations and IPA symbols, see page 309.)

Gentle Annie (p. 211)
If You've Only Got a Moustache (p. 213)

"Gentle Annie" is a sentimental ballad, in the style of Stephen Foster's other popular songs, "Beautiful Dreamer" and "I Dream of Jeannie with the Light Brown Hair." The singer stands by a tomb, lamenting that Annie will not return when the spring flowers bloom, and is comforted by wandering to the places they loved while she lived. Foster's funeral songs may seem macabre today, but during the Civil War, death was a daily part of life. His nostalgic songs of remembrance of "the voices that are gone" mix images of nature (flowers, streams, and meadows), dreams, sleep, and angels.

Foster also wrote songs of hope like "There's a Good Time Coming" and some very funny songs like "There's Plenty of Fish in the Sea." In "If You've Only Got a Moustache," Foster and lyricist George Cooper reveal the bachelor's foolproof secret to getting a girl and driving women mad.

Stephen Foster wrote nearly 300 songs that are an important part of our American history and are still popular today. His controversial "negro" songs about the pre–Civil War South ("Old Folks at Home," "Campground Races," "Massa's in de Cold, Cold Ground") are now politically inappropriate unless considered in their historical setting. Foster was born in Pennsylvania and never lived in the South, but his songs, especially "Oh! Susanna," were popular across the entire country.

El majo timido (p. 216)

A young girl waits every night for the handsome, timid boy who comes to her window. Will he have the courage to speak to her this time? Alas, no! As soon as he sees her, he runs away—again! The text by Fernando Periquet is somewhat ambiguous, so it is up to the singer to decide if she is truly amused by this nightly escapade, or if she is being sarcastic.

The composer, Enrique Granados was born in the Catalonian province of Spain. He studied music in Paris, and then returned to Barcelona to become one of the most famous Spanish composers. Many of his songs are short and playful, with a guitar-like pattern in the piano accompaniment. (For word-for-word translations and IPA symbols, see page 308.)

Con amores, la mi madre (p. 218)

In this song a young girl confides to her mother that while she slept, she dreamed of her love. "Con amore, la mi madre" was originally written by a fifteenth-century court musician in the service of Queen Isabella of Spain. Four hundred years later, the Spanish composer Fernando J. Obradors arranged the song in a modern Romantic style. It remains one of the most popular Spanish art songs, performed frequently on student recitals and recorded by famous opera singers such as Kathleen Battle, Kiri Te Kanawa, and Jennifer Larmore. Obrador's original and borrowed songs are influenced by Spanish folk music and dances. (For word-for-word translations and IPA symbols, see page 306.)

Evening Prayer (duet), from *Hansel and Gretel* (p. 221)

In the first act of Humperdinck's fairy tale opera by the Brothers Grimm, the two children, Hansel and Gretel, are lost in the woods. As nighttime descends they find a spot to sleep in the forest and pray that the angels will watch over them.

This lovely duet has been sung all over the world as a bedtime prayer and is included on some lullaby recordings. Though the opera's story has some truly gruesome elements, like abandoning children in the woods and threatening to bake them into cookies, it remains a favorite with adults and children. Perhaps it is because of Humperdinck's folk-like music or the colorful characters of the Witch, the Sand Man, and the Dew Fairy, or simply because we know how the story ends.

Summertime, from *Porgy and Bess* (p. 223)

The character of Clara has only a supporting role in Gershwin's famous folk opera, yet she gets the best song. "Summertime" is a lullaby that Clara sings to her baby in Act I, and then again as a "reprise" (repeated section) in Act II. Finally, in a very poignant scene after Clara and her husband Jake have drowned in the river, the character of Bess sings "Summertime" to the newly orphaned baby.

Gershwin suggested to Dubose Heyward that they collaborate on an opera after reading Heyward's novel *Porgy.* Heyward wrote the *libretto* (the script) for the opera and some of the song texts, including "Summertime." This tender lullaby has been recorded by thousands of classical, jazz, pop, and folk singers around the world.

Modern Major-General from *Pirates of Penzance* (p. 229)

You might say that the lyrics to Sir William S. Gilbert's comic "patter songs" were the original rap music. Patter songs depend on precise rhythmic delivery and clear pronunciation of the text, sung at breakneck speed, or as the Grove's *Dictionary* says, "getting the greatest number of words uttered in the shortest possible time." One of the most famous patter songs is the Major General's song from *Pirates of Penzance.* During the Victorian era, William S. Gilbert teamed with composer Authur A. Sullivan to create a highly successful series of operettas (comic light operas), which are still performed frequently in England and the United States. Some of the most popular G & S operettas include *Pirates of Penzance, The Mikado, H.M.S. Pinafore,* and *Ruddigore,* which features the patter song "This particularly rapid, unintelligible patter isn't generally heard, and if it is it doesn't matter."

Into the Night (p. 235)

Sopranos love to sing this romantic song about a young woman who is determined to be reunited with her love whatever the personal cost. She sets off on foot, in the middle of the night. Weary, she walks all through the night, into the morning ("The flowers lift their heads, the night is gone"), yet there is no sign of him. Resolute and strong in the last verse, she vows to follow him over land or sea. The piano part marches steadily throughout the song in lush chords underneath a beautiful melody line. This is an example of a "strophic" song, where two or more verses are set to the same melody. Strophic songs often tell a story.

Clara Edwards has been considered a "one-hit" wonder, with "Into the Night" being her best-known song. However, she published seventy-six songs, which are gradually being rediscovered. In 1948, *Etude Magazine* honored her as one of America's best-loved living songwriters. Ms. Edwards toured

Europe and the West Coast of America as a concert singer before settling in New York City.

The Hippopotamus (p. 239)

For years the humorous satirical songs of the English songwriting team Flanders and Swann existed only on stage and in live recordings of their hit revue *At the Drop of a Hat.* The show was enormously popular with London theatergoers in the late 1950s and early 1960s. Swann admits that "so-called composer that I was, I never wrote any [of the songs] down. Michael improvised [lyrics] when he felt like it, constantly improving and altering. I varied the accompaniments and laughed anew as the jokes grew. Most of the music remained in my mind." Public demand for printed versions of Flanders and Swann's songs was high, but Flanders insisted that their performances couldn't be written down. It was only after her father's death in 1975 that Claudia Flanders convinced Donald Swann to preserve "The Hippopotamus" and other songs for future generations. In the foreword to *The Songs of Michael Flanders and Donald Swan* (1977, second edition 1996) Swann writes, "The songs can be taken from these pages, and can grow again in your, the player's hands, with your or another's voice. Each singer will do what he pleases, and so he should."

I Never Knew (p. 242)

Time magazine called Ned Rorem "the world's best composer of art songs." This new American art song by Ned Rorem was commissioned by the Lotte Lehmann Foundation for CyberSing 2002, the first International Internet-based art song vocal competition. The Foundation's mission is "to spread classical song both online and in ears throughout the whole world."

Today technology is breathing new life into an art form that was nearly declared dead. The current top-selling classical vocal CDs are not opera albums but art song recording by singers such as Susan Graham, Cecilia Bartolli, Natalie Desay, and Thomas Hampson. The intimacy of the small recital hall is being replaced or enhanced by the intimacy of the recording studio, where singers are so close to the listeners that you can hear them breathe.

Live recitals are also changing as modern concert artists experiment with adding visual elements. The Lotte Lehman Foundation is championing an experiment to bring supertitles to recital halls. Already a popular feature in many opera houses, supertitles are projected images of English translations of foreign texts that allow audience members to follow the text more easily, without constantly referring to the printed program. The Lotte Lehmann Foundation is named for the famous German-born singer who refused to sing in Nazi Germany. She fled to California and continued her career as an outstanding art song and opera singer.

Come Again, Sweet Love

Music by John Dowland
(1563–1626)

For background and performance notes, see page 180.

Moderate ♩ = 88
1. Come a -
2. Come a -
gain, Sweet love doth now in - vite Thy
gain, That I may cease to mourn Thro'
grac - es that re - frain To do me due de - light, To see,
thy un - kind dis - dain; For now, left and for - lorn, I sit,
pp

cresc.
11
— to hear,— to touch,— to kiss,— to die—
— I sigh,— I weep,— I faint,— I die—
cresc.
14
— With thee a - gain in sweet - est sym - pa - thy, To see,—
— In dead - ly pain and end - less mis - er - y, I sit,—
17
— to hear,— to touch,— to kiss,— to die—
— I sigh,— I weep,— I faint,— I die—
20
rall.
— With thee a - gain in sweet - est sym - pa - thy.
— In dead - ly pain and end - less mis - er - y.
rall.

The Angler's Song

(Duet)

Words by
Isaak Walton
(1593–1683)

Music by
Henry Lawes
(1596–1662)

For background and performance notes, see page 180.

Allegro ♩ = 138
mf
Man's life is but vain, for 'tis
sub - ject to pain And sor - row, and short as a bub - ble;
(2nd time, p)
f
'Tis a hodge - podge of
bus' - ness and mon - ey and care, And care and mon - ey, and trou - ble.
(poco rit., 2nd time)

a tempo
18
mf
But we'll take no care, when the
a tempo
f
mf
25
weath - er proves fair; Nor will we vex now though it rain;
f (2nd time f)
We'll ban - ish all
31
(2nd time, poco rit.)
sor - row and sing till to - mor - row, And an - gle, and an - gle a - gain.
(Go fish - ing, go fish - ing a - gain.)*

*alternate text

Donzelle, fuggite

(Damsels, Run Away!)

Words and Music by
Francesco Cavalli
(1602–1676)

Arranged by Cynthia Lee Fox

Donzelle, fuggite procace beltà!
Se lucido sguardo vi pénetra il core,
Lasciate quel dardo del perfido amore,
Che in sidie scaltrite tramando vi sta!

Damsels, run away from [Cupid's] provocative beauty!
If a seductive glance penetrates your heart,
Escape that dart of perfidious love
That attempts to trap you!

For background and performance notes, see page 180.

Allegro ♩ = 130
1
Don -

5
zel - le, fug - gi -te pro - ca - ce bel - tà!
Fug-

13
gi - te, fug - gi - te, fug - gi - te!
Fug - gi - te, fug -
20
2nd time to Coda
gi - te, fug - gi - te! Don - zel - le fug - gi - te pro - ca - ce bel - tà!
26
Se lu - ci - do
32
sguar - do vi pén - e - tra il co - - - re,
las -

39
cia - te quel dar - do del per - fi - do a - mo - re, che in si - die scal - tri - te tra - man - do vi
46
D.S. al CODA
sta!
Don-
54
CODA

He Shall Feed His Flock

FROM *Messiah*

Music by
George Frideric Handel
(1685–1759)

For background and performance notes, see page 181.

Recitative

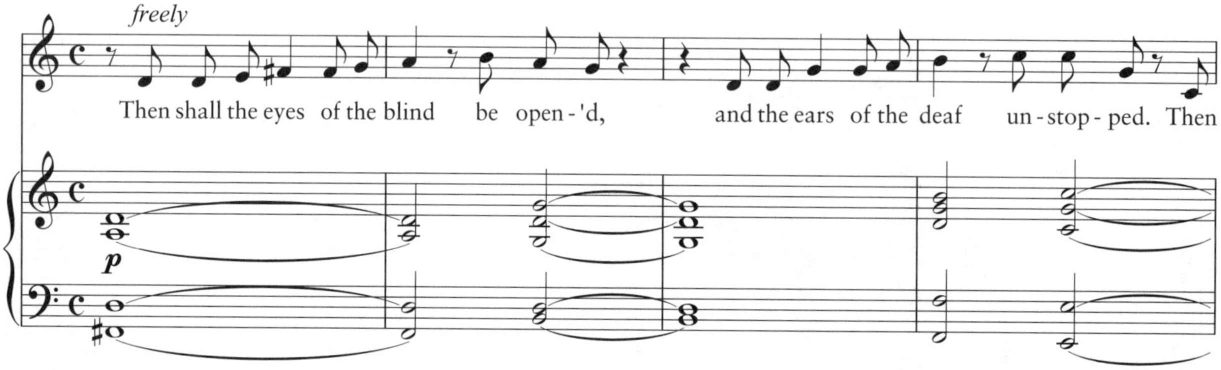
freely
Then shall the eyes of the blind be open-'d, and the ears of the deaf un-stop-ped. Then
p

5
shall the lame man leap as an hart,* and the tongue of the dumb shall sing.
f

Aria

♩. = 140

1
p

*deer

4
(,)
He shall__ feed His flock like a shep - herd, and
7
(,)
,
He__ shall__ ga - ther the lambs__ with His arm, with________ His arm,
cresc.
10
(,)
He shall__ feed His flock like a shep - herd, and
p
13
(,)
,
He__ shall__ ga - ther the lambs__ with His arm, with________ His arm,
cresc.

16
and car - ray them in His bo - som, and
p
19
(,)
,
,
gen - tly lead those that are with young, and gen - tly lead those, and
22
(,)
gen - tly lead those that are with young.

Ombra mai fù

FROM *Serse*

(LOW KEY)

Words by Nicolò Minato and Silvio Stampiglia

George Frideric Handel
(1685–1759)

Ombra mai fù di vegetabile, Cara ed amabile, soave piu!	Never was the shade of any plant Sweeter, dearer, more agreeable!

For background and performance notes, see page 181.

Larghetto ♩ = 66
p
8vb
(Intro may begin here.)
f
(8)
loco

15
p mf p
Om - - - - bra mai fù
p mf p
8vb
20
di ve - ge - ta - bi - le ca - ra ed a - ma - bi - le
(8)
25
so - a - ve più, om - bra mai fù di ve - ge -
(8)
loco
30
ta - bi - le ca - ra ed a - ma - bi - le so - a - ve

34
più, ca - - ra ed a - ma - bi - le, om - bra mai fù,
39
mf
di ve - ge - ta - bi - le ca - ra ed a - ma - bi - le so - a - ve
mf
8vb
loco
44
p
più, so - a - ve più.
p
8vb
48
(8)

Ombra mai fù

FROM *Serse*

(HIGH KEY)

Words by Nicolò Minato and Silvio Stampiglia

George Frideric Handel
(1685–1759)

Ombra mai fù di vegetabile,
Cara ed amabile, soave piu!

Never was the shade of any plant
Sweeter, dearer, more agreeable!

For background and performance notes, see page 181.

Larghetto ♩ = 66
p
8vb
f
p
(8)
(Intro may begin here.)
f
loco

15
p mf p
Om - - - - bra mai fù
p mf p
8vb
20
di ve - ge - ta - bi - le ca - ra ed a - ma - bi - le
(8)
25
so - a - ve più, om - bra mai fù di ve - ge -
(8) loco
30
ta - bi - le ca - ra ed a - ma - bi - le so - a - ve

34
più, ca - - ra ed a - ma - bi - le, om - bra mai fù,
39
mf
di ve - ge - ta - bi - le ca - ra ed a - ma - bi - le so - a - ve
mf
8vb
loco
44
p
più, so - a - ve più.
p
f
8vb
48
(8)

Auf Flügeln des Gesanges

(On Wings of Song)

Words by
Heinrich Heine

Music by
Felix Mendelssohn (1809–1847)
Edited by Walter Golde

1. Auf Flügeln des Gesanges,
Herzliebchen, trag' ich dich fort,
Fort nach den Fluren des Ganges,
Dort weiss ich den schönsten Ort.

Dort liegt ein rotblühender Garten
Im stillen Mondenschein;
Die Lotosblumen erwarten
Ihr trautes Schwesterlein.

2. Die Veilchen kichern und kosen
Und schau'n nach den Sternen empor;
Heimlich erzählen die Rosen
Sich duftende Märchen ins Ohr.

Es hüpfen herbei und lauschen
Die frommen, klugen Gazell'n;
Und in der Ferne rauschen
Des heiligen Stromes Well'n.

3. Dort wollen wir niedersinken
Unter dem Palmenbaum
Und Lieb' und Ruhe trinken
Und träumen seligen Traum.

1. On the wings of song,
dear heart, I carry you away.
Along the plains of the Ganges river,
I know the most beautiful place.

There lies a red blooming garden.
In the quiet moonlight,
the lotus blossons await
their trusted little sister.

2. The violets giggle and caress,
and look upwards at the stars.
Secretly the roses
tell fragrant fairy tales.

Jump here and listen
the clever, devout gazelles.
And in the distance
rustles the sacred stream.

3. There we want to sink low
under the palm tree,
and love, and drink in the silence
and dream blissful dreams.

For background and performance notes, see page 181.

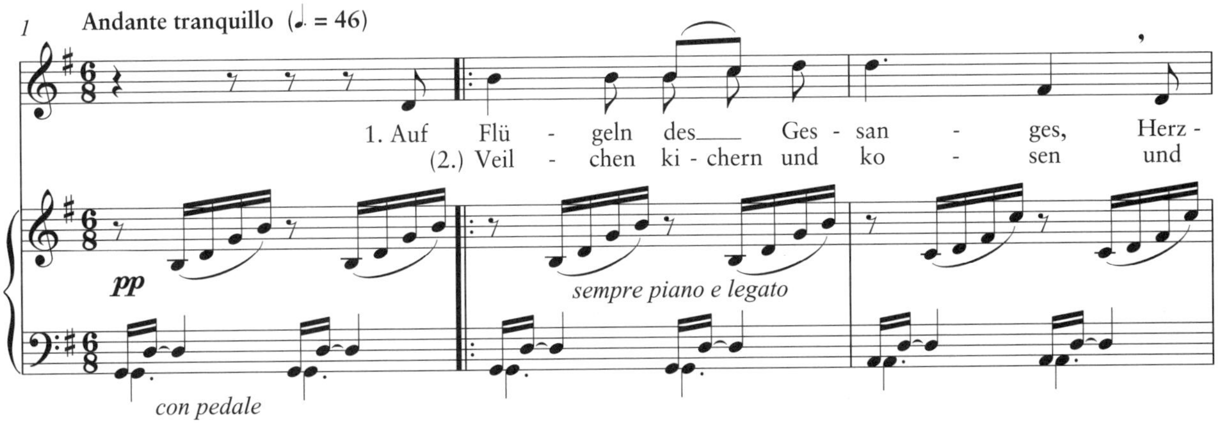
1
Andante tranquillo (♩. = 46)
1. Auf Flü - geln des___ Ges - san - ges, Herz -
(2.) Veil - chen ki - chern und ko - sen und
pp
sempre piano e legato
con pedale

4
lieb - chen, trag' ich dich fort, fort nach den Flu - ren des
schau'n nach den Ster - nen em - por, heim - lich er - zäh - len die
7
p
Gan - ges, dort weiss ich den schön - sten Ort; Da
Ro - sen sich duf - ten - de Mär - chen in's Ohr. Es
p
10
mp
liegt ein rot - blü - hen - der Gar - ten im stil - len Mon - den
hüp - fen her - bei und lau - schen die from - men klu - gen Ga -
mp
13
cresc.
schein, die Lo - tos - blu - men er - war - ten ihr
zell'n und in der Fer - ne rau - schen des
cresc.

16
dim.
p
trau - tes Schwe - ster - lein, die Lo - tus - blu - men er -
heil' - gen Stro - mes Well'n und in der Fer - ne
dim.
p
19
p
war - - - - - - - - ten ihr trau - tes Schwe - ster -
rau - - - - - - - - schen des heil' - gen Stro - mes
p
22
lein.
Well'n.
cresc.
f
dim.
25
1.
2.
2. Die
3. Dort

28
cresc.
wol - len wir nie - der - sin - ken un - ter dem Pal - men -
cresc.
31
baum, und Lieb' und Ru - he trin - ken, und
34
cresc.
f
träu - men se - li - gen Traum und
cresc.
37
dim.
p
träu - men se - - - li - gen Traum,
dim.
p

40
dim.
sel'
gen
dim.
43
Traum.
pp

Bitte

(Plea)

Words by
Nicolaus Lenau

Music by
Robert Franz (1815–1892)
Op. 9, No. 3

Weil' auf mir, du dunkles Auge,	Linger on me, dark eyes.
übe deine ganze Macht,	Practice your entire power,
ernste, milde, träumereische,	serious, mild, dream-like,
unergründlich süsse Nacht.	unfathomably sweet night.
Nimm mit deinem Zuberdunkel	With your magic darkness
diese Welt von hinnen mir,	take me from this world,
dass du über meinen Leben	that above my life
einsam schwebest für and für.	you may hover forever and forever.

For background and performance notes, see page 182.

Slow and sustained ♩ = 48
1
Weil' auf mir, du dunk - les Au - ge, ü - be
p
6
dei - ne gan - ze Macht, ern - ste, mil - de,

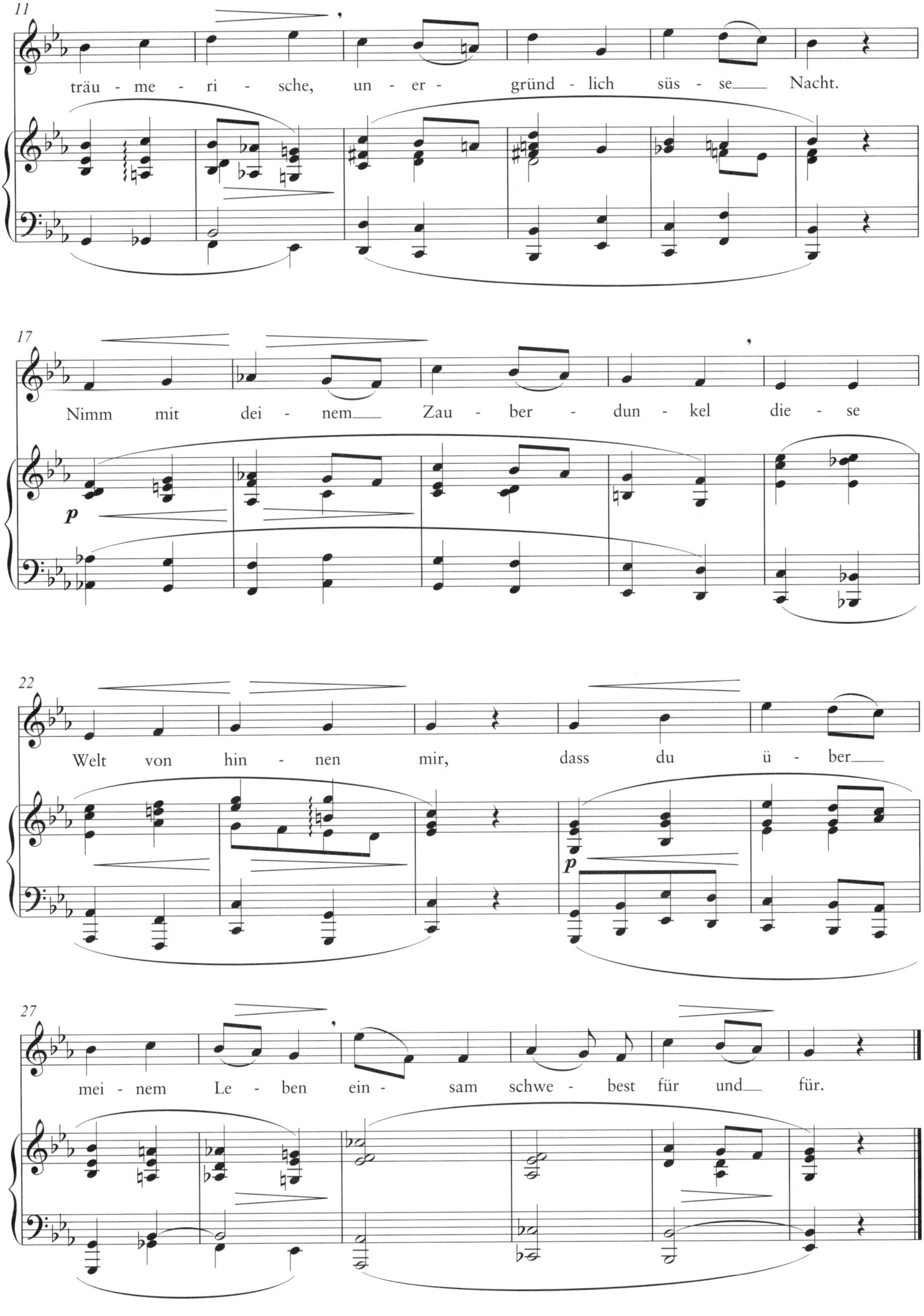
11
träu - me - ri - sche, un - er - gründ - lich süs - se Nacht.
17
Nimm mit dei - nem Zau - ber - dun - kel die - se
p
22
Welt von hin - nen mir, dass du ü - ber
p
27
mei - nem Le - ben ein - sam schwe - best für und für.

Ici-bas

(Here Below)

Words by
Sully Prudhomme

Music by
Gabriel Fauré
(1845–1924)

Ici-bas tous les lilas meurent, Tous les chants des oiseaux sont courts, Je rêve aux étés qui demeurent Toujours!	Here below (on earth) the lilacs die. All the songs of the birds are brief. I dream of summers that remain. always!
Ici-bas les lèvres effleurent Sans rien laisser de leur velours, Je rêve aux baisers qui demeurent Toujours!	Here below the lips barely touch without a trace of their velvet, I dream of kisses that remain forever!
Ici-bas, tous les hommes pleurent Leurs amitiés ou leurs amours; Je rêve aux couples qui demeurent Toujours!	Here below all the people weep for their friends or lovers. I dream of couples who remain forever!

For background and performance notes, see page 182.

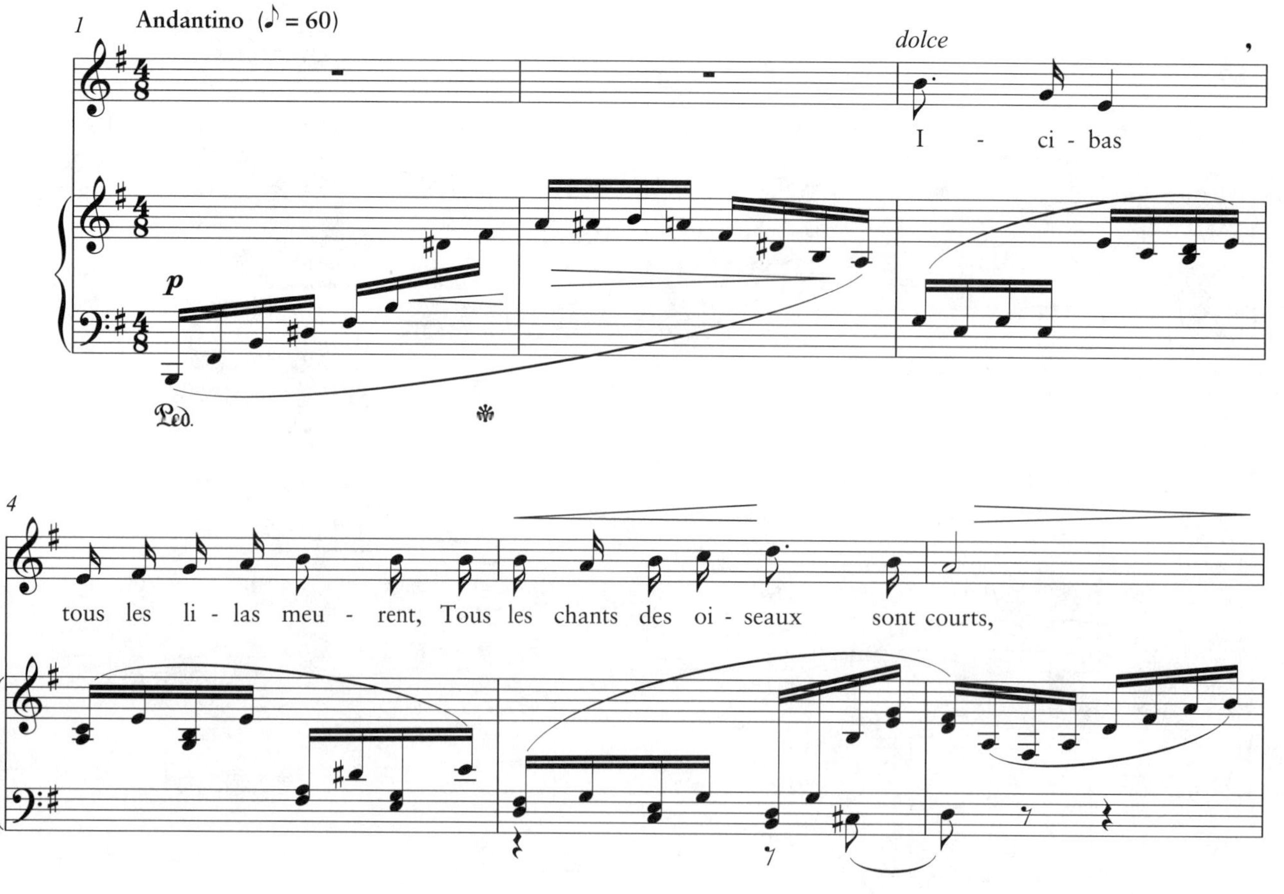
1
Andantino (♪ = 60)
dolce
I - ci - bas
p
Ped.
4
tous les li - las meu - rent, Tous les chants des oi - seaux sont courts,

7
Je rêve aux é - tés qui de - meu - rent Tou - jours!
Ped.
10
p
I - ci - bas les lè - vres ef - fleu - rent Sans
sempre p
13
p
rien lais - ser de leur ve - lours, Je rêve aux bai -
p
16
sers qui de - meu - rent Tou - jours!
Ped.

19
mf
I - ci - bas, tous les hom - mes pleu - rent Leurs a - mi - tiés ou leurs a -
dim.
Ped.
22
cresc.
mours, Je rêve aux cou - ples qui de - meu - rent,
f
25
dim.
aux cou - ples qui de - meu - rent,
p
qui de - meu -
pp
r.h.
29
rent Tou- jours!

Gentle Annie

Words and Music by
Stephen C. Foster
(1826–1864)

For background and performance notes, see page 182.

Andante mosso ♩ = 72
1. Thou wilt
come no more, gen - tle An - nie, Like a flower thy spi - rit did de - part; Thou art
(2.) roamed and loved mid the bow - ers, When thy down - y cheeks were in their bloom; Now I
(3.) hours grow sad while I pon - der, Near the si - lent spot where thou art laid, And my
gone, a - las! like the ma - ny That have bloomed in the sum - mer of my
stand a - lone mid the flow - ers, While they min - gle their per - fumes o'er thy
heart bows down when I wan - der By the streams and the mead - ows where we

12
CHORUS
heart. Shall we ne-ver more be-hold thee; ne-ver hear thy win-ning voice a-
tomb.
strayed.
16
gain When the Spring - time comes, gen - tle An - nie, When the
19
1.2.
3.
wild - flowers are scat - tered o'er the plain? 2. We have plain?
3. Ah! the
22
3

If You've Only Got a Moustache

Words by George Cooper

Music by Stephen C. Foster
(1826–1864)

For background and performance notes, see page 182.

With spirit ♩. = 72
1. Oh!
all of you poor sin - gle men, Don't ev - er give up in des -
(2.) mat - ter for man - ners or style, No mat - ter for birth or for
(3.) head may be thick as a block, And emp - ty as an - y foot
(4.) once was in sor - row and tears Be - cause I was jilt - ed you

12
pair, For there's al - ways a chance while there's life To
fame, All these used to have some - thing to do With
ball, Oh! your eyes may be green as the grass Your
know, So right down to the ri - ver I ran To
15
cap - ture the hearts of the fair, No mat - ter what may be your
young la - dies chang - ing their name, There's no rea - son now to de -
heart just as hard as a wall. Yet take the ad - vice that I
quick - ly dis - pose of my woe, A good friend he gave me ad -
18
age, You al - ways may cut a fine dash, You will
spond, Or go and do an - y - thing rash, For you'll
give, You'll soon gain af - fec - tion and cash, And will
vice And time - ly pre - vent - ed the splash, Now at

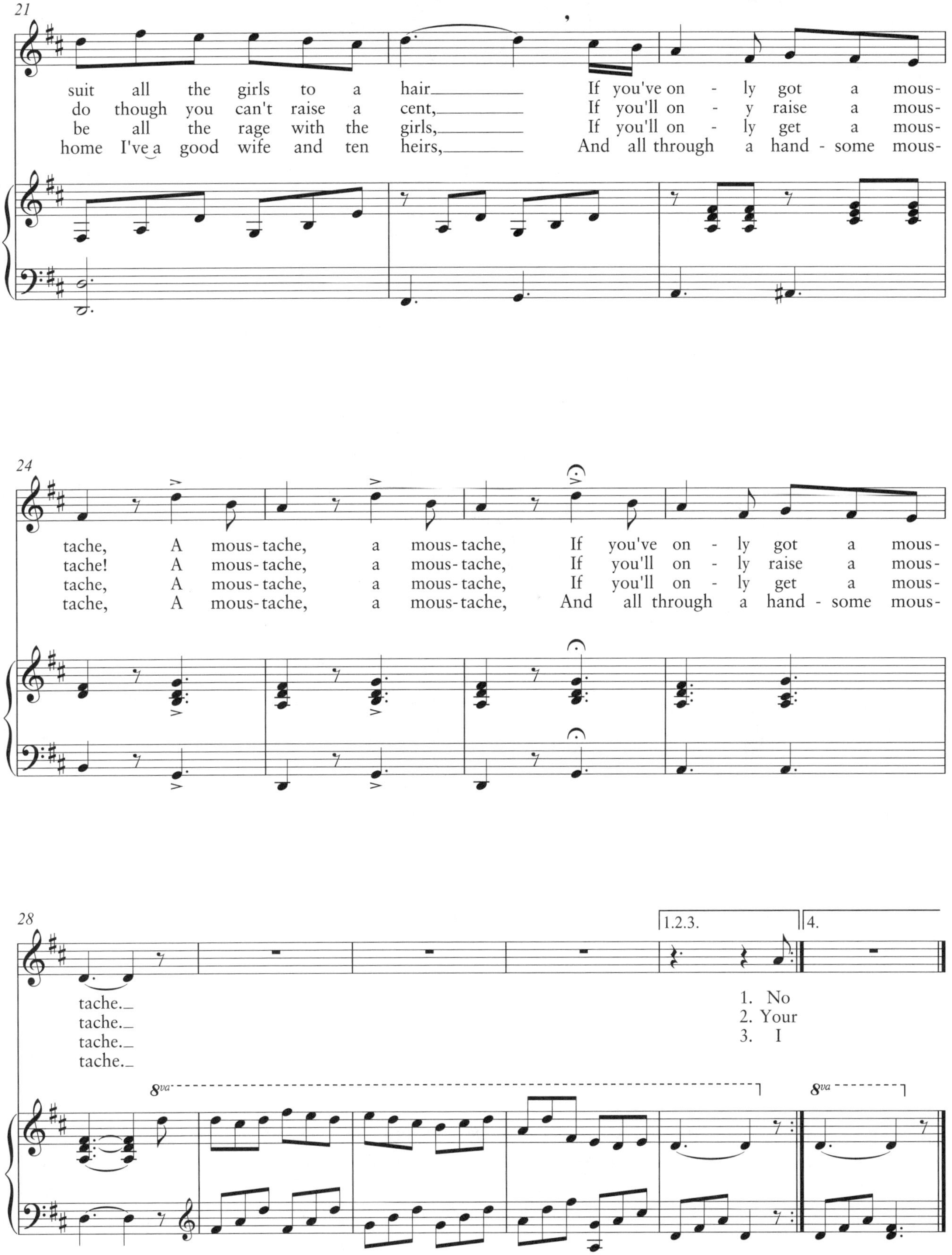
21
suit all the girls to a hair___ If you've on - ly got a mous-
do though you can't raise a cent,___ If you'll on - y raise a mous-
be all the rage with the girls,___ If you'll on - ly get a mous-
home I've a good wife and ten heirs,___ And all through a hand - some mous-
24
tache, A mous-tache, a mous-tache, If you've on - ly got a mous-
tache! A mous-tache, a mous-tache, If you'll on - ly raise a mous-
tache, A mous-tache, a mous-tache, If you'll on - ly get a mous-
tache, A mous-tache, a mous-tache, And all through a hand - some mous-
28
tache._
tache._
tache._
tache._
1.2.3.
4.
1. No
2. Your
3. I
8va
8va

El majo timido

(The Timid Suitor)

Words by
Fernando Periquet
Translation by
Noemi Lugo

Music by
Enrique Granados
(1867–1916)

Llega á mi reja y me mira	He arrives at my (window) grille and looks at me
por la noche un majo	Each night--a majo.*
que, en cuanto me ve y suspira,	Then, as soon as he sees me and sighs,
se vá calle abajo.	He goes down the street.
¡Ay qué tío más tardío!	Oh! That man is so dull!
¡Si así se pasa la vida	If this is the way he spends his life,
estoy divertida!	I am amused!

(*majo *is an untranslatable word for a handsome young man.)*

For background and performance notes, see page 182.

Allegro ♩ = 108

1

5
Lle -ga á mi re - ja y me mi - ra por la no - che un ma - jo

9
que, en cuan - to me ve y sus - pi - ra se vá ca - lle a - ba - jo.
13
¡Ay qué tí - o más tar - dí - o!
17
¡Si a sí se pa - sa la vi - da es - toy di - ver - ti - da!
21

Con amores, la mi madre

(With love, my mother)

Juan de Anchieta
(1462–1523)
Bass realization by Fernando J. Obradors
(1897–1945)

Translation by Noemi Lugo

Con amores, la mi madre, con amores me dormí;	With love, my mother, with love I slept.
Asi dormida soñaba lo que el corazon velaba,	As I slept, I dreamed what my heart concealed,
Qu'el amor me consalabe	That love consoled me
con más bien que merecí.	With more goodness than I deserved.
Adormeciome el favor que amor me dio con amor;	It put me to sleep, the one favor that love gave me;
Dio descanso a mi dolor.	The faith with which I served him
La fe con que le serví	Gave rest to my sorrow.
Con amores, la mi madre, con amores, ¡me dormí!	With love, my mother, with love I slept.

For background and performance notes, see page 183.

1
Andante mosso ♩ = 104
p
pp
Con a - mo - res, la mi
7
ma - dre, con a - mo - res me dor - mí;

13
A - si dor - mi - da so - ña - ba lo que el co - ra - zon ve -
19
la - ba, que el a - mor me con - so - la - ba
25
con más bien que me - re - cí.
A - dor - me - ciome el fa -
r.h.
31
vor que a - mor me dio con a - mor;

37
Dio des - can - so a mi do - lor.
La fe con que le ser -
43
ví
Con a - mo - res, la mi ma - dre, con
pp
49
a - mo - res me dor - mí!
55

Evening Prayer

Duet from *Hansel and Gretel*

Engelbert Humperdinck
(1854–1921)

For background and performance notes, see page 183.

Moderato ♩ = 80
Gretel
When at night I go to sleep, Four - teen an - gels
Hansel
When at night I go to sleep, Four - teen an - gels
p

watch do keep, Two my head are guard - ing, Two my feet are guid - ing,
watch do keep, Two my head are guard - ing, Two my feet are guid - ing,

11
Two are on my right hand, Two are on my left hand, Two who warm - ly
Two are on my right hand, Two are on my_ left hand,
poco cresc.
16
cresc.
cov - er, Two who o'er me hov - er, Two to whom 'tis giv - en To
cresc.
Two who warm - ly cov - er, Two who o'er me hov - er, Two who guide my
cresc.
21
poco rit.
Tempo
guide my steps to Hea - - ven.
steps to Hea - - ven.

Summertime

from *Porgy and Bess*

(High Key)

Words by
DuBose Heyward

Music by
George Gershwin (1898–1937)

For background and performance notes, see page 183.

1
Allegretto semplice, freely
p
mf espress.
mp
6
rit.
p
Moderato ♩ = 76
Bm6 (much expression) Bm6 C♯m6
Sum - mer - time an' the liv - in' is
rit.
r.h.
pp
10
Bm6 C♯m6 Bm6 C♯m6 Bm6 Em7 Em7/G Em7/G poco rit. B
mp
eas - y, Fish are jump - in', an' the cot - ton is
3
3
3
poco rit.

a tempo
14
F♯ C♯7 F♯ F♯6 F♯7 Bm6 C♯m6 Bm6 C♯m6
high. Oh, yo' dad - dy's rich, An yo' ma is good -
mf
r.h.
18
Bm6 C♯m6 Bm6 E7 D Bm E A9sus
look - in', So hush, lit - tle ba - by, don' you
3
22
Bm E9(♭5) Bm6 C♯m6/B E9 E9(♭5)(no 3rd)
poco animato
poco rit.
3
cry. One of these
8va
poco animato
poco rit.
Tempo I
26
Bm6 C♯m6 Bm6 C♯m6 Bm6 C♯m6 Bm6 C♯m6 Bm6
morn - in's you goin' to rise up sing - in', Then you'll

30
Em7 Em7/G Em7/B B F♯ C7 F♯ F♯6 F♯7
spread yo' wings an you'll take_the sky. But 'till that
3
34
Bm6 C♯m6 Bm6 C♯m6 Bm6 C♯m6 Bm6 E7
morn - in' there's a noth - in' can harm you With
3
38
D Em E A9sus Bm E A9sus
(,)
mp
Dad - dy an' Mam - my stand - in' by.
mp
42
D Dm/G C F♯7(add D♯) Bm Bm6
dim.
dim.
8va
ten.

Summertime

FROM *Porgy and Bess*

(LOW KEY)

Words by
DuBose Heyward

Music by
George Gershwin (1898–1937)

For background and performance notes, see page 183.

1
Allegretto semplice, freely
p
mf espress.
mp
6
rit.
p
Moderato ♩ = 76
Fm6 (much expression) Fm6 Gm6
Sum - mer - time an' the liv - in' is
rit.
r.h.
pp
10
Fm6 Gm6 Fm6 Gm6 Fm6 B♭m7 B♭m7/D♭ B♭m7/D♭ poco rit. F
mp
eas - y, Fish are jump - in', an' the cot - ton is
3
poco rit.

a tempo
14
C G7 C C6 C7 Fm6 Gm6 Fm6 Gm6
high. Oh, yo' dad - dy's rich, An yo' ma is good -
mf
r.h.
18
Fm6 Gm6 Fm6 B♭7 Ab Fm Bb E♭9sus
look - in', So hush, lit - tle ba - by, don' you
3
22
Fm poco animato B♭9(♭5) Fm6 Gm6/F B♭9 B♭9(♭5) (no 3rd)
poco rit.
cry. One of these
3
8va
poco animato
poco rit.
Tempo I
26
Fm6 Gm6 Fm6 Gm6 Fm6 Gm6 Fm6 Gm6 Fm6
morn - in's you goin' to rise up sing - in', Then you'll

30
B♭m7
B♭m7/D♭
B♭m7/F
F
C
G♭7
C
C6
C7
spread yo' wings an you'll take_the sky. But 'till that
(3)
34
Fm6
Gm6
Fm6
Gm6
Fm6
Gm6
Fm6
B♭7
morn - in' there's a noth - in' can harm you With
3
38
A♭
B♭m
B♭
E♭9sus
(,)
Fm
mp
B♭
E♭9sus
Dad - dy an' Mam - my stand - in' by.
mp
42
A♭
A♭m/D♭
G♭
C7(add A)
Fm
Fm6
dim.
dim.
8va
ten.

Modern Major-General

from *Pirates of Penzance*

Words by
Sir William S. Gilbert
(1836–1911)

Music by
Sir Arthur Sullivan
(1842–1900)

For background and performance notes, see page 183.

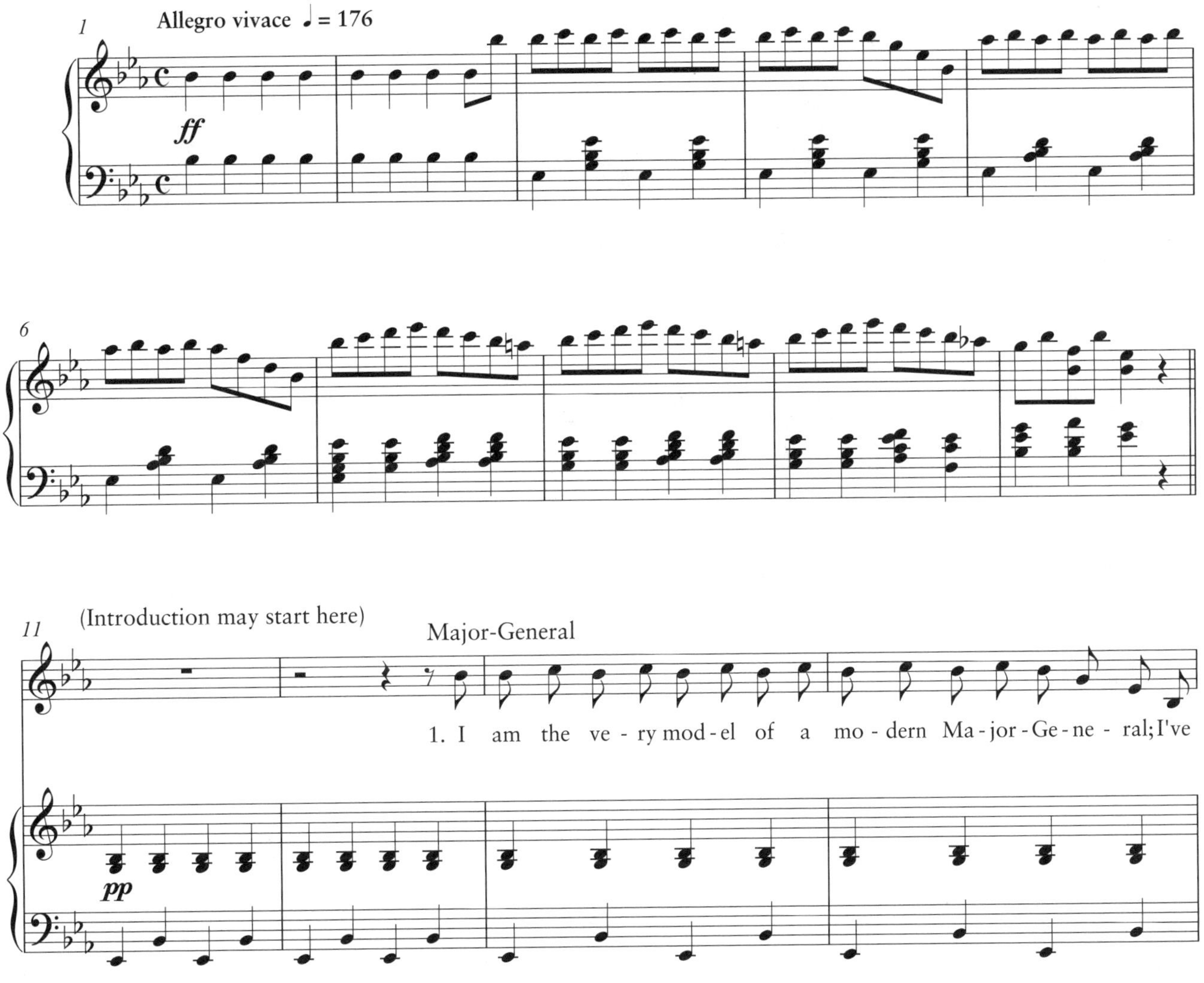
1
Allegro vivace ♩ = 176
ff
6
11
(Introduction may start here)
Major-General
1. I am the ve - ry mod - el of a mo - dern Ma - jor - Ge - ne - ral; I've
pp

15
in - for - ma - tion ve - ge - ta - ble, a - ni - mal, and mi - ne - ral; I know the kings of Eng - land, and I
18
quote the fights his - to - ri - cal, From Ma - ra - thon to Wa - ter - loo, in or - der ca - te - go - ri - cal. I'm
21
ve-ry well ac-quaint- ed, too,with mat-ters ma - the-ma - ti - cal; I un-der-stand e - qua- tions, both the
24
sim - ple and quad - ra - ti - cal: A - bout bi - no - mial The - o - rem I'm teem - ing with a lot o' news,

27
*
With many cheerful facts about the square of the hypo-ten-use;
Chorus
With
With
30
many cheerful facts about the square of the hy-po-ten-use, With
many cheerful facts about the square of the hy-po-ten-use, With

*trying to think of a rhyme

32
ma - ny cheer - ful facts a - bout the square of the hy - po - ten - use, With
ma - ny cheer - ful facts a - bout the square of the hy - po - ten - use, With
34
ma - ny cheer - ful facts a - bout the square of the hy - po - ten - po - then - use.
ma - ny cheer - ful facts a - bout the square of the hy - po - ten - po - then - use.
fz
37
Major-General
I'm ve - ry good at in - teg - ral and dif - fer - en - tial cal - cu - lus; I
pp

40
know the sci - en - ti - fic names of be - ings a - ni - mal - cu - lous. In short, in mat - ters ve - ge - ta - ble,
43
a - ni - mal, and mi - ne - ral, I am the ve - ry mo - del of a mod - ern Ma - jor - Ge - ne - ral.
f
Chorus
In
f
In
46
short, in mat - ters ve - ge - ta - ble, a - ni - mal, and mi - ne - ral, He is the ve - ry mo - del of a
short, in mat - ters ve - ge - ta - ble, a - ni - mal, and mi - ne - ral, He is the ve - ry mo - del of a

49
mo - dern Ma - jor - Ge - ne - ral.
mo - dern Ma - jor - Ge - ne - ral.
ff

52

Into the Night

Words and Music by
Clara Edwards
(1880–1974)

For background and performance notes, see page 183.

Tranquillo ♩ = 68
mp
Si - lent - ly in - to the
con pedale
night I go, In - to the fra - grant night, I know not where; The path is
strange my wea - ry steps are slow I do not find you
l.h.

10
mf
there. I turn my gaze toward the
dolce
mf
13
morn - ing sun As from the east he comes thro' the dark and the
cresc.
15
mf
dew; The flow - ers lift their heads the night is gone But
mf
18
mf
where are you? The
dolce

21
count - less wea - ry steps I do not heed Tho' they be
mf
23
o - ver land or bound - less sea; I care not where the road may
f
cresc.
26
lead If I but come a - gain at last to thee.
mf
l.h.
dim.
29
Si - lent - ly in - to the night I go, In - to the
p

32
star - ry night of heav - en - ly blue; What mat - ters where the road may
cresc.
mf
35
lead If I but come a - gain at last to you!
l.h.
p
38
p
(,) pp
Si - lent - ly, si - lent - ly
pp
ppp
41
rit.
I come to you!
rit.
morendo
Ped.

The Hippopotamus

Words by
Michael Flanders
(1922–1975)

Music by
Donald Swann
(1923–1994)

For background and performance notes, see page 184.

1
Heavily, in the region of 𝅗𝅥. = 58
f
mf
1. A bold Hip - po - po - ta - mus was
(2.) fair Hip - po - po - ta - ma he
(3.) more Hip - po - po - ta - mi be -

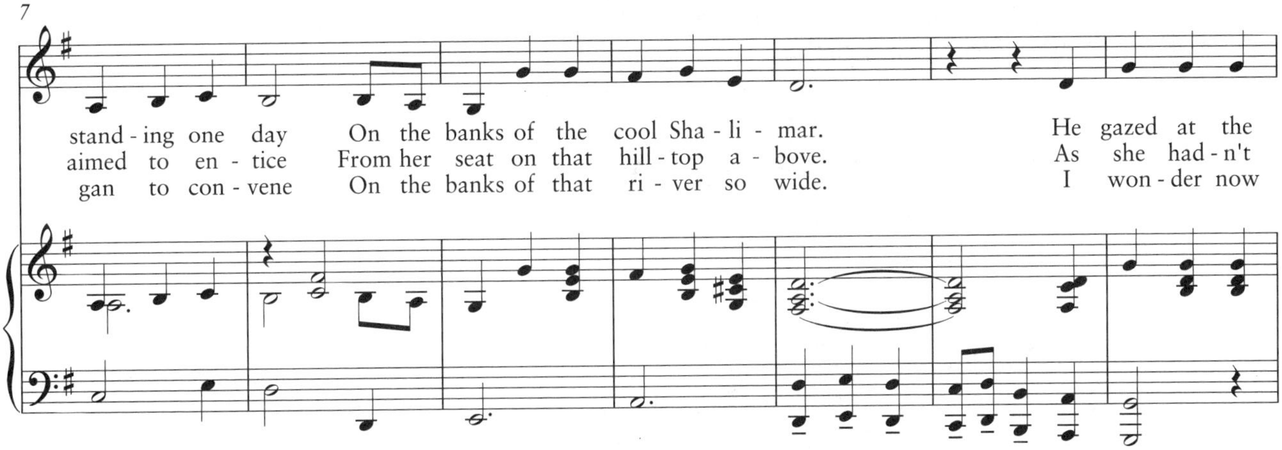
7
stand - ing one day On the banks of the cool Sha - li - mar. He gazed at the
aimed to en - tice From her seat on that hill - top a - bove. As she had - n't
gan to con - vene On the banks of that ri - ver so wide. I won - der now

14
bot - tom as it peace - ful - ly lay By the light of the e - ven - ing star.
got a ma to give her ad - vice, Came tip - toe - ing down to her love.
what am I to say of the scene That en - sued by the Sha - li - mar side?
20
A - way on the hill - top sat comb - ing her hair His fair Hip - po -
Like thun - der the fo - rest re - e - choed the sound Of the song that they
They dived all at once with an ear - split - ting splosh Then rose to the
26
po - ta - mine maid; The Hip - po - po - ta - mus was
sang as they met. His i - na - mo - ra - ta ad -
sur - face a - gain, A re - gu - lar ar - my of
31
no ig - no - ra - mus And sang her this sweet ser - e - nade:
just - ed her gar - ter And lift - ed her voice in du - et:
Hip - po - po - ta - mi All sing - ing this haunt - ing re - frain:

37
REFRAIN
Mud, mud, glo - ri - ous mud, Noth - ing quite like it for
43
cool - ing the blood! So fol - low me, fol - low, down to the hol - low And
49
1.2.
there let us wal - low in glo - - ri - ous mud!
55
3.
rit.
2. The
3. Now glo - - ri - ous mud!
mf
rit.
8vb

I Never Knew

Words by
Lotte Lehmann
Translated by Judy Sutcliffe

Music by
Ned Rorem
(b. 1923)

For background and performance notes, see page 184.

𝅗𝅥. = 40 (♩ = 120)
mf
I nev - er knew how much
love - li - ness lives in the bare and leaf - less trees,
Nor that
gold and sil - ver lov - ing - ly weave them - selves In - to bronze web - bing in
mp
cresc.

21
(,)
which buds_ dream of com - ing, spring- drunk ex - u - ber - ance;
28
f
I nev - er knew these best__ gifts strewn be - fore us, I
ff
f
cresc.
35
(,)
nev - er had time, could nev - er rest, was al - ways driv - en like a
ff
41
mf
hunt - ed an - i - mal. But now_ the hunt - er is my____
f
mf

48
rit.
mp
quar - ry.
I've
55
a tempo
(,)
caught what hunt - ed me, Time and to -
mp
61
(,)
day up - on its wings it has re - newed my
mp
67
Slower
rit.
world.
p
pp

PART III

How the Voice Works

The first part of this book is devoted to getting you involved in and enjoying the art of singing. The goal of this section is to help you understand the fascinating process and precision with which your voice produces sound, and some of the logical reasons for using specific techniques. Included here is a discussion of elementary vocal anatomy, additional exercises, and "finding out for yourself . . ." sections.

The human voice is fascinating to study. The more we know about it, the more we marvel at all its possibilities for producing sound. As a singer, you need to have a working knowledge of the major parts of your voice. It will help you be sensible about using your voice and keep you from panicking when anything goes awry.

CHAPTER SEVEN

Muscles and Physical Alignment

While we are being sensible, it is also useful to be logical about the human body. What follow are some hints about how to read and think about the anatomy of the voice.

Structure

Every building has a blueprint and a skeletal structure. This is what keeps it from collapsing. The same is true of the human body. Always look at the skeletal structure first to give you vital clues to how the body functions. These clues will give you important information about possible movement and support for joints, including those in the vocal skeleton.

To get a good idea of how a joint can move, look at how cartilage and/or bones fit together. For example, bones with rounded ends usually fit into bones with concave ends—some shallow, some deep. By looking at their shapes you can begin to decide what possibilities of movement there are and where there might be restrictions. Next you can begin to look at where, logically, a muscle would need to be located to move that joint.

Muscles

Skeletal muscles create movement of the body—not ligaments and membranes. When a muscle contracts, a joint changes position. Any move we make takes a signal of intent from the brain. The message is then sent to the muscle via nerve fibers and it is given the equivalent of an electric charge. The muscle then shortens or contracts. When the brain stops sending the signal and the charge stops, the muscle relaxes. This will give you a clue about highly tense or nervous people who can never either sit or stand still. Being "wired" is a good way to describe these people. In the case of hyperactivity, the brain rarely stops sending messages to the muscles. The muscles remain partly contracted and take energy away from what you really want to do—in your case sing. The body needs to replace tension with appropriate muscle use.

Muscles have to cross over joints and shorten or contract to move them. To determine the action of a muscle, you need to know where it is attached and in which direction the fibers are running. (You also need to know that muscles only contract to create an action. They do not push or expand.) By noting the direction of the fibers you can determine the direction of possible action of the muscle. Therefore, when you are looking at anatomical illustrations on a flat page, you can determine the action with a certain amount of logic rather than trying to memorize every muscle and its action. It is helpful to know that in general, muscles are named according to where they are located in the body, their shape, or their actions. Their Latin names are routinely used in texts, but don't let that deter you.

In order for muscles to contract and move a joint in one direction, muscles on the opposite side of the joint must relax. Sometimes muscles do not let go completely because they are still receiving a signal. When this happens, there is restriction of movement. A tug–of–war between opposing muscles creates muscular antagonism. When this kind of antagonism is used to stabilize a joint to help its performance, it is known as synergy. For example, when standing on one leg, the muscles on opposite sides of your thigh must help stabilize your hips. However, it is the unwanted antagonism that creates the problems. Using more muscles than you need when you are singing can make singing difficult for you, especially when a joint that needs flexibility becomes locked.

All this is a simple introduction and explanation for a very complex topic. For more information you can refer to anatomy books and Internet sites that have more detailed discussions of the human body.

Physical Alignment

Freeing your body and posture is not just for singing; it has a direct relationship to your physical balance, energy, health, voice, breathing, and image. The word *posture* conjures up memories of someone saying "Get your shoulders back and stand up straight." These verbal admonitions are given in great seriousness and with good intention, but they are not always very helpful, creating more problems than they solve. Many who are told to get their shoulders back as children poke their heads forward and tense their upper backs. You can walk down the street and easily pick out those people who may have been given that postural direction. Correcting posture means working with how it feels, not just verbal instructions.

Finding out for yourself . . .

Stand with both feet firmly on the floor and observe the following by becoming aware of the sensations in your body:

1. Where is my center of gravity?
2. Does my body feel heavy or light? (This has nothing to do with how much you weigh.)

3. Is my weight equally distributed between both feet?

4. What happens to my body when I want to rise on my toes?

5. Can I feel my whole foot on the floor?

6. Do my shoulders feel level?

7. Do my hips feel level?

8. Is there pressure anywhere along my spine?

9. Where is my breathing centered?

Experiment by rocking back and forth until the body finds a new feeling of balance. Learn to feel your balance first and then check in the mirror for confirmation.

Remember: How you think you look and how you actually look, are usually different.

A balanced, free, and flexible posture is fundamental to efficient vocal production and lovely voice quality. The alignment of the breathing mechanism—the chest, the voice box (larynx), and throat (resonator)—is the starting point for healthy singing. Correcting a voice without generating good postural balance first is like trying to build a sturdy, stable house around crooked framing.

A healthy human being is capable of maintaining balance against gravity with minimal effort, or with varying degrees of difficulty. As a child of two or three you probably had perfect alignment and balance with the head poised beautifully over the shoulders and hips. Notice young children around you; they normally exhibit this balance. They use few muscles and little energy to maintain this stance. Later, as children begin to develop various inefficient postural habits from sitting in chairs for long periods of time to imitating various role models from family or peers, they call into play more muscular energy and brain function. This creates an energy-draining situation in which many unnecessary muscles are needed to maintain balance. Such posture is known as collapse, not relaxation.

One postural habit that drains energy is pushing the head forward rather than aligning it over the shoulders (see Figure 7.1). This can happen when you spend long hours in front of a computer or over a desk with a slumped back or carry a heavy book pack on your back. When the head hangs forward, a huge strain is put on the muscles that run from the skull to the shoulders. These muscles contract strongly just to keep your head from falling off, so to speak. As a result of this constant contraction, the spine is pulled out of place at the top of the back, the shoulders ache, and the head hurts from the tug of the muscles on their insertion points on the back of the skull. Making it worse, to counterbalance the head as it pushes forward, the bottom goes backward. This is the way poor postural habits contribute to pain and potential injury.

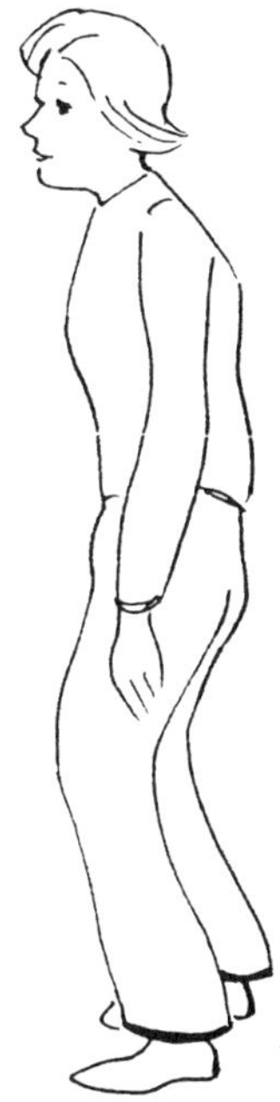

Figure 7.1: Poor posture

Experts in physical function, including those who study biomechanics and other techniques such as Alexander, have agreed on the following description of good posture. When a plumb line is dropped beside you, it falls through the ear, the point of the shoulder, the highest part of the hip-bone, just behind the knee cap and barely in front of the ankle (see Figure 7.2). How well do you fit this description?

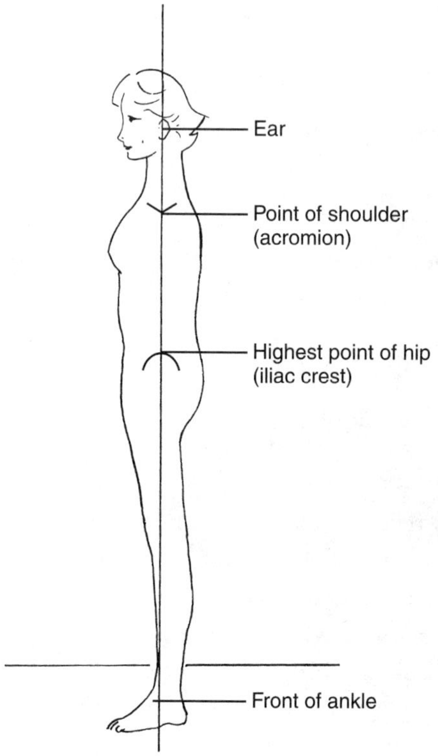
Ear
Point of shoulder
(acromion)
Highest point of hip
(iliac crest)
Front of ankle

Figure 7.2: Efficient alignment

GUIDELINES FOR GOOD PHYSICAL BALANCE

Here are some generally accepted guidelines for establishing good physical balance. Some of these are repeated from Part I with added detail.

- Feel as if the soles of your feet are superglued to the floor.
- Feel your neck lengthen by allowing the crown (cowlick area at the top-back) of the head to move upward without disturbing the tilt of the chin. It is important to begin with the head rather than some other part of the body. The whole spine has a chance to lengthen when you begin at the top.
- Make sure your knees are gently loose. Locked knees tend to contribute to an overly arched back. Loose knees will give the tail a chance to drop down and lengthen the back.
- Feel the ribs of the lower back move backward over the hips. (When the back is locked you will not be able to feel this.) You can encourage lower rib movement by placing the backs of your hands on them and

inhaling into the hands and pushing them backward with the breath (see Figure 7.3).

- Balance in the centers of your feet. Check your balance by rising on your toes without disturbing the rest of your body.

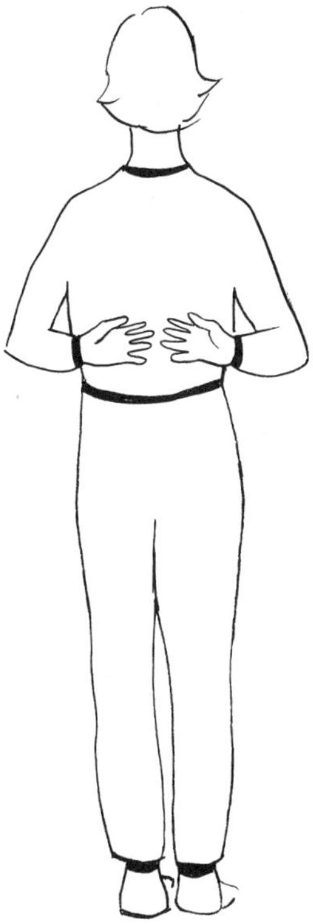

Figure 7.3: Placing hands on lower ribs

More ways to improve your posture:

1. Leave sticky note reminders to yourself by the telephone, on your mirror, on your music, on the piano, or any place your eyes fall during the day. When you are preoccupied with lots of other things, you need visible reminders. Do this for a few weeks and your body will begin to tell you when to adjust your posture. It will no longer care for the old one.

2. Feel as if there are two triangles that form your back: one with its apex on the spine just below the ribs and its base along the base of the spine and hip joints (see Figure 7.4) and the second with its apex on the spine just below the ribs and its base across the top of the shoulders. As you sit or walk, imagine that you get taller by expanding both triangles in opposite directions.

3. Lie on the floor with knees bent and your head on a book. (Make sure that your chin is not tipped toward the ceiling or pulled down onto your neck.) Gravity will help pull your back down. Breathe into the arched part of the back so that it reaches the floor. This is a good way to relax after a strenuous day of practice and study.

4. Get help from outside sources such as Alexander technique, yoga, martial arts courses, Feldenkrais work, Body Mapping, or Pilates.

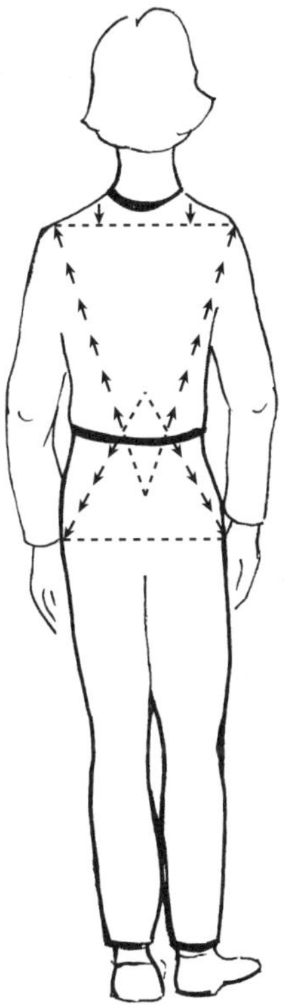

Figure 7.4: Triangles of the back with imaginary lines of direction
(Suggested by G. MacDonald.)

CHAPTER EIGHT

Breathing

Breath is the essence of life and sound, and normally breathing is a subconscious process. The regulation of the body's chemical balance depends on breathing. Also, air is the medium of transport for sound.

During low-energy activity, like sitting and reading or watching television, we need little air. For activities that require more energy, like singing and dramatic speech, we generally use more muscular effort and therefore need more air. However, you may need less air than you think for singing, particularly when your alignment and the balance of muscle use and airflow are maintained.

Airflow is a matter of balance between the pressures of the air outside and inside the chest. When we breathe out, a negative pressure is created inside the chest, leaving a space for the breath to then re-enter and equalize the pressure. This is an ongoing pattern that exists until we die. The air comes in without effort when the mouth is slightly open and the neck and larynx are free of muscular tension.

For now, remember the two most important things: (1) use the most physically and vocally efficient way of breathing, and (2) keep the air moving rather than attempting to hold it back. There are many theories regarding breathing for singing—some bordering on the strange and exotic. However, efficiency of breath is the ultimate factor in vocal health and quality of sound.

Subconsciously, we take about 24,400 breaths a day. If you had to take each breath consciously, you would have time for nothing else. When people walk or march while singing, they take air in without thinking about how they do it, and it seems to work with no problem. The breathing process happens below the level of consciousness without our interference. However, when we become conscious of the need to take in air while singing, we can develop many misconceptions and worries.

The perceived need to control air, the fear of running out of breath, and a sense of near panic or nervousness have caused the greatest breathing problems for singers. These fears and concerns among singers have led to general misuse of the breath and a misunderstanding about the physical process of breathing. The body and brain are capable of regulating the breath when the analytical-critical mind does not interfere with the automatic processes of the body and the vocal mechanism. The body behaves in a logical way, and this applies to breathing.

Note: There are good singers who breathe badly. They sing well in spite of themselves and might sound even more wonderful with a better technique. Most of us are not so fortunate, so pay attention and develop good habits from the beginning. Efficient breathing is not just for "classical" singing; pop singers could improve immensely from work on their breathing as well. You might be surprised to know how many noisy breath sounds have to be removed in the editing and processing of their recordings.

Let's begin with some simple concepts first. In normal, quiet, or passive breathing, the chest must expand to let air in and diminish in size to let it out. This is accomplished subconsciously with minimal physical effort. People breathe in many ways according to their postural habits and physical health. However, for singing, there are only efficient and inefficient ways of breathing. The efficient way was discussed briefly at the beginning of this book. We will now look at it in more detail so you can understand what is happening.

EFFICIENT BREATHING

1. The body is physically balanced and poised for action.
2. The intake of air is silent—no gasps!
3. There is no visible muscle tension—especially not in the face, mouth, neck, shoulders, or chest.
4. The feeling of breath begins deep in the lower part of the body.
5. The focus is on sensing the action of the lowest ribs in the back and the lower part of the abdomen in the front.
6. The abdomen and ribs are flexible and available to respond to the demands of singing.
7. The muscles of the abdomen are able to work with reasonable effort to help the air flow out without interference by the chest or neck.

Inhalation

When you look at a skeleton, you will see that the largest open space of the chest is at the bottom of the rib cage (see Figure 8.1). So it makes sense that when we want to create more space for air we need to expand in that area. This is precisely what happens in natural and efficient breathing.

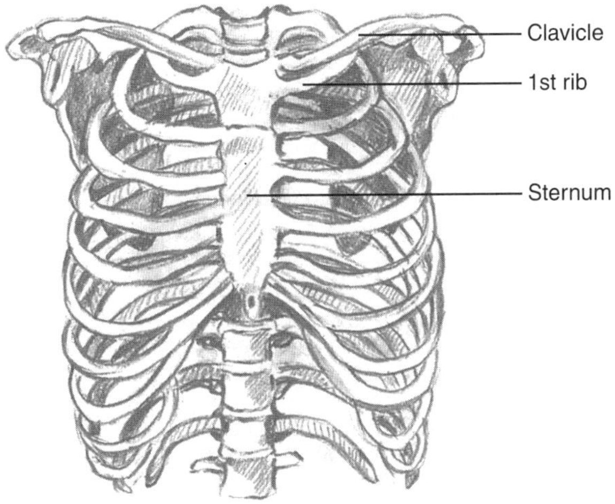
Clavicle
1st rib
Sternum

Figure 8.1: Rib cage

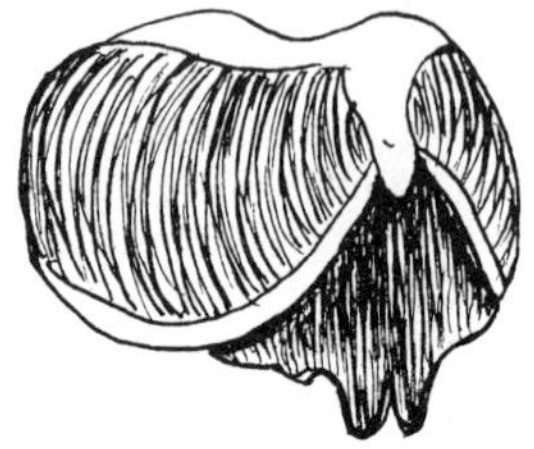

Figure 8.2a: Diaphragm as a "hat"

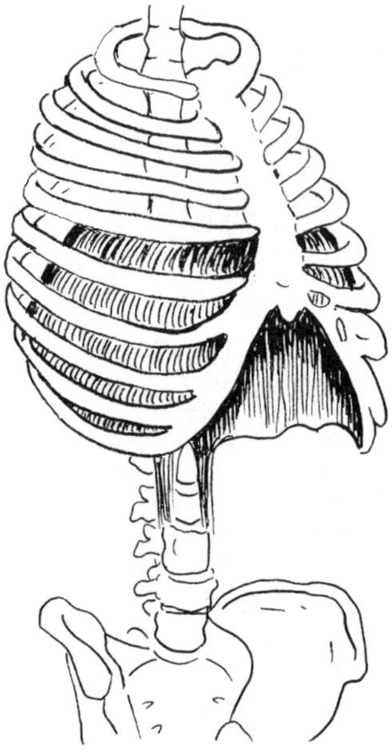

Figure 8.2b: Diaphragm placed in rib cage

A very large dome-shaped muscle called the diaphragm occupies the lower part of the rib cage (see Figure 8.2a). The diaphragm is so "fabled" in singing lore and so unfamiliar in appearance to most people that they are amazed when they finally see the real thing in a science lab. It is the most important muscle of inhalation (inspiration) and acts as a partition between the chest and abdomen. Picture it this way: Imagine inserting into an empty skeleton a large, strangely shaped muscular hat that has its lower brim stuck around the bottom edges of the rib cage and the spine at the level of the last rib (see Figure 8.2b). The top part of the dome is tendonous and located centrally just below the heart; it does not have the capability to move very much. (Your heart has enough work to do without jumping up and down every time you breathe.)

The edges and main body of the diaphragm are formed of thin muscle and the center is a thin, flat tendon. When the diaphragm contracts, it moves downward, displacing the lower ribs and the organs and soft structures below it. It is not capable of moving below the ribs, including those in front. It does not invert. The action of the diaphragm causes the abdomen to expand and the lower ribs to move outward. This abdominal expansion is caused by organs being displaced and has often caused people to mistake it for the diaphragm itself. When the body is in good alignment, this action will happen easily without specific attention paid to the diaphragm. Without such alignment, efficient breathing becomes difficult to master.

Twelve pairs of small muscles elevate the ribs from behind and help the diaphragm. Each of these muscles runs from projections on the sides of the vertebrae (transverse processes of the spine) down to the angle of the rib below (see Figure 8.3). They make up what are called the *levator costarum*. This puts them in a good position to raise the ribs slightly and swing them outward. The effectiveness of this movement relies on the freedom and flexibility of the back. A rigid back will hinder these muscles from doing their job.

Numerous other muscles attached to the neck, rib cage, and back also work to maintain stability during the breathing process. The muscles between the ribs

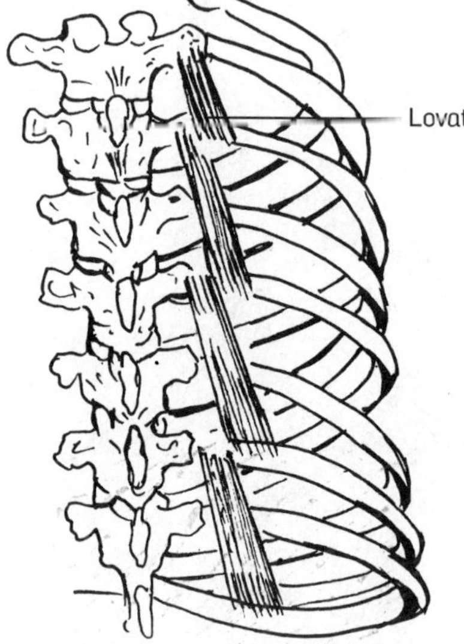
Lovator costarum

Figure 8.3: Levator costarum muscles (posterior view)

(intercostals) are often mentioned as contributing to inhalation and exhalation. However, they are most effective as stabilizers of the ribs. All these muscles seem to work very well when we stand properly. Only the primary muscles have been included in this discussion in order to leave your mind relatively uncluttered. More detailed knowledge can be obtained through reading some of the texts mentioned in the "Further Reading" section at the end of the book.

Finding out for yourself . . .

With a partner, experiment with some common but inefficient inhalation patterns.

What happens to the body when you take breaths in the following ways and then sing? What happens to the quality of the sound? Into what physical patterns does each exercise force the action of breathing? Carefully watch the chest and abdomen during these experiments.

1. Take a breath with the tummy held in tightly.
2. Take a breath with the back held rigidly.
3. Take a breath with the back overly arched (but not exaggerated).
4. Take a breath while slouched in a chair.

Why are these patterns less useful for good singing?

Now feel the difference in the vocal tract and chest when you inhale low in the body with good alignment and a released head and neck. Describe the difference in how you feel and look. Ask your partner to describe the difference in the vocal quality.

Exhalation

Because most people assume you have to take air in to get it out, inhalation is usually discussed first. Ideally, singers think first of exhaling, and then of allowing the inhalation to be a reflex action. It is just as easy to think of breathing out to breathe in. After all, the body is just creating a cyclic balance. Exhaling during the introduction of a song and then allowing a reflex breath a beat or two just before you sing is a more secure approach. Most people panic during an introduction, and go through a pattern of breathing in and out, and somehow are never ready when it is time to sing, hence the last-minute gasp.

Exhalation during minimal physical activity is a simple matter of releasing the muscles of inspiration (such as the diaphragm) and letting the elastic recoil of the lungs and gravity do the rest. This is done for us by the subconscious. For singing, we need to use more muscular effort, and it is best accomplished by the muscles of the abdomen.

The abdominal muscles form a kind of girdle around the abdomen and are located in the best place to facilitate breathing without interfering with the vocal tract. There are three paired muscles (*transversus abdominis* and the *internal* and *external obliques*) that form this girdle and a fourth set, the "six-pack" (*rectus abdominis*) that goes up and down the mid-line of the abdomen from the ribs to the pubic bone. The muscles that form the abdominal girdle tend to work as a unit for breathing. They contract and cause the abdominal contents to move toward the back and the diaphragm, thus helping the diaphragm to return to its original position and to send air out of the lungs (see Figure 8.4).

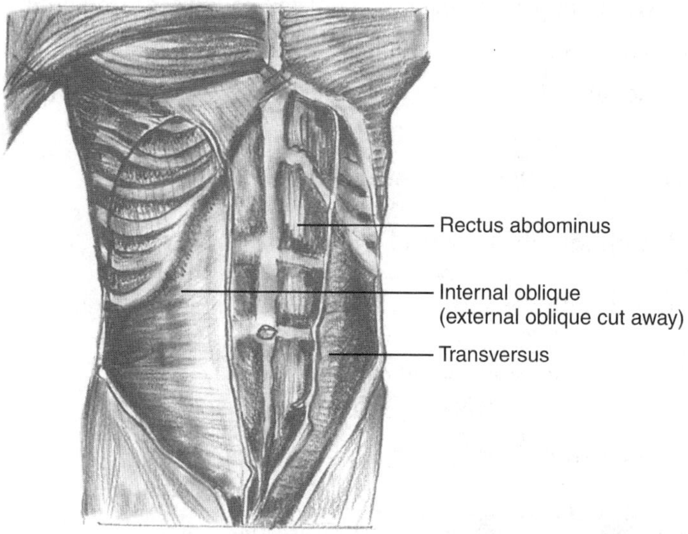
Rectus abdominus
Internal oblique
(external oblique cut away)
Transversus

Figure 8.4: Abdominal muscles: obliques and rectus abdominus

Normally, the action of the rectus muscle is to bring the rib cage and pelvis closer together, as in curling forward. However, some singers use it sparingly and gently to add a little top-up breath pressure or emphasis to a phrase or note.

If you have done "abs" workouts in a gym, you will know that you can contract your abdominal muscles in different areas. Various kinds of sit-ups help to develop the upper or lower abs. *Where* the singer chooses to activate the abs is very important. The most efficient area is the lowest one near the pelvis. Contracting the muscles in this area sends pressure toward the diaphragm and lower back ribs from below. Using the middle or the top abs tends to cut the singer in the middle and send energy up and down at the same time. Inefficient use of the muscles of exhalation can cause unwanted tensions to transfer to the neck, throat, and jaw. The better you maintain your good posture, the easier it will be to use the more effective lower part of the abdomen for exhaling. Collapsing the body will cause the air to release too quickly and you will pay the price by running out of breath.

Finding out for yourself . . .

Playing with balloons

Imagine that a blown-up balloon represents your whole abdominal area. Draw the rough outline of the pelvis, sacrum (fused bones that form the lowest part of the spine), and lower ribs on it. The top of the balloon represents the diaphragm and the lowest part the pelvic floor muscles (sometimes called the pelvic diaphragm).

Note what happens when you push on the top of the balloon—remembering that in reality, the bony parts will not move.

What happens when you hold the front tightly and try to push the top down? This is the equivalent of holding in the abdomen and trying to take a good breath. In this situation, the diaphragm cannot really descend in this situation and the chest is forced upward.

What happens when you squeeze the top of the balloon?

What happens when you squeeze the lower part of the front of the balloon? Notice particularly what happens to the top. It tends to enlarge and spread. This is similar to what happens to the diaphragm and lower ribs when you use the lower part of the abdomen to help send the air back out.

BALANCING BREATH AND MUSIC

There are days when singing seems easy and effortless; on other days it seems like hard work. The easy days probably occur when the body, breath, and voice are working as a unit rather than fighting each other. The first months of learning to sing can seem like a battle between old and new habits. However, it will all prove worthwhile when you finally achieve good coordination; it is easy to sing and the resulting "high" or being in the singing "zone" is satisfying. That is when singing can become addictive.

A number of things are happening when the coordination is good: There is a balance of pressures in the abdomen, chest, at the level of the vocal folds (vocal cords), and in the mouth that help the singer maintain steady airflow appropriate to the music and phrasing of the text.

These pressures include (1) the lower abdomen contracting up toward the lower ribs at the back, slowing the return of the diaphragm and ribs; (2) the flow of air meeting resistance of the vocal folds as they close for phonation (see Chapter 9), keeping a certain amount of pressure in the chest and resistance to the diaphragm (see Figure 8.5); and (3) the exhaled air hitting the palate, teeth or even lips and moving back toward the vocal folds creating back pressure in the mouth. These pressures are the product of coordinated muscle action and breath. They are not goals in and of themselves. When any

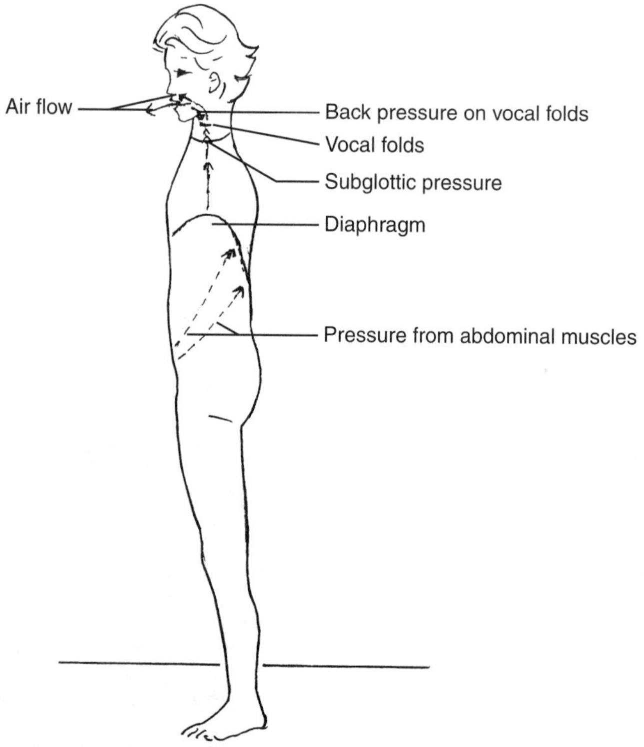
Air flow
Back pressure on vocal folds
Vocal folds
Subglottic pressure
Diaphragm
Pressure from abdominal muscles

Figure 8.5: Balance of pressures while singing

one of these areas is out of sync, you can have difficulty with airflow and phrasing. In the *Finding out for yourself* box above you were playing with balloons. Go back and look at this again. It can give you a sense of the physical buoyancy that happens when you sing well.

Poor Breathing Habits

After reading (or singing) all this information, it would be ideal if you had no poor habits. As that is rarely the case, poor habits must be addressed. Watch the breathing of singers in concert and on TV and video. You will see examples of some of the most common faults, discussed next.

Collapsing physically when beginning to sing

Look in the mirror at your upper chest. Sometimes the downward movement that happens at the beginning of a phrase is quite obvious and at other times it is very subtle. Such a movement is very inefficient for breath control and sound quality.

Gasping

This is simply counterproductive. It locks your body and larynx and makes a dreadful noise. Too many singers have been told that they need large amounts of air. This causes them to end a musical phrase by gulping air in immediately.

This gasp at the end of exhalation is a common habit causing the vocal folds to clamp shut and create excess pressure in the chest. Singers are then unable to recover in time for the next phrase.

Remember your wide breathing pipe discussed earlier. It cannot be squeezed at the level of the larynx. Let your air flow easily as you sing and allow it to cease moving by stopping the abdominal pressure. Leave yourself reminders everywhere so that good breathing becomes a habit. This is also important for centering and creating peace in yourself. Breathing techniques are used in many types of meditation.

Be careful in your conversations with friends. You do not have to gasp and heave your chest when you are enthusiastic and excited. Excitement without a gasp is the key thought.

Exercise . . .

Choose a song you know and patiently sing each phrase separately so you can make sure your breaths have no associated gasps:

Using your hands (at the level of your neck and upper chest), indicate the stable width of your breath channel (see Figure 8.6).

Breathe out before you begin. When you inhale to sing the first phrase, imagine that it is through that very wide channel.

At the end of each phrase you sing, allow the breath to go out through the wide channel. It does not matter how long it takes. The rhythm and timing of the breaths will be distorted in this exercise. Do this for every breath that you take in the song.

After you have done this with no physical and breath tension, sing several phrases together in their correct rhythm. When there are no gasps, continue singing the song the same way.

Figure 8.6: Imaginary breathing pipeline

Taking in more air than you need

Five short notes do not need twenty-five notes' worth of air. You cannot save it. Take what you need and use all of it. Otherwise you will tank up, close the vocal folds to hold it in, create a tremendous pressure in your chest, and feel as if you do not have enough air. No one wants to sing feeling like that!

CHAPTER NINE

Making Sound

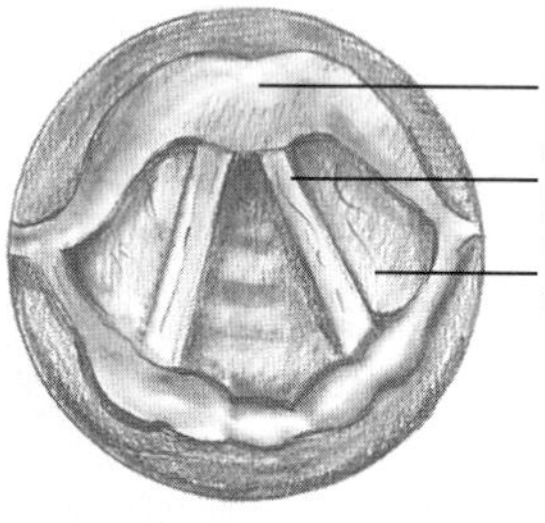

Epiglottis
Vocal ligament
Vocalis muscle

Figure 9.1: Vocal folds viewed from above

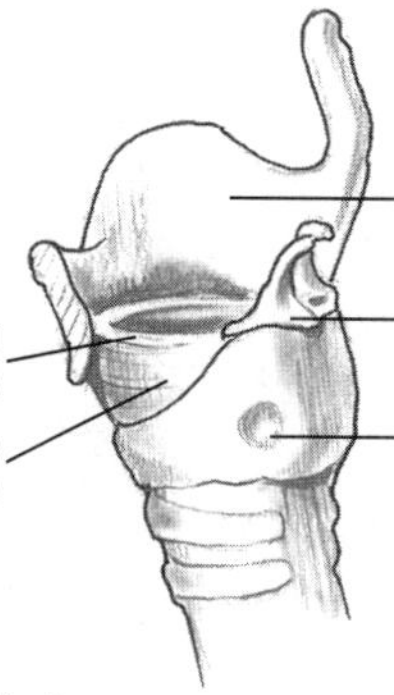

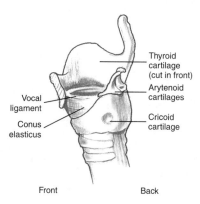

Thyroid cartilage (cut in front)
Arytenoid cartilages
Cricoid cartilage
Vocal ligament
Conus elasticus
Front
Back

Figure 9.2: Cartilages of the larynx

Sound is made and amplified in the vocal tract, which consists of the voice box (*larynx*) and throat area all the way up to the soft palate (and the nose, for nasal sounds). The initiation of the voiced sounds we make comes from the vibration of two folds of muscle, housed in the larynx (Adam's apple) that sits on top of the windpipe (*trachea*) (see Figure 9.1). These folds are commonly (and incorrectly) known as the "vocal cords." When relaxed, they are about the size of your thumbnail and a little longer than that when stretched for higher pitches. If you have ever blown up a balloon, pulled the opening wide to release the air, and listened to the resulting squeal, you will have a good idea of how the vocal folds work.

The larynx consists of several cartilages and is a housing for the vocal folds that are activated by airflow from the lungs (see Figure 9.2). The sound is then modified and amplified by resonating in the "vocal tract" (the *pharynx* or throat and mouth). Alterations in the position of the larynx will affect the shape of the vocal tract, change the voice quality, and possibly affect the efficiency of the vibration of the vocal folds. When air is sent through these folds with the intention of making sound, they vibrate, creating the sound and the pitches we use for speech and singing. The cleaner and more efficiently these folds vibrate, the clearer and healthier the sound. The number of times the vocal folds vibrate per second determines the pitch. For example, for A 440 (the A immediately above Middle C), the folds vibrate 440 times per second.

The larynx is suspended and supported in the neck from in front, behind, above, and below by groups of paired muscles (see Figure 9.3). It is not stuck in the neck but is able to move freely when we swallow and speak. You can put your finger on your larynx and feel its movement when you swallow. While the larynx can be looked at as a separate unit, it never functions in that manner; the connections are too complicated. It has a complex relationship with the throat (pharynx), soft palate, tongue, jaw, neck, and chest. The position of the neck and chest, movement and tension of the tongue and jaw, and flexibility or constriction of the muscles of the pharynx all contribute to laryngeal efficiency and affect tone quality.

The vocal folds act as a sensitive valve and guardian for preventing foreign material from entering the lungs. They close tightly when we swallow or cause us to cough when anything other than the smallest imaginable particle tries to enter.

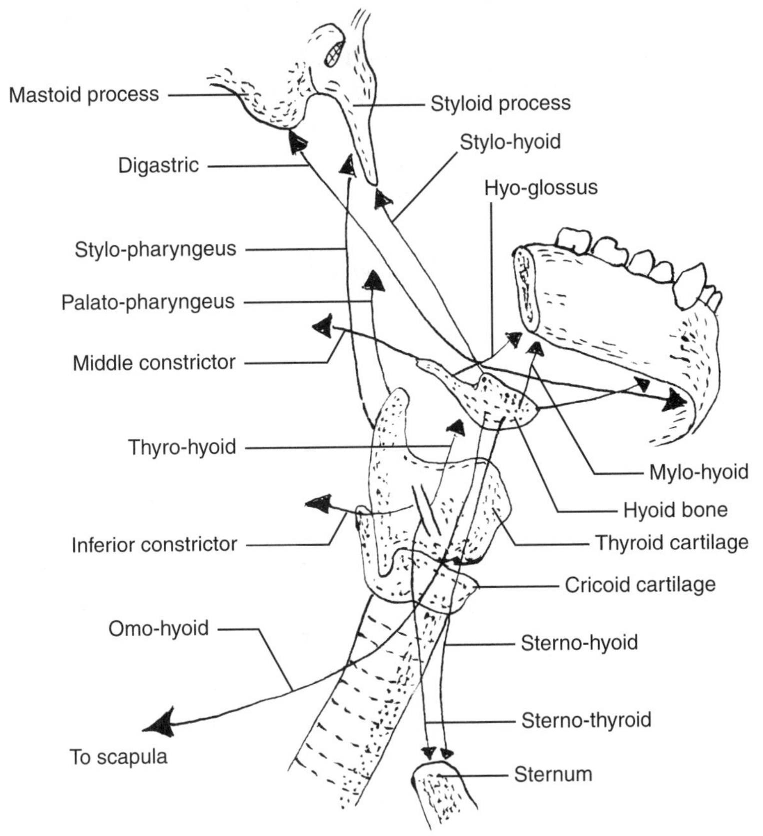
Mastoid process
Styloid process
Stylo-hyoid
Digastric
Hyo-glossus
Stylo-pharyngeus
Palato-pharyngeus
Middle constrictor
Thyro-hyoid
Mylo-hyoid
Hyoid bone
Thyroid cartilage
Inferior constrictor
Cricoid cartilage
Omo-hyoid
Sterno-hyoid
Sterno-thyroid
To scapula
Sternum

Figure 9.3: Diagram of muscles suspending the larynx

You have probably experienced the powerful coughing reflex that occurs when something goes down the wrong way. Swallowing raises the larynx, shortens and narrows the throat, and causes the vocal folds to react by closing tightly to prevent food from going down into the lungs. Singing demands the opposite physical situation from swallowing—a wide-open air passageway with no constriction or hindrance to the balance of the larynx in the neck or its ability to vibrate freely.

STRUCTURE OF THE LARYNX

Knowledge of the basic anatomy of the laryngeal mechanism is useful for dispelling some of the mystery of that "box" inside us that enables us to speak and sing. Like the rest of the body, its skeletal structure supports the movements of the muscles needed for us to make sound. The main structure of the larynx consists of four cartilages and a bone (see Figure 9.4):

- The cricoid looks like a signet ring with the highest part at the back. It sits on top of the trachea and forms a stable base for a pair of small arytenoid cartilages. On both sides of the cricoid there is a small joint formed with the lower horns of thyroid cartilage.
- The two arytenoids look like two small pointed hats and sit atop the back of the cricoid. Attached to them are the vocal folds, the muscles that move the vocal folds together and apart, and the vocal ligament.
- The thyroid cartilage is shaped somewhat like a shield, is open at the back, and has upper and lower horns. It serves as an anchor for the

vocal folds and forms a joint with the cricoid on each side. There are muscle attachments to the hyoid bone, the sternum, the pharynx, underneath the skull, and the palate. This complicated set of attachments forms part of the sling in which the larynx hangs.

Note: Most of the muscles attaching to the thyroid come from above.

- The hyoid bone is shaped like a horseshoe (sitting horizontally), is located between the jaw and thyroid cartilage, and is considered part of the laryngeal structure. It has complicated attachments and is suspended in the neck by muscles and membranes that attach to the thyroid cartilage, sternum, scapula, jaw, tongue, pharynx, and skull (see Figure 9.4).

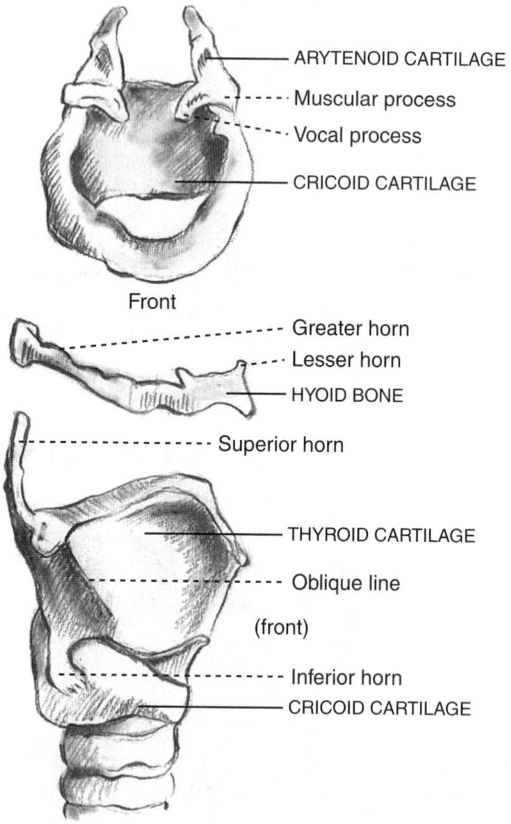
ARYTENOID CARTILAGE
Muscular process
Vocal process
CRICOID CARTILAGE
Front
Greater horn
Lesser horn
HYOID BONE
Superior horn
THYROID CARTILAGE
Oblique line
(front)
Inferior horn
CRICOID CARTILAGE

Figure 9.4: Skeleton of the larynx

Finding out for yourself . . .

One of the best ways to understand the larynx is to make a 3-dimensional clay model of the cartilages. It is not the artwork that is important; it is the process. By going through the process of making this model, you will gain a very different understanding and appreciation of the structure. This will then give you the basis for understanding how the muscles work.

1. Build the cricoid cartilage as a base. Look carefully at its shape before you begin. (Some people like to build a solid trachea for it to sit on, but this is not necessary.)
2. Now look very carefully at the shape of the arytenoid cartilages and create them. Note their relative proportion to the cricoid and thyroid. It is worth measuring your picture or diagram to determine the ratio. Now set them on the back of the cricoid cartilage.
3. Next build the thyroid cartilage. Again, look carefully at its features and dimensions. Exactly where is the joint of the thyroid and cricoid on each of these cartilages?
4. You may wish to add the vocal folds that attach to the vocal process of the arytenoids and the inside front of the thyroid.
5. The epiglottis can now be attached to the inside front of the thyroid cartilage just above the attachment of the vocal folds.
6. The hyoid bone can now be made. You will probably need some toothpicks to hold it in place.

You now have a structure to work with. As you learn more about the muscles, you can take something like small ribbons and cut them in the shape of the muscles and stick them on with pins.

Important Muscles of Phonation

To make sound, the vocal folds need to come together. To breathe, they need to open. To create higher pitches, the vocal folds must be able to stretch. To accomplish all this some small muscles do a lot of work without our having to think much about it. They are placed in very logical positions to execute these skilled movements.

First, let's define a vocal fold more precisely. A vocal fold consists of a muscle (the *vocalis* or *thyro-arytenoid*) that runs from the front of the arytenoid cartilages (vocal process) to the inside of the back of the thyroid cartilage. The muscle is covered with mucous membrane and there is a ligament on the inside edge of each fold known as the vocal ligament. This ligament is the loose end of a structure called the *conus elasticus* (Figure 9.2), a tough ligament-like structure that looks a little like a tent. It arises from the top of the sides of the cricoid cartilage and forms a support for the vocal folds, with the upper free edge becoming the vocal ligament. When your voice is healthy, this ligament looks pearly white. Generally speaking, the vocal folds are thick and loose when relaxed or singing on low notes; they are stretched as you move higher in pitch.

Muscles that move the vocal folds apart

On the back of the cricoid cartilage are two muscles that move the vocal folds apart (abduct them) for breathing. These muscles run from the base of the cricoid up and outward to insert on the outside (lateral side, muscular process) of the bases of the arytenoid cartilages. They are logically called the *posterior crico-arytenoids*. When these muscles contract, they swing the arytenoids wide taking the vocal folds with them (see Figure 9.5).

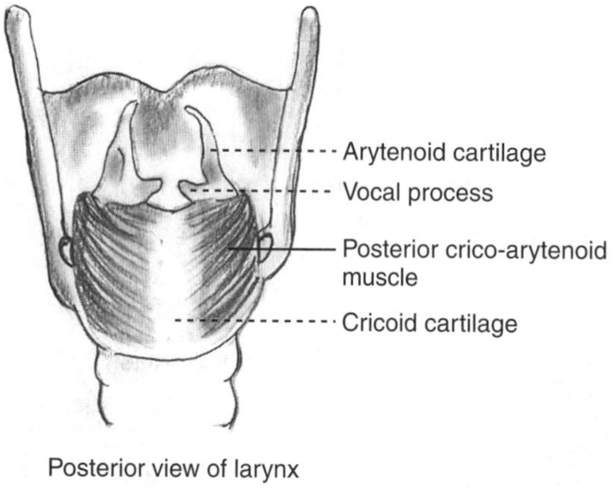
Arytenoid cartilage
Vocal process
Posterior crico-arytenoid muscle
Cricoid cartilage
Posterior view of larynx

Figure 9.5: Posterior crico-arytenoid muscles

Muscles that bring the vocal folds together

It takes two sets of muscles to fully close (adduct) the vocal folds for phonation. Running from the upper edge of either side of the cricoid cartilage are muscles that attach to the sides (muscular processes) of the arytenoids. These muscles are called the lateral crico-arytenoids. When they contract they swing the front of the arytenoids (vocal processes) together causing the vocal folds to meet in the center (see Figure 9.6). However, the meeting is not complete; this leaves a small chink between the arytenoid cartilages where air can escape. To complete the process and ensure a clear, clean sound, the arytenoids must slide toward each other and close the gap. The muscles that contract to do this are a group called the interarytenoids—all very logical.

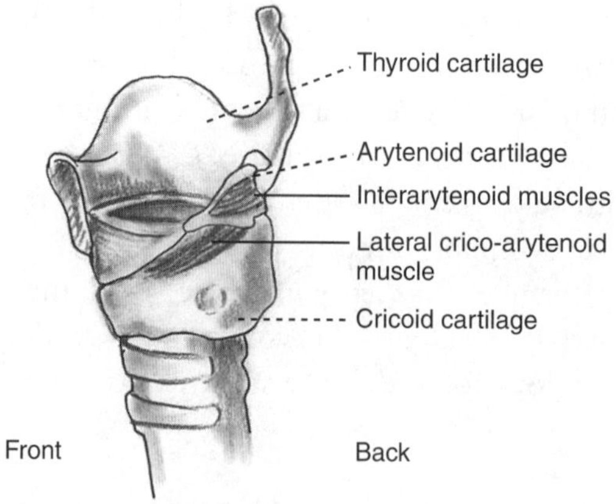
Thyroid cartilage
Arytenoid cartilage
Interarytenoid muscles
Lateral crico-arytenoid muscle
Cricoid cartilage
Front
Back

Figure 9.6: Interarytenoid muscles and lateral cricoarytenoid muscle

Muscles responsible for pitch changes

The vocal folds are relaxed for the lowest pitches and are lengthened to create higher pitches. Common sense tells us that there need to be muscles in place to cause the thyroid and cricoid cartilages to move apart and create the stretch. The pair of muscles that performs this task are the cricothyroids, running from the front of the cricoid to the lower front edge and horns of the thyroid. When they contract they tilt the thyroid cartilage forward and the cricoid backward a little, creating a pull on the vocal folds (see Figure 9.7). When the lengthening of the folds is done smoothly and evenly with no extra tension in the throat and larynx, the pitch change happens easily. At the highest pitches, the vocal folds are fully stretched and the vocal ligament vibrates. When the vocal folds are not stretched, they are thick. This configuration produces the low, heavier sounds (sometimes called "chest" voice). When the folds are stretched, the sounds are higher and lighter. It is when you sing the high notes with a very heavy sound that "muscular arguments" (antagonism) can occur and create uneven changes in the sound.

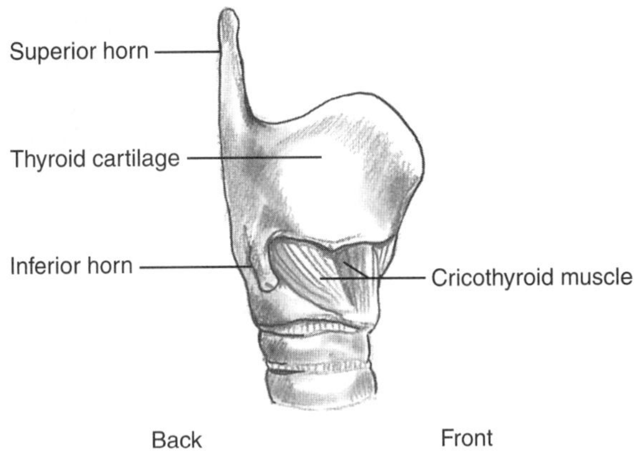
Superior horn
Thyroid cartilage
Inferior horn
Cricothyroid muscle
Back
Front

Figure 9.7: Cricothyroid muscle

A note about pitch

While the vocal folds are responsible for initiating the pitch, they are not the only determining factor for singing *on pitch*. Poor vocal technique can cause a singer to go out of tune by going flat (too far below the pitch) or sharp (too far above the pitch). Extraneous tension of the tongue, jaw, and neck can pull your larynx out of line and hinder the efficiency of the vocal folds. This can cause the vocal folds to vibrate awkwardly so that the voice is "out of tune" with itself. Some singers have been accused of having poor musical ears when that is not the case at all.

The vocal folds themselves tend to be passive in that they have other muscles moving them most of the time, either stretching them or moving them toward or away from each other. When they (the vocalis muscles) contract, they become bulkier and shorten the distance between the thyroid and arytenoid cartilages. This can cause them to act as antagonists to the muscles working to open and close them, and make the voice heavy sounding.

Note: If you had to think about all the muscles we have discussed, you would not be able to function as a singer. It would be like analyzing all the muscles in your arm before you swung at a ball. The ball would be long gone by the time you swung the bat. Fortunately, the body is more clever than we are and manages to regulate all of this by the intention to sing, by imagination, and by good physical alignment. It is when we have a problem that we need to address something specific. The larynx has been researched more than any other area of voice because scientists and doctors can see and analyze this area best. However, remember that the larynx is mainly the initiator of the voice that begins the sound and furnishes the pitches.

Sounds Made by the Vocal Folds

The initiation of sound

The initiation of vocal sound is called the onset or attack. For a clear sound, the vocal folds need to touch each other cleanly and gently. This happens when the muscles of breathing, the airflow, and the onset of sound are well coordinated. When the folds close with a lot of pressure, they can beat on each other and create little explosions of sound (glottal attacks). The sound this makes is usually tight and irritating to the ears. Continual abuse like this can cause growths on the folds called nodules.

Inefficient coordination can also cause the sound to be too breathy. This happens when the folds do not close well and air leaks out. It is all right to make a deliberately breathy sound for some popular styles, but a consistently breathy sound is indicative of poor vocal balance. And do not confuse breathiness and hoarseness. Hoarseness is discussed in the chapter on vocal health.

Quality within the vocal range

Sometimes in inexperienced singers, the lower voice will seem rich and strong and the upper voice will sound small and thin. In these singers the change in quality can be obvious. This happens when the highest and lowest areas of the vocal range are not connected by smooth coordination of the vocal mechanism. Generally it is desirable to have an even sound in classical music, but consistency is less important to nonclassical singers who happily use much more variety of vocal sounds in their singing. Pop singing, jazz, and many other styles are more adventurous with sound and may not be so concerned about equal quality throughout the range.

In vocal literature you will find these differences in sound referred to as vocal registers. A balanced voice produces a sound that is even from the bottom to the top of the singer's vocal range. Many of the nonclassical styles emphasize a sound that is closer to normal speech quality, and they use extremes of range for effect. This is true of most female and some male singing. However, it is current fashion for male soloists and groups to use a lot of light high sound that mainly involves the vibration of the vocal ligaments and edges of the vocal folds.

It is important to understand that most people have a speaking voice that is close to the lowest pitches of the voice. Because this is the sound we hear most of the time, we become accustomed to that quality. This can make the higher qualities sound high and thin, or even like yelling, to the ears of singers when they first begin to sing healthily. The more you practice and the more you use audio and video feedback, the faster you will rid yourself of that concept.

Faulty perceptions of the singer can cause imbalance as well. An example of this might be the alto who is trying to sound like her perception of an alto, and therefore putting a lot of pressure on the voice by singing heavily. This can happen also to nonclassical singers who try to sing in a heavy, throaty voice throughout their range. When this occurs, it puts quite a strain on the vocal folds and can cause a break in the voice and even physical damage.

Note: It is easy to get hung up on creating an even sound *inside your head.* This is one of the jokes played on you by the acoustics of the voice. When you allow your inner hearing or analytical-critical brain to dominate control of the sound, the joke is on you because it does not come out that way to the audience. Singers who do this find it hard to believe that they are being fooled—but fooled they are. For the singer, the motor is inside the body and all the mechanics can be heard. Good singing can be very noisy internally and will sound and feel very uneven and buzzy to you. This is why it is imperative to have a teacher with good eyes and ears, or audio, and preferably, video feedback.

Vibrato

As beginning singers develop an easily produced sound, they often feel and hear their voices become pulsating and "wavy." The common response is, "Does that make me sound like an opera singer?" There is a fear that the voice is becoming too stylized, and the reference in this case is negative. However, you need to know that the voice has a natural vibrato that contributes to the pleasantness of the sound. It is a factor that successful pop singers use frequently.

The vibrato is an acoustic phenomenon that occurs in most voices. It was so valued by instrumentalists that they have mimicked it in their playing. It is like waves or ripples of sound. These waves can be fast or slow (frequency), deep or shallow (amplitude), and narrow and wide (variance)—much like the ripples in water. They add beauty to the sound and are acceptable to the ear as long as they vary no more than a quarter of a tone on either side of the pitch. An amplitude that is too wide will produce a sound that varies too much around the pitch and is unpleasant to the listener.

When these waves of sound are too fast and too close together, they are like a bleat—usually caused by pushing the voice too much from the throat. This bleat can occur when you try to restrict airflow at the level of the larynx rather than use the breathing muscles appropriately. When the frequency of the vibrato is too slow and wide, a wobble is heard. This can be caused by a number of factors from poor breath management to muscle fatigue. Comics like to mimic opera singers by producing a big fat sound with a wobble. It does not have to be that way. Note that it is not useful for the singer to think of controlling the vibrato. The keys to even sound are good alignment, efficient muscle use, deep breathing, and consistent airflow.

The ideal vibrato has consistent, even acoustic waves. They are not perfect like a computer, which can generate perfect waves but not beautiful vocal sounds. The ear prefers a vibrato that occurs from five to eight times per second and varies a semitone around the pitch. Any voice or acoustics lab can show you exactly how all the variants of the vibrato look spectrographically.

Straight sound

Some types of music demand less vibrato and more speech-like sound. Certainly speech quality is used in a variety of nonclassical styles such as pop, jazz, rap, rock, and some world music. An acoustic reading will demonstrate that this sound irons out the peaks and troughs of the vibrato. There is nothing wrong with a straight sound as long as it is not blatant, strained, or tight. Every singer needs variety of sound and expression. When you use your imagination, you will be surprised at the spontaneous response of your voice in color and quality.

When you sing in a choir, you may hear the conductor ask the singers to produce a straight tone with less vibrato. Conductors find it difficult to get a balanced matched sound when there are so many diverse vocal techniques in the choir. It is the conscientious singers who follow the directions and the not-so-concientious ones who keep their vibrato; invariably the straight tones get straighter and the vibratos increase, thus defeating the purpose. Your training in the basic principles of good singing with work on posture and breath will cause many of the issues of vocal imbalance to go away.

Finding out for yourself . . .

Many schools have voice or acoustics labs with spectrographs or oscilloscopes. Experimenting on these machines while making various tones can be very enlightening for the singer. You may even have a software program on your computer that will do this for you. Visit the acoustics or language lab in your school or some place nearby and experiment with well-coordinated vocal attacks, breathy sounds, deliberate vibrato, and straight tones.

CHAPTER TEN

Voice Quality and Resonance

Each person has his or her own unique vocal signature or vocal quality. This is why you can recognize people simply by hearing their voices. As children learn to speak, they mimic the muscular speech patterns of close relatives, peers, and the local community. Regional speech patterns are referred to as dialects or "accents." Your accent is a result of the infinite variety of shapes formed in the throat or the pharynx and the movement patterns of the tongue and jaw.

While the sound is initiated in the larynx, the quality of sound depends on the shape of the pharynx. The pharynx (throat) is highly flexible and capable of forming many different shapes. Each variation in shape will cause your voice to produce a different voice quality.

Finding out for yourself . . .

Find a way to watch or listen to three or four singers with different styles—country-western, jazz, gospel, pop. Note particularly what they do with the vowel sounds, and their lips and jaws. See if you can discover what makes them different.

Imitate several of these styles. What do you have to do to sing that way? What changes do you feel in your throat when you do it?

The pharynx serves a dual purpose by acting as an air and a food passageway. For breathing it needs to be relaxed and spacious; for swallowing it closes around the food and squeezes it down into the esophagus. When you swallow, the whole pharynx is pulled up and narrowed to squeeze the food down. This brings the larynx up with it. Therefore the whole throat becomes short and narrow—not a good space for singing. When the muscles of the pharynx relax, the space is wide and long—the optimum for the most resonance and a freely produced sound. People sing in many gradations between the closed and open throat.

Finding out for yourself . . .

Put your finger on your larynx and swallow. Note what happens. Now sing something in the position of the "swallow." What does it sound like?

With your finger still on your larynx take a nice breath with your mouth open. What happens now? Sing something with that feeling of space.

Structure of the Pharynx

The pharynx is a muscular sleeve-like structure that hangs from the base of the skull and attaches itself to various bones and cartilages along the way. It has openings into the nose, the mouth, and the larynx, and then it becomes completely circular and continues as the esophagus.

Divisions of the pharynx

Anatomists and acousticians usually divide the pharynx into three main sections: the nasal pharynx, the oral pharynx, and the laryngeal pharynx (see Figure 10.1). The nasal pharynx is located between the base of the skull and the soft palate. The soft palate (the soft part located at the end of your hard palate) can move up and close off the nose as in making non-nasal sounds or swallowing, and it can be lowered for nasal sounds or breathing (you will have a chance to experiment with this later).

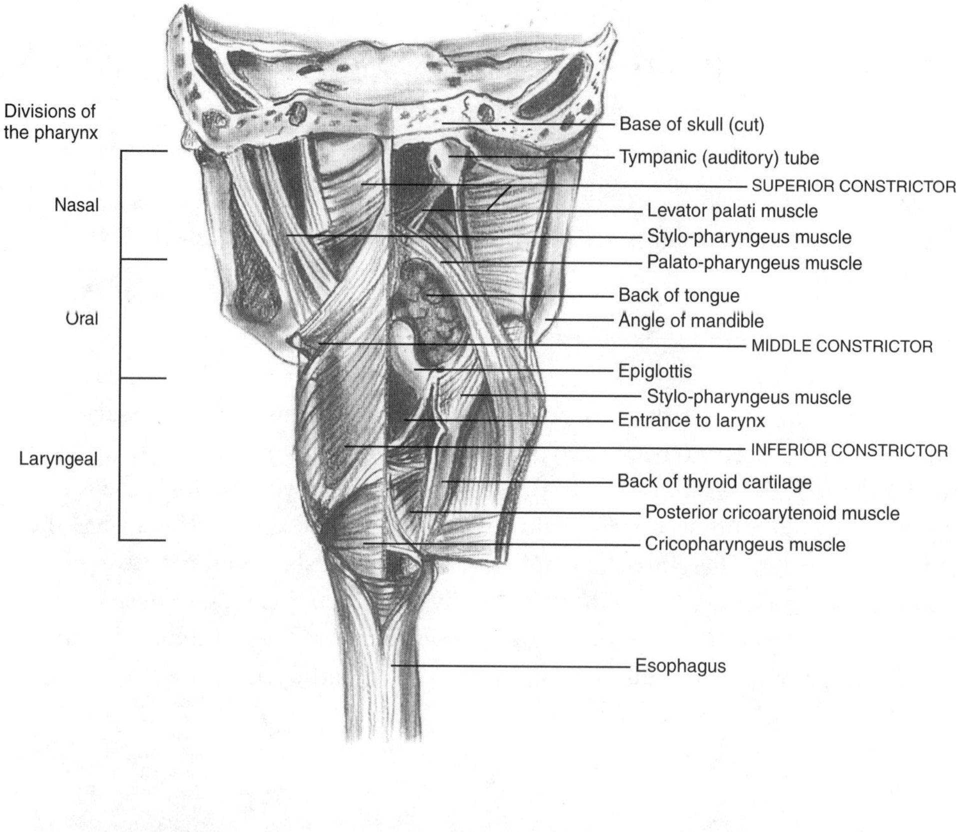
Divisions of the pharynx
Nasal
Oral
Laryngeal
Base of skull (cut)
Tympanic (auditory) tube
SUPERIOR CONSTRICTOR
Levator palati muscle
Stylo-pharyngeus muscle
Palato-pharyngeus muscle
Back of tongue
Angle of mandible
MIDDLE CONSTRICTOR
Epiglottis
Stylo-pharyngeus muscle
Entrance to larynx
INFERIOR CONSTRICTOR
Back of thyroid cartilage
Posterior cricoarytenoid muscle
Cricopharyngeus muscle
Esophagus

Figure 10.1: Pharynx (from behind)

Finding out for yourself . . .

You can find your soft palate by running your tongue along your hard palate until you reach the soft flexible part at the back.

You can feel the soft palate lower when you sniff or sneeze. You can feel it rise when you yawn or try to blow through closed lips.

The oral pharynx begins at the level of the soft palate and continues to the level of the middle of the epiglottis near the back of the tongue. This area is the most flexible and subject to many different shapes. Because the soft palate can move up and down and your tongue and larynx can move as well, the oral pharynx can get taller, wider, narrower, shorter, and so on. It is the place where most of your vocal resonance occurs.

The laryngeal pharynx is the area from the middle of the epiglottis to the lower border of the cricoid cartilage. This area is credited with contributing to the acoustic part of the voice responsible for its carrying power. In pedagogy books it is referred to as the "ring" of the voice.

These three areas are continuous but are usually described separately to help explain the structures better. Now we can look at more details.

Bones and cartilages to which muscles of the pharynx attach

The key to understanding the pharynx is to look at the bony structure to which the muscles attach (see Figure 10.2). In the illustration there are arrows pointing to the base of the skull, the pointed process that hangs from the skull (styloid

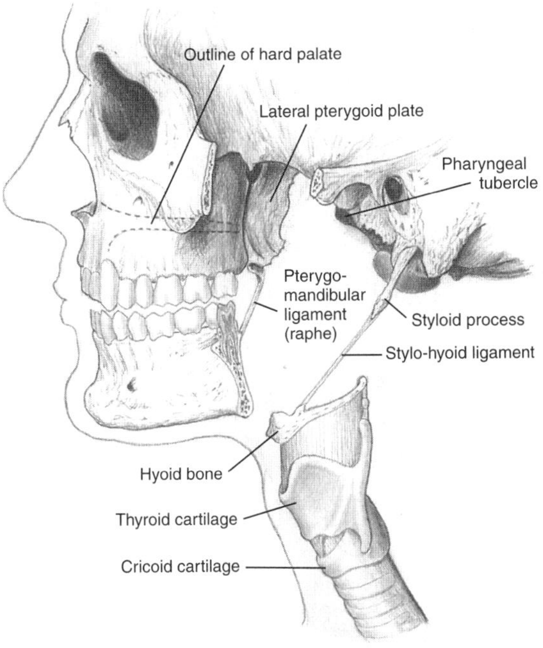
Outline of hard palate
Lateral pterygoid plate
Pharyngeal tubercle
Pterygo-mandibular ligament (raphe)
Styloid process
Stylo-hyoid ligament
Hyoid bone
Thyroid cartilage
Cricoid cartilage

Figure 10.2: Bony structure of the pharynx

(With permission of Springer-Verlag and M. Bunch. From *Dynamics of the Singing Voice*, M. Bunch.)

process), the ligament from the styloid to the hyoid bone (stylo-hyoid ligament), the hyoid bone, and the thyroid and cricoid cartilages. Seeing these will help you understand the complex relationship between the muscles of the pharynx and the other structures of phonation.

Important muscles that form the pharynx

Let's look again at the actions of the pharynx from a logical standpoint. We know that to swallow something the muscles need to contract and narrow the back of the throat in order to squeeze the food down. We also know that the larynx comes up under the tongue as part of the same action. What muscles are contracting to cause these actions to happen?

The pharynx is considered to have two layers of muscles: an outer circular layer and an inner longitudinal layer. The outer layer squeezes the food down in swallowing and the inner layer pulls the pharynx and larynx up. The outer circular layer consists of three paired constrictor muscles (inferior, middle, and superior). The lowest part of the inferior constrictor, called the crico-pharyngeus, forms the beginning of the esophagus. The constrictors arise from bones, ligaments, and cartilages at the sides and meet in the center at the back. The crico-pharyngeus simply begins on one side of the cricoid cartilage and continues to the other side forming a sphincter-like opening (see Figure 10.3). When the constrictors contract, they exert a pull on the least stable area—in this case, the back of the throat—and cause a narrowing of the throat.

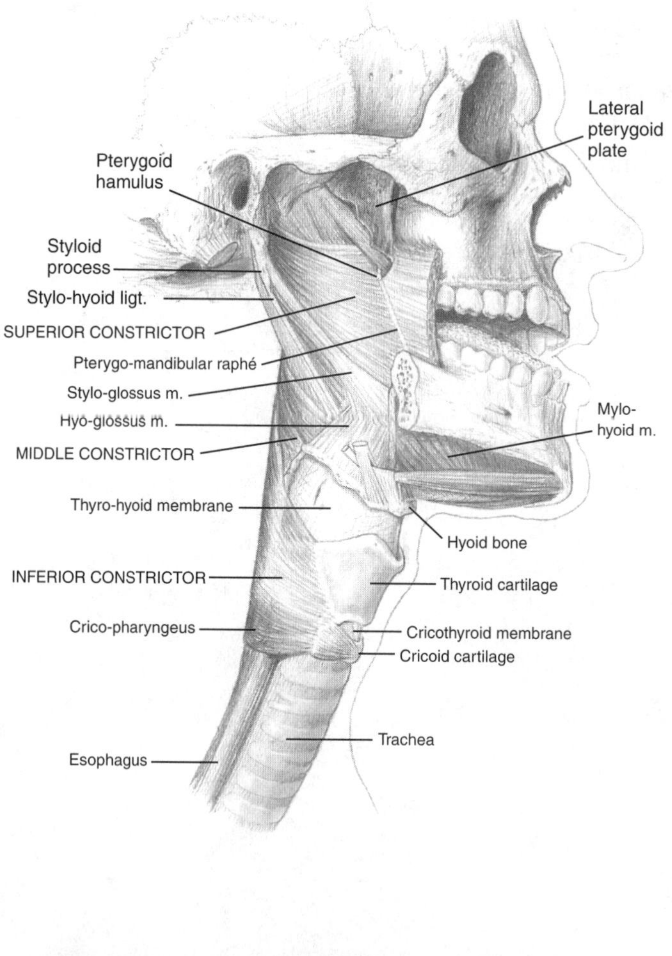
Lateral pterygoid plate
Pterygoid hamulus
Styloid process
Stylo-hyoid ligt.
SUPERIOR CONSTRICTOR
Pterygo-mandibular raphé
Stylo-glossus m.
Hyo-glossus m.
MIDDLE CONSTRICTOR
Mylo-hyoid m.
Thyro-hyoid membrane
Hyoid bone
INFERIOR CONSTRICTOR
Thyroid cartilage
Crico-pharyngeus
Cricothyroid membrane
Cricoid cartilage
Trachea
Esophagus

Figure 10.3: Muscles of the pharynx

(With permission of Springer-Verlag and M. Bunch. From *Dynamics of the Singing Voice*, M. Bunch.)

The second layer of muscles runs up and down and forms the longitudinal layer. These muscles run from the skull (styloid process—stylo-pharyngeus) and the palate (palato-pharyngeus) to the back of the pharynx and thyroid cartilage (see Figure 10.1). When they contract they shorten the space by pulling up the back of the throat and the larynx.

Notice that we have been discussing the muscles that make the pharynx narrow and short. This is not an ideal configuration for singing or speaking. Are you becoming aware that in order to have a wide, long pharynx you must release or relax these muscles?

SOFT PALATE

The palate has been mentioned above. It is not considered part of the pharynx, but through shared muscles the two are linked intricately. The soft palate is very flexible and is capable of moving up and down. It closes off the back of the nose during swallowing to prevent food from entering the nasal passages. In efficient vocal production, the palate does the same thing to prevent air from going into the nose and causing an unwanted nasal resonance. The raising of the soft palate also creates more resonance space in the throat. The palate will be lowered during intentional use of nasal consonants or sounds.

Note: Good singing can feel "nosy" without being nasal. If you wish to check whether your sound is nasal, hold your nose while singing non-nasal consonants. For example, sing something like "all is light." There are no nasal sounds and the voice will be clear if the palate is up. However, if air is escaping through the nose you will get an exaggeration of the nasality.

Finding out for yourself . . .

Stand in front of a mirror and look at your soft palate while saying [a] and a nasal [ã]. You will see the palate move up and down as you say each one alternately.

Sing a phrase of a song while holding your nose. When the palate is up, the sound will be clear. However, when the palate drops for the nasal consonants you will sound like you have a very bad cold and blocked nasal passages.

Muscles of the soft palate

Four main muscles form the soft palate: two that are above it and two below it. There is a pair of muscles that lifts the palate (levator palati) and a pair that widens it (tensor palati) (see Figure 10.4). The levator muscles come from the skull and pull the palate up. The tensor muscles are a little more complex. They have an attachment to the Eustachian tube and are thought to help adjust pressure in the inner ear.

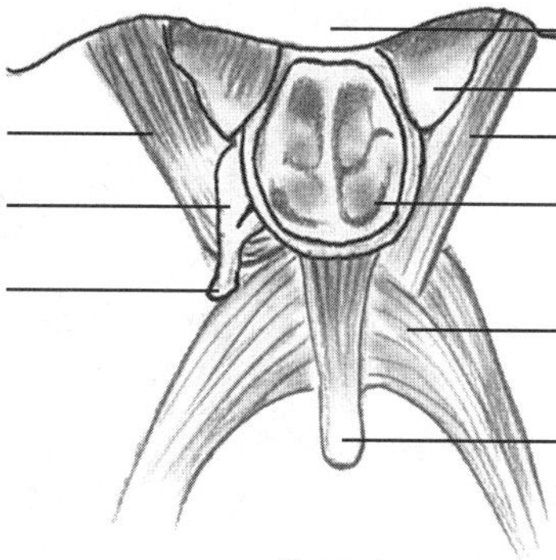
Base of the skull
Auditory tube
Tensor palati muscle
Levator palati muscle
Pterygoid plate
Back of the nose
Hamulus
Palato-pharyngeus muscle
Uvula
Posterior

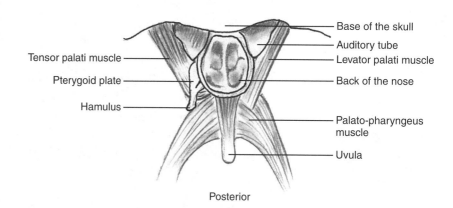

Figure 10.4: Muscles of the soft palate (posterior view)

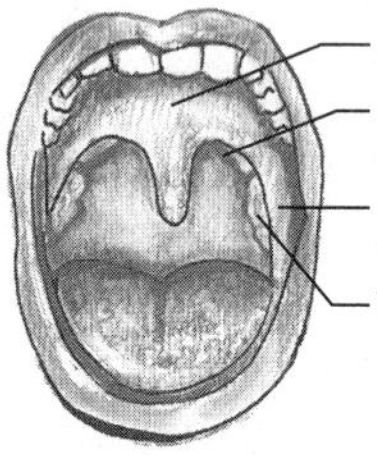
Soft palate
Palato-pharyngeal arch
Palato-glossal arch
Tonsil

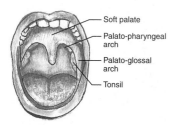

Figure 10.5: Inside the mouth

Two muscles go down from the palate to the sides of the tongue at the back. They are named, logically, palato glossus (glossus means tongue). You can see these muscles when you open your mouth and look in a mirror. On each the side of your tongue is a fold that forms an arch with the uvula hanging down in the middle (see Figure 10.5). That fold is the palato glossus muscle. Behind that fold is another one that is formed by the other two palatal muscles that go from the palate down to the back of the pharynx and the superior horns of the thyroid cartilage.

You can begin to see some of the complex relationships that exist in the head and neck (see Figure 10.6). The tongue and palatal relationship is a particularly important one. When a singer has the habit of tensing the tongue or pulling it down in the back to make sound, the soft palate can be prevented from going up because the palato glossus is acting as an antagonist to the levator palati. The sound that results is a bit garbled and not too pleasant.

Finding out for yourself . . .

Stand in front of a mirror and observe your soft palate. When you take a surprise breath, the palate will probably go up. However, when you deliberately pull your tongue down, notice what happens to the soft palate.

Relationship Between Pharynx and Larynx

The first illustration in this chapter demonstrated the relationship of the skull, jaw, hyoid bone, and larynx. When these structures are in alignment, the muscles of the pharynx and the position of the larynx is freely suspended in the neck. They are in position to respond easily to what is asked of them. When the head or jaw pushes forward, this alignment is distorted and the pharynx and larynx are put at a disadvantage. The roles of the tongue and jaw are explained in Chapter 11, which discusses articulation. Your posture is the key to allowing the muscles of the throat to respond to the sound you wish to make.

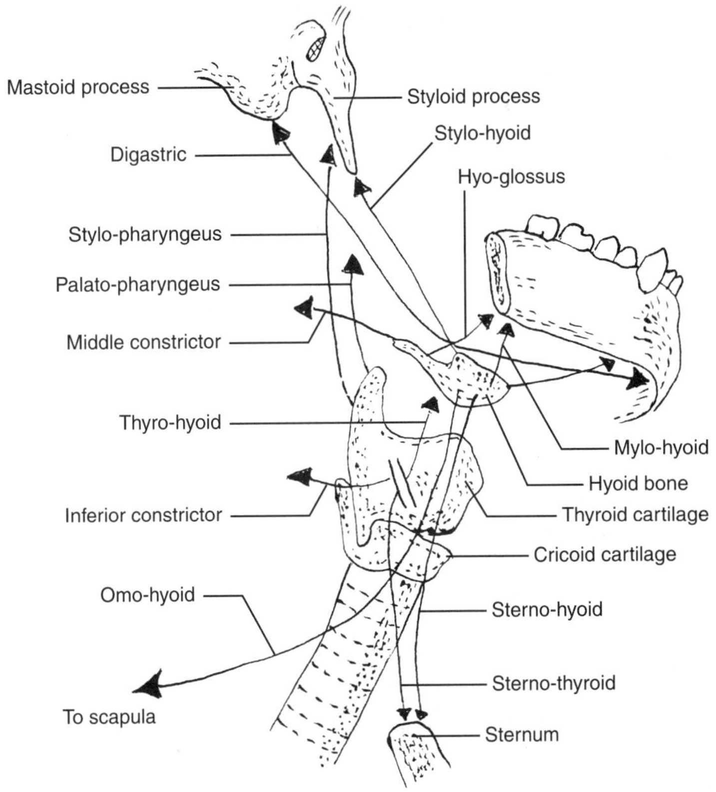
Mastoid process
Styloid process
Stylo-hyoid
Digastric
Hyo-glossus
Stylo-pharyngeus
Palato-pharyngeus
Middle constrictor
Thyro-hyoid
Mylo-hyoid
Hyoid bone
Inferior constrictor
Thyroid cartilage
Cricoid cartilage
Omo-hyoid
Sterno-hyoid
Sterno-thyroid
To scapula
Sternum

Figure 10.6: Directions of muscle pull on larynx and hyoid bone

ACOUSTIC DECEPTION

It is worth repeating that how you think you sound and how you actually sound can be very different. The reason is that you have so much feedback inside your head. Your bones act as conductors of vibration. Your larynx buzzes, and sound bouncing around your throat can be noisy and deceptive. Interestingly, your audience does not hear all of this.

Your acute sensitivity to the mechanical workings of your instrument can cause you to have a very unbalanced idea of your own sound. Do you remember the first time a recording of your voice was played back to you? Most people respond to this by saying: "I don't sound like that, do I?" And the answer is, "Yes, to the rest of the world you do." This is why a teacher or video feedback is so important—particularly at the beginning of your study. In time you will learn your own voice well enough to have a better idea of your external sound. However, as long as you sing, outside feedback will be very important to you.

EVEN TONE

Many singers, especially classical ones, aspire to create a beautiful, even sound throughout their ranges, but trying to do this by exerting excessive control over everything in the throat and mouth results in an even sound inside the head and an uneven or tight one to the listener. With freedom and consistent vowel sounds, your voice will be consistent throughout.

Creating Vocal Variety

It is not necessary for you to consciously manipulate the muscles in your throat to color sound. This will only create tension and an undesired vocal quality. Your expression and vocal color will respond to your understanding of the text and to your imagination and energy. Focusing on and deeply understanding your message will go a long way toward creating the vocal effects you want—whether they are dark, bright, light, or heavy. You can sing any song in a variety of characters—old, young, king, queen, witch, or any other you desire.

What Is a Resonator?

A resonator needs to be hollow and have an opening for the sound to escape. In singing, your throat acts as the primary resonator with help from the nose (nasal sounds) and mouth. There are many anecdotes regarding resonators of the voice—including the great line from the comedienne, Anna Russell, who said, "Singers have resonance where their brains ought to be." The sinuses are often credited with adding resonance. You may feel their vibration but it is inaudible to the audience. And the tiny openings of the sinuses are not large enough to qualify for a resonator. Even when your sinuses are blocked with an infection or cold, you can sing without a sinus sound. While this honky sound can be heard when you speak, it rarely comes through when you sing because singers are more conscientious than speakers about raising the soft palate.

Vocal Problems and the Pharynx

Tension is the main problem associated with the pharynx. Tension will narrow the space of the throat and cause the larynx to rise under the tongue. The quality of the sound is then compromised. Because we swallow many times during a day, it is easy to get caught somewhere between the full swallow and full relaxation of the throat. Don't get caught in a tense swallowing position when you need to be relaxed for singing.

Misalignment of the head and shoulders is another major contributor to poor tone quality and to potential vocal damage. Pushing the head forward toward the microphone or audience is extremely common and exaggerated in the pop singing world where singers manage to copy the bad habits of famous singers rather than the good ones. Even nonclassical singers need to keep their heads over their shoulders!

Your Speaking Voice

How many times have you heard someone sing well and then speak poorly? Some singers work very hard to create optimum quality in singing and then become completely slovenly when speaking. Your speaking voice needs the same careful attention that you give to your singing. The same principles and habits of good singing discussed in this book apply to speaking. Bear this in mind.

Using good speaking habits may feel artificial to you at first, but keep working at it. The change will not be drastic; you will probably sound clearer and articulate your words better. Using good speech habits will make it much easier for you to sing.

Chapter Eleven

Articulation and Expression

Music alone can convey many emotions, but it is words that enhance and underline the emotions in vocal music. In the first section of this book, you were asked to learn the text of your song before learning the tune. It was one indication of how important words are to the music. Typically, composers begin with a text and then set it to music. With some of the more improvised forms of music, such as jazz, rap, and pop, music and words are often created concurrently.

Words are meant to be heard and understood. This sets the singer apart from instrumentalists. Therefore, it is vital that the text of the music be clear, efficiently produced, and expressive. Physically, this means that the structures of articulation—the soft palate, jaw, tongue, and lips—have to be loose and available to respond to the text. Tension in any of these areas restricts their movement and makes it difficult to articulate quickly and easily. This is where speech habits can help or hinder your ease of singing. Poor speech habits will become exaggerated when you begin to sing. This does not mean you need to create an entirely different voice—simply that you correct any poor habits.

Finding out for yourself . . .

You can feel the various actions of the jaw by doing the following:

Put a finger in or just in front of your ear and gently and slowly move your jaw forward, backward, downward, upward, and sideways. Make sure that you are not moving your lips instead. Many people with a tight jaw will compensate by doing strange things with their lips.

Next, with a partner, deliberately sing with your jaw in these positions:

- Forward
- Backward
- Clenched
- Deviated to one side
- Loose and hanging freely

What is the difference in sound in each position?

When someone complains about not being able to understand the words, the singer usually responds with increased muscular effort with the jaw and lips. It is common for singers to think that they need to exaggerate the movement of the lips and jaw to make the sound clearer. Nothing could be further from the truth. Over-exaggeration of consonants and vowels causes unwanted changes in the shape of the throat, distortion of the words, and singing that is off pitch. Rap and patter songs—fast, wordy, theater songs such as those by Stephen Sondheim or Gilbert and Sullivan (see "Modern Major-General," p. 229)—demand rapid, almost shotgun speed of articulation. For this you need loose lips and jaw, and a flexible tongue. It would be extremely difficult to sing fast music with lots of words with a tense jaw or lips.

Structures of Articulation

Let's take a closer look at the structures that help us to articulate. As in the case of the pharynx, these structures are heavily involved with the process of eating, particularly chewing. The muscles involved are very powerful because they are used so much.

The jaw

The jaw bone, or mandible, is shaped a bit like a horseshoe with long upward portions at the ends, and it hangs from the skull by means of ligaments and muscles. Those upward portions form a joint with the skull on each side just in front of the ears (see Figure 11.1). Most of the muscles of the jaw are used for

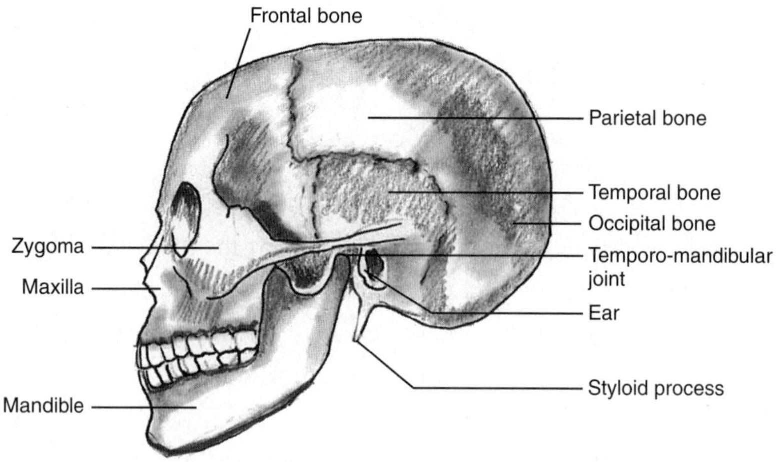
Frontal bone
Parietal bone
Temporal bone
Occipital bone
Zygoma
Temporo-mandibular joint
Maxilla
Ear
Styloid process
Mandible

Figure 11.1: Skull, jaw, and temporo-mandibular joint

chewing (muscles of mastication) and are responsible for moving it up and down, forward or backward, or side to side. Since you spend the majority of your time with your mouth closed (unless you breathe through your mouth or talk incessantly), the muscles that elevate the jaw are active continually. Therefore, to allow them to relax and let the jaw hang freely during singing or speech require concentration and willpower on your part.

MUSCLES THAT MOVE THE JAW

Two powerful muscles elevate the jaw. The first (*temporalis*) is located in the area of your temple and above and behind the ear. You can feel the action of this muscle by spreading your fingers just above and behind your ear and slowly moving your jaw up and down. As you move your jaw up and down, you can feel the temporalis contract and become bulky under your fingers. It occupies most of the area above your ears and attaches very strongly to the jaw (see Figure 11.2).

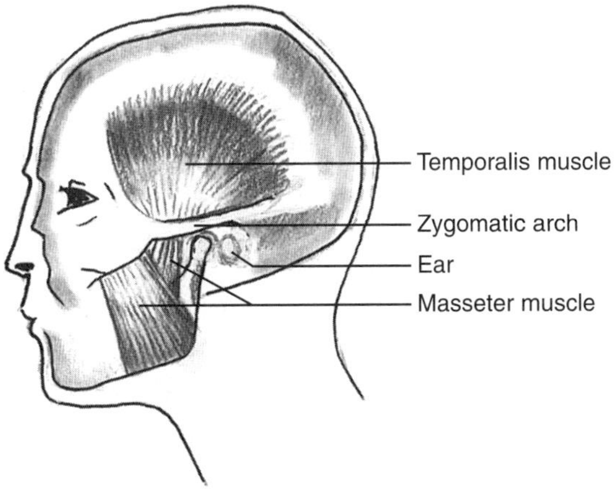
Temporalis muscle
Zygomatic arch
Ear
Masseter muscle

Figure 11.2: Temporalis and masseter muscles (schematic drawing)

Note the directions of its fibers: Some are straight up and down while others slant backward. This tells you that the muscle is capable of both elevating and retracting the jaw.

The second set of muscles that elevate the jaw is located between the cheekbone and the angle of the jaw (*masseter*) (see Figure 11.2). It becomes bulky when you grind your teeth. You can feel its action by placing your fingers along the side of your face and grinding your back teeth—gently (see Figure 11.3).

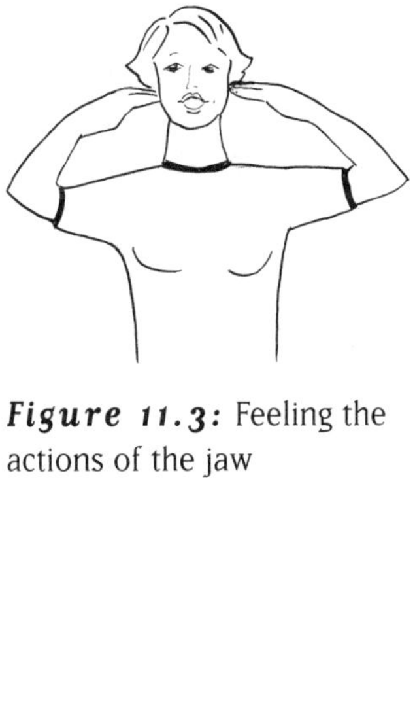

Figure 11.3: Feeling the actions of the jaw

Muscles on either side of the skull that attach to the joint area of the jaw (*lateral pterygoids*) cause side to side movements (see Figure 11.4). They coordinate with one another, that is, one is active and the other is passive depending upon which side of the jaw is moving. When they act together, they help protrude the jaw or bring it forward. There is another set of pterygoid muscles (*medial pterygoids*) that elevates the jaw or can work with the lateral pterygoids to protrude it.

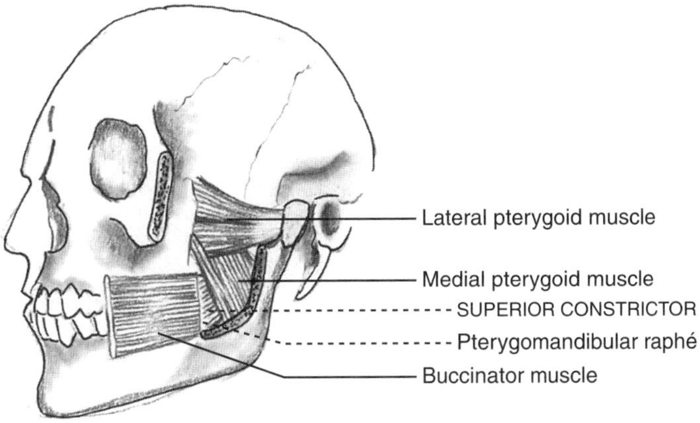
Lateral pterygoid muscle
Medial pterygoid muscle
SUPERIOR CONSTRICTOR
Pterygomandibular raphé
Buccinator muscle

Figure 11.4 Pterygoid muscles

PROBLEMS RELATING TO THE JAW

The jaw has many complex relationships with the skull, the pharynx, tongue, and larynx. Therefore, when the jaw is displaced forward or jammed open, the whole vocal tract is affected. A number of regional (southern and other) speech patterns include slightly moving the jaw forward for consonants—particularly the ch and j consonants. (If you watch very closely, many people pronounce these consonants with a slight forward movement of the jaw.) The jutting jaw is unnecessary and it causes vocal havoc. It pulls the back of the throat forward, tends to raise the larynx, and makes it difficult to use the tongue efficiently.

A number of things can cause the jaw to deviate to one side as it opens. Chewing mainly on one side will strengthen the muscles on that side and tend to pull it in that direction. Also, people who have poor hearing in one ear will tend to open the mouth in the direction of the good ear. They can hear themselves better that way.

One enormous problem relating to the jaw is that of over-opening it. When the mouth is open too wide, the back of the throat tends to close. It becomes physically impossible for the tongue to reach the palate so the consonants and vowels become distorted. Ideally the jaw just hangs—freely available. The energy yawn exercise in Part I is good for releasing the jaw.

Muscles of the Tongue

While the jaw and hard palate provide the stable structures for articulation, the tongue, lips, and soft palate do most of the work. The tongue, in particular, carries a large part of the responsibility for the production of vowels and consonants. It is composed of several groups of muscles (see Figure 11.5) that come from the skull, soft palate, mandible, hyoid bone, and some intrinsic ones that have no bony attachments.

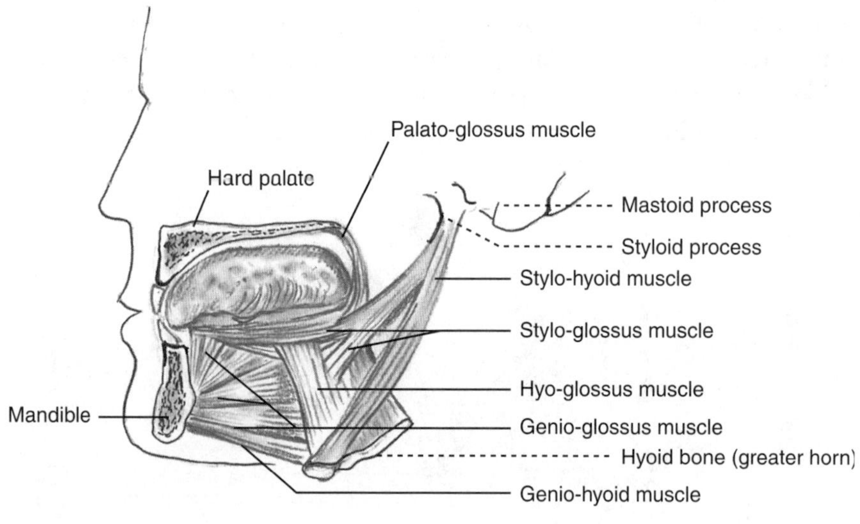
Palato-glossus muscle
Hard palate
Mastoid process
Styloid process
Stylo-hyoid muscle
Stylo-glossus muscle
Hyo-glossus muscle
Mandible
Genio-glossus muscle
Hyoid bone (greater horn)
Genio-hyoid muscle

Figure 11.5: Muscles of the tongue

The muscles that attach to the skull pull the tongue back and up (*stylo-glosssus*); those attaching to the hyoid bone (*hyo-glossus*) pull it down at the sides at the back (a common American speech pattern that is not helpful for singing); and those attaching to the soft palate (*palato-glossus*) can either pull the back of the tongue up or act antagonistically to the elevators of the soft palate. Tension in any of these muscles is not helpful at all.

A muscle having several bundles (*genio-glossus*) makes up the bulk of the tongue. These bundles act together to protrude your tongue. When acting separately they can draw parts of the tongue downward.

Other acrobatic movements such as grooving the tongue or turning it over are attributed to the small intrinsic muscles that are located between the other muscles. Some of these movements may be hereditary.

Finding out for yourself . . .

With a partner sing a few phrases in the following ways:

- With your normal singing pattern
- With the tongue pulled down as if trying to flatten it
- With the tongue tip returning to the edge of the lower teeth each time
- Flicking the tongue in and out of your mouth as you sing

How do you compare the various voice qualities produced in this exercise? What have you learned about your own habits?

PROBLEMS ASSOCIATED WITH THE TONGUE

In this age of close-up television, it is easy to see what a singer does with the mouth and tongue. Many good singers show a flat tongue that is a natural characteristic for them. However, this is not the same as deliberately pulling the tongue down. When done purposely, there is excess tension, the soft palate is pulled down, the pitch is poor, and the tone is garbled. You can experiment with this by putting your thumb in the soft area under your jaw (under the tongue) and checking for tension. If there is no tongue tension it will be loose and your thumb will not encounter resistance; with tension there will be a lump. You can feel this when you pull down the back of the tongue.

SPEECH PATTERNS THAT CONTRIBUTE TO TONGUE TENSION

Two of the most obvious characteristics of the American dialect or accent are the backed [a] (made by pulling the back of the tongue down) and the tense [r]. Pulling down the back of the tongue creates a kind of garbled, strangled [a] that interferes with easy vocal production. Singers who want to learn to sing any of the European languages often despair at learning a correct, vocally pure [a] sound.

The American [r] is famous—or infamous—and imitated by anyone wanting to sound American. It is a problem because the tip of the tongue curls backward and completely changes the vocal quality—for the worse. While country-western, folk, and pop singers may love it, it is not useful for other styles and creates many vocal problems. We sustain sound on vowels and when the tongue slowly curls while you are singing a vowel, the distortion becomes obvious. You can try this out with a friend by singing and exaggerating the "rrr."

Some performers have too much tension in the tongue when they sing. When this is so, the inner sound can be perceived as loud and feel gratifying to the performer. However, the audience is getting a very different perception. This is another area in which there can be poor acoustic perception. A good tape recorder will let you know whether the audience would perceive your sound in the same way.

The soft palate

The soft palate was mentioned in the chapter on vocal quality. Because the soft palate is interlinked muscularly with the tongue and pharynx, movements of the jaw and tongue can cause its ideal function to be compromised. The whole area around the soft palate, tongue, and jaw can create a lingering problem because it is difficult to know where to put the blame when something is not quite right. Create a checklist for yourself when you cannot find out what is causing you difficulty. Always begin with posture and breathing, then check the mirror for any deviations of the jaw, tongue, and lips. Become a vocal sleuth.

The lips

One of the first things you learned to do as a child was to enjoy games with adults by making funny faces. Playing with different lip configurations and making sounds like "raspberries" was all part of the fun. We would lose much of our expression if we had little or no possibility of movement of our lips. The feel-good effect that a smile has on your own body and on others is well known. We prove it every day.

The lips are part of a large group of muscles that belong to facial expression. The muscles that form the lips come from the cheekbones, the face next to the nose, and the area near the upper teeth and the jaw; they form a muscle that encircles the mouth (sphincter). These muscles are in position to move the lips to create expressions such as smiling, frowning, puckering, sneering, pouting, and many other variants (see Figure 11.6). Their names usually reflect their

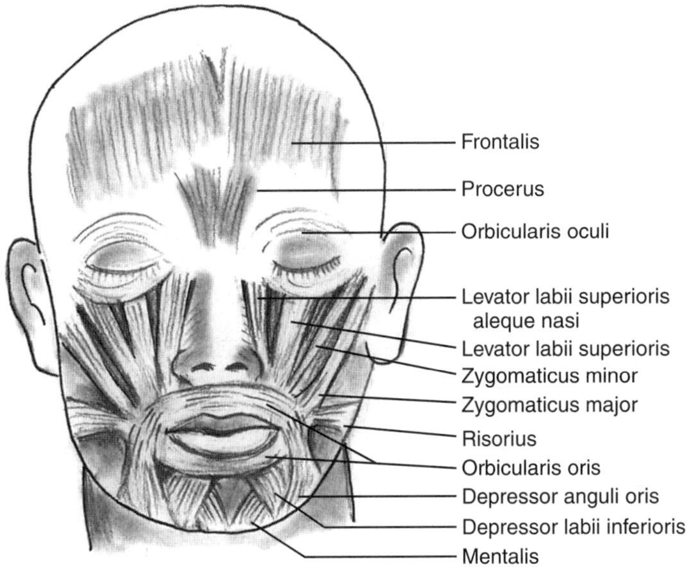
Frontalis
Procerus
Orbicularis oculi
Levator labii superioris aleque nasi
Levator labii superioris
Zygomaticus minor
Zygomaticus major
Risorius
Orbicularis oris
Depressor anguli oris
Depressor labii inferioris
Mentalis

Figure 11.6: Muscles of facial expression

actions (for example, the *levator anguli oris* means the elevator of the angle of the mouth).

The lips, together with the tongue, are responsible for most of the consonants we use. Therefore, like the rest of the vocal mechanism, they need to be flexible and free. Try singing a very fast song with tense lips. You will soon find that the rhythm and phrasing get slower and slower. Your jaw will begin to ache because tense lips will inhibit its movement.

MUSCLES OF FACIAL EXPRESSION

The muscles of facial expression are a very magical group of thin muscles that have few or no bony attachments. They lie just under the skin of the face and enable us to express our feelings and emotions. These muscles are in the scalp (for those of you who can wrinkle your scalp), the forehead (we see these when people look worried or intense), radiating from the ears (some people can wiggle their ears), and around the eyes, the lips, and the chin.

You probably know people who say everything with the same facial expression. What effect does that have on the sound and your gut reaction to what they are saying? The exercise on page 284 demonstrates what happens when the facial expression and words are not matched.

Finding out for yourself . . .

This is an exercise to be done in pairs.

Choose one or two lines of a song that you can sing over and over (each person is to chose a different song). Get your partner to fill in the form as you sing the same lines each time in the following ways:

	HOW DOES IT LOOK?	HOW DOES IT SOUND?	WHAT'S YOUR GUT REACTION?
1. with furrowed brows			
2. with staring eyes			
3. with alive, seeing eyes			
4. with lips protruded			
5. with lips tense			
6. with an overly broad smile			
7. with a frown (a downturned mouth)			
8. with the jaw jutting forward			
9. with the jaw jammed downward each time you open to sing			
10. with the jaw hanging freely			

The exercise described above is good for indicating what happens when we have speech or singing habits that are fixed for everything we sing. Both the tone and the intended message are affected. It can be very funny, yet give a seriously flawed message when you have any of those habits.

VOWELS AND CONSONANTS

The building blocks of languages are vowels and consonants. Without vowels there would be no way of sustaining sound—unless you want to spend your life humming. Consonants enable us to define the sound and communicate meaning and language. We have discussed the main physical structures of articulation and how they work individually. Now let's look at how they combine to produce vowels and consonants.

Vowels

The position of the tongue, with some help from the lips, is mainly responsible for shaping the vocal tract and creating the resonances that are recognized as vowels. Fine movements of the tongue and its position in the mouth make all of the vowels and their various hybrids. The role of the tongue may come as a surprise to you if you have learned exaggerated movements of your lips and jaw as part of your speech patterns and regional dialects. Regional speech dialects can include some strange vowel shapes and sounds. For example, some dialects can include several vowel sounds together when only one is needed for singing. (Two vowel sounds used together make up a *diphthong;* three vowel sounds are a *triphthong.*) And they can make sounds that were intended to be diphthongs into one sound. For example, the vowel sound in the word "fine" is a double vowel, [aɪ], but often pronounced [a].* This happens on many occasions in speech and must be corrected in singing. The full sound of each word is important in classical singing. Other styles incorporate more everyday use of language sounds. However, it is still important for the words to be understood.

Singers who adjust their vowel sounds for optimum singing are often said to sing "without an accent." American singers often comment that British singers (such as the Beatles . . .) lose their British accent when they sing. In fact, the prevailing pop song accent at the moment is American.

Singers can create very uneven vowel sounds by exaggerating mouth and lip positions. (This distorts the vocal tract.) There is a common misconception that the vowels are made by the lips. Notice what happens to the quality when you sing an [i] sound with wide smiling lips. It will become very bright compared to the vowels that are made mainly by the position of the tongue. The pictures below indicate the tongue positions for the main vowels: [i], [a], [o], and [u] (see Figure 11.7). Any changes in the tongue position while you are singing a vowel will begin to distort it or change it, and may confuse the audience about what you are singing.

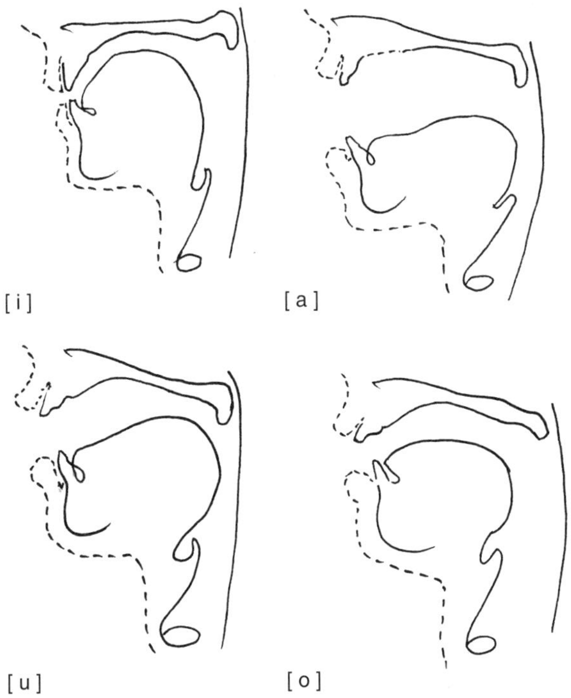
[i]
[a]
[u]
[o]

Figure 11.7: Tongue positions for [i] (beet), [a] (father), [u] (boot), [o] (boat)

* For a guide to the International Phonetic Alphabet, see Appendix B.

Finding out for yourself . . .

With a partner or a mirror do the following:

Sing the vowels on one pitch with

- exaggerated mouth and lips for each one
- different jaw positions for each vowel
- a finger between the teeth with no jaw or extra lip movement

Try to sing an [i] with a flat tongue. What happens to the sound?

Consonants

Clear words are the result of efficient pronunciation of consonants. Slovenly consonants and speech habits can be the downfall of good vocal communication—even in nonclassical styles. Good articulation of consonants requires an efficient, coordinated movement of lips and tongue, with little or no action from the jaw. (*Note:* the jaw needs to close only for sounds such as [sh], [j], [ch], [s], and [v].) All movements are articulated centrally, along the middle of the face. When any of the consonants are produced physically off-center the sound becomes distorted. This is called "chewing" the sound.

Consonants are classified according to how they are physically made, and whether they are voiced or unvoiced (see chart below). You can experiment with these by pronouncing [p] and [b], [v] and [f], [d] and [t]. These are all pairs that are physically alike, yet one is made with vocal sound and one without.

CLASSIFICATION OF CONSONANT SOUNDS

Physical action	Examples	
	Voiced	Voiceless
Upper and lower lips	b. m*	p
Upper teeth and lower lip	v	f
Upper teeth and tongue	th (thing)	th (this)
Alveolar ridge (just behind teeth) and tongue tip	d, n*, l, z**,	t, s**
Alveolar ridge — palate boundary and tongue blade	z (seizure)	s (she)
Hard palate and tongue blade	j	
Soft palate and back of the tongue	g	c, k, q
Glottis (opening between vocal folds)	h	

*Nasals **Fricatives (noisy, escaping breath)

Some consonants are more like vowels. These include the w and y. The r has been discussed earlier in connection with the tongue.

Note: When the tip of the tongue deviates to the side of the teeth to make an s, air escapes out the other side of the mouth and gives you a lisp. This is not useful for singing. In fact, any deviation from the center of your mouth by the tongue or lips will distort the consonants or vowels. You can correct this with some patient work in front of a mirror by making sure the tip of your tongue stays in the middle when you are pronouncing your words.

Finding out for yourself . . .

You can find out just how clear your consonants are by doing the following:

First, sing a song your usual way.

Next, place the tip of a finger centrally between your upper and lower teeth and gently close the teeth on your finger. Do not change this to do the exercise below.

Sing the song again with finger inserted.

Did you find that you were trying to chew your finger?

Rest assured, you are able to pronounce your words this way. There may be some minor distortion of the consonants that require the lips to touch in the front. However, they will be making contact with your finger for that sound, and it is usually clear enough for the purposes of this exercise.

Another important thing to learn from this exercise is that you can sing most of your song without the need of excessive jaw movements. Crucially, the back of your throat and soft palate will begin to respond appropriately because you have not dragged them out of place by over-opening your mouth. Over-opening the mouth can cause the back of the throat to narrow rather than widen.

Attention to articulation can pay huge dividends in singing. It can help your vocal technique and enable your audience to take part in the song. While the discussion above has been quite technical, it will serve as a guide and reference for you if you have any problems.

Expression and Words

Expression of your message comes from your imagination, understanding of the text, and motivation. Mindless manipulation of text and concentration on the forming of words will not help you communicate with your audience. Your listeners need meaning if they are to be moved by your singing.

If you do not know this word, spend some time thinking about it: *onomatopoeia.* It relates to how the sounds of words mimic their meaning. The words *buzz* and *hiss* are good examples. The sounds of all words are important. Pictures, symbols, and sounds came before the actual words. It is important to remember this when you rehearse your music. In Part I, Chapter 4, a lot of space was given to the importance of the text and how to approach it. It is worth going back and rereading that section. Revisit the exercise of miming the words with your hands. The clarity of diction, meaning, and motivation will begin to happen for you.

CHAPTER TWELVE

Maintaining a Healthy Voice

If someone gave you a car when you first learned to drive and told you that it had to last your whole life, how would you treat it? Your body was given to you at birth and it lasts for your lifetime. How are you treating it? Your voice is directly affected by how you treat your body. Your general health and sense of well-being will always have an effect on your voice, so treat your body well.

A singer is a "vocal athlete"; you will sing better if you are in shape. Being in shape comes from appropriate physical exercise, mental focus, good nutrition, and a reasonable amount of sleep. Being an athlete or a singer requires responsibility and wisdom in the way you take care of yourself.

IMPORTANT HEALTH HABITS

A positive attitude

Many research studies have shown the effects of positive thinking on the immune system. It is true that we create our own reality. A positive attitude about your goals, your abilities, your body, and your singing is step one toward vocal health. Striving for perfection is laudable; kicking yourself for not being perfect is the best way to achieve little. Find a way to be positive.

Visualization was discussed in the Part I of the book. This is an indispensable tool for achieving what you want. It takes no time—only a second to see yourself being able to do what you want to do technically, physically, and for your life.

Another tool is meditation. It is a fine way to still a hyperactive mind. There are many forms of meditation, from total silence to the chanting of mantras (repeated words or sounds). A group silence is very powerful and can refresh you as much as a short nap. Learn to practice "traffic control" by simply stopping what you are doing at several points during the day and experience silence for one or two minutes. Such a discipline can make a huge difference to your study and practice. Meditation is known to focus the mind, to still the body, and even to lower blood pressure. Many people are practicing meditation to alleviate their stress. The "being still" exercise in Part I is a quick way to get into a meditative state.

Sleep

The body needs sleep for healing itself and regrouping. You can lose sleep for just so long before the body and mind become sluggish and the mind is unable to think clearly. That's why sleep deprivation is used as a form of torture. Sitting in front of a computer all day and night is a recipe for developing poor sleeping patterns. While different people need varying amounts of sleep, the important thing is to get sound, restful sleep most nights. Some things that contribute to healthy sleep patterns are moderate exercise during the day, relaxation and quiet time before going to bed, maintenance of regular hours, and no heavy meals, caffeine, or alcohol just before bed.

Nutrition

To return to the analogy of a car, what would happen if you mixed the oil and gas in your car with a bit of dirt and water? The car would work for a short time, but after a while would stop. Your body is more tolerant of what you put into it for a while. Eventually, however, it will complain and threaten to stop working well. Your body works hard to keep itself balanced chemically, and everything you take in either sustains or alters that balance.

The first thing your body needs is plenty of water. More than 70 percent of your body is water and what is lost on a daily basis needs to be replenished. Pure water is needed, not just any form of fluid. (Other fluids tend to be regarded as food by the body and treated differently from water.) For singers, the lubrication of the throat and vocal folds is important. So keep your water bottle handy whenever possible.

Like everything else, however, having to drink water can become a kind of obsession. So make sure you are well hydrated *before* important events like concerts. Seeing a singer drinking water on stage can be very off-putting and distracting for the singer and the audience. Drink your water offstage during the intermission or during breaks. Carry it onstage only if you are having some kind of vocal problem or sore throat.

Foods that contain high water content are considered very healthy. This includes most fruits and vegetables, but a diet of only fruit and vegetables does not give us enough muscle-building protein. Protein comes in many forms, so you are able to choose freely from meat, cheese, yogurt, milk, nuts, seeds, and legumes (beans, lentils, etc.). Grains and some fat are important as well. No matter what your budget, healthy food options are available. Food supplements and vitamins may help when there is little fresh produce. *The key is always balance.*

Exercise

There is appropriate exercise for everyone's level of fitness. The simplest thing you can do is walk. It is not unusual for those who live in large cities to walk at least a mile or two a day. In most cities and towns, though, walking to work or school is not a viable option and a car is essential. This is why gyms and local sports clubs are so popular.

Today many forms of exercise are available that work with the mind as well as the body. Some of the most effective forms of exercise and techniques for singers are these:

- Alexander Technique, a way of balancing mind and body through developing efficient habits for daily living
- Feldenkrais, a very effective way to correct your body through micro-movements
- Pilates, exercises for balancing the body and correcting physical problems, especially alignment and the abdominal muscles
- Tai Chi, a beautiful, flowing Eastern martial art form
- Chi Gung, a combination of movement, breathing, and meditation
- Dance in many forms such as jazz, ballroom, salsa, tap, ballet, circle dancing, and square dancing

Your school or community may offer many of these forms of exercise.

Active exercises that jar and shake the body or make you pant and gasp can be fun and use up lots of energy, but they may not be helpful just before you sing. Jogging in cold air just before a lesson is not a good idea. More is not always better. Be sensible.

Healthy vocal habits

Your vocal health will be enhanced or damaged on a daily basis depending on how you use your voice for speaking and singing. By paying attention to your posture and breathing you can keep yourself out of vocal trouble.

Part I included information on how to practice. Go back and remind yourself of that information now. Wisely spent rehearsal time is vital to your vocal health and learning. Short practice sessions are advisable for the beginning singer. Just as you would not go out and run a mile or run for an hour if you had not run before, you would not sing for an hour either. Being methodical and patient is the best way to learn to sing well.

HABITS THAT CAN HARM YOUR VOICE

Poor voice use

At the top of the list of vocal abuse is yelling at sports events. Prolonged yelling puts a lot of pressure on the vocal folds and causes them to swell. The resulting hoarseness is called laryngitis (inflammation of the larynx). It is analogous to spraining your ankle—except that it is your voice. Since you can't wrap it up and protect it, you have to be quiet until the swelling has subsided. Unbounded enthusiasm is commendable, but vocalizing it is not recommended for singers. Remind yourself that the team cannot hear you individually. Therefore let the rest of the crowd do your yelling for you. Ring a bell, blow a horn; just don't yell.

Talking over loud noise and dance music is another way to create vocal problems. There is a catch-22 situation here. There is music playing and people talk over it. Someone then can't hear the music so the volume is turned up. People talk even louder. The music is turned up again. And so it goes on until everyone is shouting. The next morning there are scores of people who are hoarse, have very tired throats, and are somewhat deafened.

Another source of vocal abuse is constant throat clearing. People who do this are often unaware of their habit. Clearing the throat makes the vocal folds virtually explode air out and can cause damage in the long term. This can be a nervous habit to call attention to yourself as well. Ask your friends to let you know if you are constantly clearing your throat. It is common for speakers to clear their throats just before they begin to speak and nervous singers to do this before they sing. Most of the time clearing the throat is not necessary. When you feel the urge to clear, it is best to swallow or drink water instead.

Airborne substances that impair the voice

The job of the vocal folds is to protect your lungs. These folds are so sensitive that inhaling anything larger than 3 microns (much smaller than a speck of dust) in diameter causes you to cough. As further protection, there are tiny hairs called *cilia* attached to the cells that line the windpipe and lungs. They beat upward to clear any debris from your lungs. Airborne or inhaled toxins that are tiny are able to pass by the vocal folds and inflict untold damage on the cells that line the respiratory tract and imbed themselves in the cellular structure of your lungs. Over time the cells lose their protective capacity and disease processes have a clear path. This is particularly true if you smoke anything.

The toxicity of cigarettes is well documented and new evidence regarding cannabis is frightening. Both smoking and passive or second-hand smoking are considered unhealthy. The message for singers is this: *Don't smoke!* It is not helpful to your health or vocal career.

Living in air pollution is not helpful either. We do not always have a choice about where we live and work—smoky nightclubs or toxic big cities may be unavoidable. Make it a point to live in the cleanest environment possible. Keep your personal environment free of smoke, fumes, dust, and damp. At least you will avoid compounding the problem by adding your own pollution.

Ingestion of toxic substances

Your body is working constantly to maintain its chemical balance. When you introduce substances that alter that balance, the body works hard to get rid of them. The broad category of recreational drugs is considered destructive to the body in general—especially in large amounts.

ALCOHOL

Moderation is always a good rule to follow. Drinking six beers one night and none for the next six nights does not constitute moderation—even if the average is one. Your liver is the organ responsible for clearing toxins from your body, and six beers can create mass panic in your liver. You can read many studies about alcohol. Some of these recommend a glass of wine every night; others tell you it is deadly. However, all tend to agree that getting drunk kills brain cells, slows your responses for nearly twenty-four hours, and plays havoc with your liver. Too much alcohol makes it difficult to sing on pitch or respond easily to your music.

Alcohol has a drying effect on the mucous membranes that line the throat and larynx. Over a period of time the dryness can become chronic and the husky, "drinker's voice" emerges. For those serious about their singing, heavy drinking is not an option. Contrary to thought, it does not help you sing better. It can cause you to *perceive* that you are singing better, but it is more likely to relax the muscles enough to create pitch problems.

NARCOTICS

There are times when we all want to escape the unpleasantness of life in some way. However, drugs like cocaine, opium derivatives, ecstasy, and any other variations will only defer our problems; they don't solve them. A performer, like an athlete, needs all senses and facilities available for the best performance.

Common Problems That Need Professional Help

The following section includes a general discussion of some common issues and typical problems encountered by singers. It is not intended to be a definitive medical statement or a tool for diagnosis, but is purely intended for information. For more specific knowledge, consult a specialist, refer to materials such as those listed in *Further Reading,* or search the Internet. When you have any doubts about the way you are feeling or singing, it is best to consult a health professional.

Hoarseness

Hoarseness is a big catch-all term that can cover a multitude of vocal problems. It occurs when there is any kind of swelling on the vocal folds that causes them to touch with uneven surfaces. It becomes a problem only when it does not go away. Then you have to begin to search for possible causes.

The following can cause temporary hoarseness:

- Poor speech habits
- Over-singing or singing too loudly
- Air conditioning
- Air travel

- Central heating with low humidity
- Singing too long
- Constant throat clearing
- Drinking too much alcohol
- Medications such as antihistamines that dry the throat
- Medications like aspirin and ibuprofen that cause local bleeding
- Smoking
- Fatigue
- Your menstrual period
- Sore throat
- Cold or flu

Attending to vocal technique, drinking plenty of water, getting a good night's sleep, and humidifying your environment can help most of those problems. If you experience hoarseness after practicing or a choral rehearsal, it will normally go away after a few hours. It is not unusual to over-sing in a choral situation. However, if there is hoarseness after every rehearsal, you would do well to go to your teacher and look at what you might be doing vocally to cause this.

Air travel

The incredible dryness experienced during flying can cause all kinds of respiratory symptoms. You are advised to drink lots of water. It is wise to breathe through a wet cloth or mask during the flight as well. This can make all the difference in the way you feel when you land.

Excess fluid during menstrual cycles

During the menstrual period it is common for excess fluid to be present in many of the tissues of the body. This includes the vocal folds as well. This swelling makes you feel heavy and dull. You may even sound hoarse from the swelling on the vocal folds. It is best to sing gently on those days and take easy physical exercise when you can. Often singing makes you feel better.

More than hoarseness

As a general rule, when you are hoarse for more than two weeks, you need to seek professional advice. There can be any number of benign causes for this, so it is best not to be your own diagnostician. The problem can be systemic or localized in the vocal or respiratory tracts.

ALLERGIES

We seem to be living in an allergy-filled environment most of the time. There are so many types of allergies—from dust, pollen, perfume, and smoke to food intolerances and reactions to medicines—that determining the ones that you are sensitive to is not always easy. It is not fun to live with streaming eyes and stuffy noses, or with gallons of phlegm. If the allergy is seasonal, then you can get some relief in the off season. When your symptoms continue unabated, it is time to see a doctor or other health practitioner.

LARYNGITIS

Laryngitis is inflammation of the vocal folds and surrounding tissue. It can be viral or bacterial. You can tell the difference by the color of what you are coughing up. If it is greenish and foul-looking, it is usually bacterial and some medication might be in order. You can help yourself by keeping the throat moist at all times. Drinking lots of water and keeping your room humidified is important for your comfort. (Make sure you clean your humidifier periodically. That dampness can harbor all kinds of bugs and bacteria.) Inhaling steam is suggested by many doctors as a treatment for laryngitis and is highly effective in the healing process.

SINUSITIS

The sinuses may be too small to act as resonators and affect our singing positively, but they can certainly cause a lot of discomfort when they are infected. A sinus infection can cause headaches, make you feel heavy-headed, and create a postnasal drip that also causes you to be hoarse. Again, bringing up foul-colored mucus implies infection and indicates the need for professional help. Decongestants can allay the symptoms but may cause excessive drying of the throat. It is unwise to take decongestants over a long period of time.

PERSISTENT SORE THROAT

Like hoarseness, sore throats can stem from a variety of problems. They can be symptomatic of viral or bacterial infection, tonsillitis, sinusitis, and postnasal drip. When you have a sore throat, it is wise to maintain short rehearsals and take good care of your voice. If you overwork your voice while you have a sore throat, you run the risk of developing hoarseness.

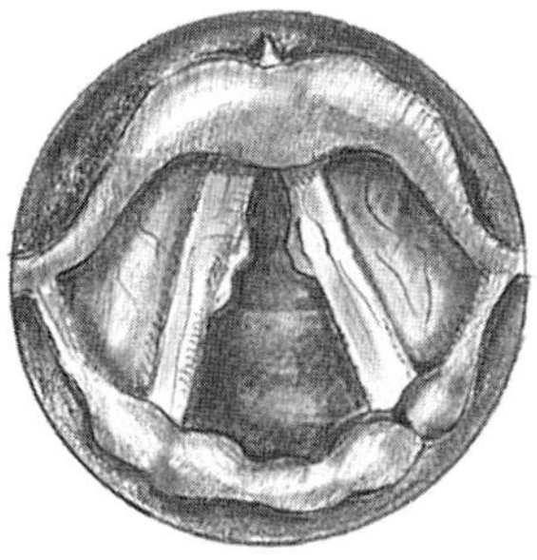

Figure 12.1: Vocal nodules

VOCAL NODULES

When people sing or speak with excessive tension or poor vocal technique, they abuse the vocal folds. The vocal folds bang together and create a swelling like a callus or a corn on the inner edges (see Figure 12.1). This may begin as a blood clot and slowly develop into something firmer and larger. The swelling or nodule prevents the vocal folds from touching cleanly and allows excess air through the resulting chink. The symptom is constant hoarseness or breathiness in the speaking and singing voice. There is loss of vocal range and a tendency for the voice to sound breathy, weak, and tired.

When nodules are discovered early enough, they can be corrected by voice and/or speech therapy. The ear, nose, and throat specialist will probably suggest that they be surgically removed if they are large and hard. Good vocal technique is the way to prevent and correct for vocal nodules. Removing the nodules surgically will only remove the symptoms and may leave scar tissue. Vocal nodules will return if you continue the same vocal habits. Many a budding singing career has been ruined by poor technique—no matter what the singing style.

Hoarseness will usually be the first symptom of vocal abuse. There are very few pain fibers in the larynx and it has no obvious way of letting you know you are in trouble. If you are having constant throat pain and vocal fatigue, you need to do something immediately.

VOCAL FATIGUE

Your voice can be overworked over a long period of time to the point of muscle fatigue. Tired vocal muscles, like any other muscle of the body, simply refuse to do what you want. One symptom of vocal fatigue is a wobble in the sound. By the time vocal fatigue sets in, the vocal folds are usually very damaged. This is a serious symptom and is not easily corrected. It is not a likely problem for you at the beginning of your vocal studies, but it is important for you to remember that your voice will not stand constant abuse without eventually rebelling. Classroom teachers yelling over noisy students and anyone shouting over constant noise are prone to this problem. Changing your work environment may be necessary if you want your voice to last your lifetime.

ACID REFLUX

Acid reflux is more common in older than younger people. However, it can happen to any one at any age. Reflux typically happens during sleep when stomach acids are regurgitated. The acid secreted is a very potent hydrochloric acid that irritates and burns everything it touches. If you have ever wondered what the burning sensation was when you have vomited, it was this acid. It is not pleasant and is very harmful to the larynx. The symptoms of acid reflux include waking up with a burning sensation in the throat that goes away during the day, foul breath (more than your normal bad breath), and hoarseness. People with this problem are usually given special diets, instructed not to eat a heavy meal late at night, advised to keep the head more elevated than the feet at night, and given medication to neutralize the acid. If you think you have reflux, see your doctor.

Deafness

Many people live in noisy environments—with busy streets, traffic, loud TVs and stereos, personal stereos and headphones, slamming doors, and loud concerts. We have become almost immune to the amount of loud noise that constantly surrounds us. It is slowly making us deaf.

The eardrum functions to protect the ear and transmit sound signals to your brain, and its protective capacity is damaged every time you overload it with loud sustained noise. After a rock concert, it takes the ear several days to recover from the trauma. You may notice that you hear poorly the day after attending such concerts. Wearing earplugs to these concerts is worth your consideration.

Loud noise is causing people to develop partial hearing impairment because of exposure to the excessive decibel levels of dance clubs, personal stereos, TVs, and other sources of noise. Some clubs are known to have sound at the decibel levels of a jet plane. Sound is considered harmful when it reaches ninety decibels. A jet plane takes off at 120 decibels. That is approximately thirty decibels over the hearing health limit. (Decibels go up by the power of ten, so you can work out just how loud 120 decibels might be.) The ears are an important part of singing. They are traumatized by long sessions of loud music. If your hearing is impaired, your singing could be affected because sensitivity to language, vocal feedback, and pitch perception will be reduced.

Optional treatment

A number of options are available for treating some of the health problems discussed above. In addition to standard medical treatment, many people find help in homeopathy, naturopathy, acupuncture, nutrition, and other therapies. If you find you are taking medication on a long-term basis, it would be wise to seek further answers regarding your problem.

Summary

This chapter has been devoted to the prevention of vocal ill health. Your voice is a precious and important aspect of your communication. Trying to communicate without sound is an extremely frustrating and slow process. There are few if any jobs in which no talking is involved. Singing or speaking while under vocal duress is counterproductive and vocally risky.

A positive spirit and a healthy lifestyle are the two most important things you can do for yourself and your voice. Paying attention to your attitudes, general health and fitness, and practice habits will enhance your vocal health and give you the confidence to use your voice and your body wisely for the rest of your life.

Epilogue

Now that you have finished *singing* this book, you are ready to explore more refined areas of vocal performance. You have been given the basic knowledge and repertoire for establishing an easily produced sound and a musically intelligent interpretation. You can use the principles in this book to sing in any musical style that interests you.

You have also been given the tools to discover things about your voice for yourself. While your singing teacher is very important for guidance and advice, learning to sing is a shared responsibility. In the end, only you can feel what is happening inside your body. Do not neglect its messages.

Ask for clarification when you have a question; it is not a sign of stupidity. Intelligent people ask questions and strive for understanding. While there is not an answer to every question, there are at the same time few mysteries. If we can let go of preconceptions and dogma and be open to new information and have the courage to explore, there is usually some logic at work. Where there is mystery, enjoy it and revel in the wonder of it all. Music and singing have space for magic and the mysterious.

The spirit that you bring to your singing will add huge amounts to the physical and musical skills you already have. It brings that little bit extra, and anyone can have spirit.

Singing is a joyful thing to do and it does not need to be classed as a skill for the specially gifted. It is part of the spirit of being human—and you have every right to "sound your spirit."

APPENDIX A

Worksheet for Preparing the Text of Your Song

You will have to use your own imagination to answer many of these questions. Fill in each one of them before memorizing the text. This applies to every song you sing, independent of the style. Remember that you choose the characters, their costumes, colors, and materials; you design the set down to the last detail. By filling in this worksheet, you will find that you really know the words and the song. The more imagination you use, the more compelling your singing will be.

1. How many characters are there? (This includes the narrator.)
2. Name each character and describe the following:
    a. What color are the eyes and hair? What is the height, weight, and age?
    b. What is the skin like to touch? Is the woman wearing perfume?
    c. Is the hair long, short, straight, or curly? Is it silky, thick, or thin? Is the man bald? Does he have a beard or moustache? If so, what color?
    d. Describe in great detail the clothes each character is wearing—the colors, specific materials, type of shoes, and any accessories.
    e. What is the personality like? Is the character sweet, mean, kind, loving?
3. What is the setting? Describe in detail the scenery around the character(s):
    a. Describe the type of house or interior, including curtains, wallpaper, and furniture. What can you see out the windows?
    b. If outside, describe the ground, the sights, smells, sounds, types of trees and flowers, colors, and depths of colors.
    c. Are there mountains, the sea, desert, streams and rivers? If so, give *full* descriptions. For example, is it on a beach? If so, what is the sand like? Are there sea grasses blowing in the breeze? How does the sea smell? sound? look? Is it calm or rough?

d. Which season is it? What is the air like? Is it soft, a spring breeze, or stormy? Are there any smells in the air such as flowers, the sea, or cooking?

4. What is the main message of each character?

5. What is the message of the whole song *in one sentence?*

6. What is the one thing you want your audience to take away from hearing you sing this song?

APPENDIX B

Introduction to IPA: Pronunciation of Vowels and Consonants

The *International Phonetic Alphabet*, or IPA, was created in the late 1880s by a group of French language teachers who wanted to help students learn the sounds of unfamiliar languages. IPA is a series of symbols that represent individual sounds (or phonemes) that are used in languages. IPA is not tied to a specific language, and those who familiarize themselves with the symbols can learn to pronounce any language on earth. The International Phonetic Alphabet is a valuable tool for singers because you must first learn to speak a word before you can sing it. IPA has been widely adopted by singers and singing teachers, language teachers, and publishers of dictionaries. This partial list of IPA symbols includes those most commonly used by singers.

Many of the symbols such as [t] [p] [d] [k] [o] are already familiar to Americans while others like [æ] [ə] [ŋ] [θ] will look rather strange at first. Let's begin by looking at some basic *vowel sounds.*

Vowels

closed [i]	long ee	"ee" as in bee, receive, green, jeans
open [ɪ]	short ih	"ih" as in sit, pretty, list, busy
closed [e]	pure ay	"ay" as in dictate, day, weigh, filet
open [ɛ]	open eh	"eh" as in bed, air, when, friend
broad [æ]	short a	"a" as in has, plaid, act, plant
bright [a]	bright ah	*Spanish:* madre; *French:* parle; *German:* Halle
dark [ɑ]	tall ah	"ah" as in father, dark, hot, pasta
closed [o]	pure oh	"oh" as in stone, moat, go, hotel
open [ɔ]	open oh	"aw" as in haughty, dog, saw, cause
open [ʊ]	open oo	"oo" as in hook, should, put, book
closed [u]	pure oo	"oo" as in pool, blue, noon, you
short [ʌ]	short uh	"uh" as in cup, shut, rough, flood
schwa [ə]	neutral uh	"uh" as in second syllable of little, even *German:* blume; *French:* jeune
closed [y]	long umlaut u	"oo" + "ee," *German:* für; *French:* pur
open [ʏ]	short umlaut u	"oo" + "ee," *German:* mütter
closed [ø]	long mixed o-e	"ay" + "oh," *German:* schön; *French:* adieu

open [œ]	mixed	"aw + eh," similar to bird, earth, her *German:* möchte; *French:* fleur
glide [j]	y	"yuh" as in yellow, union, punitive *Italian:* piu; *German:* jah; *French:* bien
glide [w]	w	"wuh" as in water, we, quick, one *Spanish:* bueno; *French:* oui; *Italian:* qui
American [r]	er	"er" as in red, year, car, court
glide [y]	quick[y]	*French:* lui, nuit

Many *consonants* in IPA are pronounced just as we pronounce them in American English: [b] [d] [f] [g] [h] [k] [l] [m] [n] [p] [s] [t] [v] [y] [z].

Other consonants merit their own unique symbols.

Consonants

unvoiced [ʃ]	sh	"sh" as in shadow, shine, machine *German:* schön; *French:* riche; *Italian:* lasciatemi
combined [tʃ]	ch	"ch" as in church, chili, itch *Spanish:* mucho; *Italian:* cielo; *German:* deutsch
voiced [ʒ]	soft zh	as in treasure, leisure, azure *French:* jeune, je, gymnopedi
combined [dʒ]	hard j	"juh" as in jelly, huge; *Italian:* giuro
soft [ç]	ichlaut	soft blown "ch" as in human, *German:* ich
hard [x]	achlaut	hard blown "ch," *German:* ach, Bach
unvoiced [θ]	soft "th"	"th" as in Thanksgiving, theater, with; *Castillian Spanish:* corazon
voiced [ð]	hard "th"	"th" as in these, writhe, then
liquid [ŋ]	ng	"ng" as in sing; *Italian:* ancora; *German:* bang
n tilde [ɲ]	ñ	"en-yah" as in onion; *Italian:* sogno; *French:* cigne
liquid [ʎ]	[lj]	"el-yah" as in million; *Italian:* voglio, egli; *Castillian Spanish:* ballena
flipped [ɾ]	single flip	"r" flipped as in British: very; *Italian:* caro; *Spanish:* Maria; *German:* sehren; *French:* repos
rolled [rr]	rolled "r"	"rrrr" as in *Italian:* crudele, amor; *French:* horrible; *Spanish:* rojo
voiced [β]	voiced "b"	*Castillian Spanish:* verlaba

ITALIAN

A rule of thumb in Italian is to flip the [ɾ] when it is between two vowels: *cara, Figaro.* Roll the [rr] when it is before or after a consonant, or at the beginning or ending of a word: *amor, pronto, morte, ruggiadose.* Some words contain both rolled and flipped "r"s: *brillare.*

Some consonants that are aspirated and rather noisy in English—[t], [k], [p]—are very soft in Italian. They implode rather than explode. Also, in Italian be aware of double consonants, such as *sebben, fuggite, donzelle.* Take a little time to "stick" on the double consonants, without stopping the flow of the musical phrase. Differentiation between single consonants and double consonants will make your pronunciation more authentic and fun.

Latin and Spanish

The Latin rounds and group songs in *The Singing Book* are pronounced very much like Italian. One major exception is that the [t], [k], and [p] are aspirated. Spanish also has a lot in common with Italian pronunciation, including many similar vowels and soft [t], [k], and [p]. Unlike Italian, the "r"s at the beginning of Spanish words are rolled. Differences in Spanish pronunciation between Latin America and Spain (Castillian) are noted in the IPA for the individual songs.

French

In the French language there are special vowels called *nasal vowels.* These vowels resonate in both your mouth and in your nose, and are sung with a slightly lowered soft palate. The "n" in nasal vowels is not pronounced. There are no English language equivalents to these nasal vowels, so you will need to experiment with the new sounds.

[ɑ̃]	nasal [ɑ]	as in blanc, enfante
[ɛ̃]	nasal [ɛ]	as in main, Sainte
[ɔ̃]	nasal [ɔ]	as in bon, tombe
[œ̃]	nasal [œ]	as in parfum, un

To practice saying all four French nasal vowels, speak "A fine white wine" in French: "Un bon vin blanc." It is helpful to think of French as a very "round" language. Most American singers don't use their lips enough when singing French. Pucker up and also remember to keep the [t], [k], [p] consonants soft.

German

In contrast, the German language is full of noisy, aspirated consonants. When singing in German, go ahead and explode the [t], [k], [p], [ts], [x], and [ç]. Especially when singing words like *nicht* and *nacht,* you will need to shorten the vowels to allow plenty of time to blow air through the "ch." For singing, be sure that you don't gargle the [x] and [ç] in your throat. It's more like a cat's hiss or the way we say "huge" or "human" in English. The [x] is a bit farther back in your mouth than the [ç]

Also, be aware of "glottal" stops (places where the vowels begin with a popping sound) in German. Usually when a word begins with a vowel you will need to precede it with a slight pause for clarity, for example, "und ich." Americans are quite familiar with the gentle "grunt" of a glottal stop. Say "Oh, my!" and notice the percussive sound of the [o].

The more familiar you become with the symbols and sounds of the International Phonetic Alphabet, the easier and more enjoyable it will become to sing in foreign languages. You can also use the symbols to remind you of vowels you want to sing in English. For example, if you tend to sing "binch" instead of "bench," you can simply jot [ɛ] above the word.

IPA is a very practical language tool and can help you sing languages accurately. Practice speaking your texts aloud, and do your best to avoid a monotonous, robotic delivery. Once you have translated your text and learned your IPA pronunciation, speak the poetry with emotion and facial expression. When you know exactly *what* you are saying and *how* to say it, then the melody and accompaniment will add the final threads to your musical tapestry.

IPA and Word-for-Word Translations for Songs

Ah! si mon moine voulait danser! (p. 86)
Ah! If my monk wanted to dance!

[a] [si] [mɔ̃] [mwan] [vulɛ] [dɑ̃se]
Ah! si mon moine voulait danser!
Ah! If my monk wanted to dance!

[œ̃] [kapyʃɔ̃] [ʒə] [ly] [dɔnəɾɛ]
Un capuchon je lui donnerais,
A hood I would give to him,

[dɑ̃sə] [mɔ̃] [mwan] [dɑ̃se]
Danse, mon moin', danser!
Dance, my monk, to dance!

[ty] [nɑ̃tɑ̃] [pɑ] [la] [dɑ̃sə]
Tu n'entends pas la danse,
You don't hear the dance,

[ty] [nɑ̃tɑ̃] [pɑ] [mɔ̃] [mulɛ̃] [lɔ̃] [la]
Tu n'entends pas mon moulin, lon la.
You don't hear my mill, (tra-la).

[ty] [nɑ̃tɑ̃] [pɑ] [mɔ̃] [mulɛ̃] [maɾʃe]
Tu n'entends pas mon moulin marcher.
You don't hear my mill to walk.

Auf Flügeln des Gesanges (p. 201)
On Wings of Song

[aof] [flygəln] [dɛs] [gəzaŋəs]
Auf Flügeln des Gesanges
On wings of the songs/chants

[hɛɾtslipçən] [trak] [iç] [diç] [fɔɾt]
Herzliebchen, trag' ich dich fort,
Heart dear little, carry I you away,

[fɔɾt] [nax] [den] [fluɾən] [dɛs] [gaŋɛs]
Fort nach den Fluren des Ganges,
Along after the plains of the Ganges,

[dɔɾt] [vaes] [iç] [den] [ʃønstən] [ɔɾt]
Dort weiß ich den schönsten Ort.
There know I the most beautiful place.

[dɔɾt] [likt] [aen] [ɾotblyəndəɾ] [gaɾtən]
Dort liegt ein rotblühender Garten
There lies a red blooming garden

[ɪm] [ʃtɪlən] [mondənʃaen]
Im stillen Mondenschein;
In the quiet moonshine;

[di] [lotosblumən] [eɾvaɾtən]
Die Lotosblumen erwarten
The lotus blossoms expect

[iɾ] [tɾaotəs] [ʃvɛstəɾlaen]
Ihr trautes Schwesterlein,
their trusted little sister,

[di] [faelçən] [kɪçəɾn] [ʊnt] [kozən]
Die Veilchen kichern und kosen,
The violets giggle and caress,

[ʊnt] [ʃaon] [nax] [den] [ʃteɾnən] [ɛmpoɾ]
Und schau'n nach den Sternen empor;
And looks after the stars upwards;

[haemlɪç] [ɛɾtsɛlən] [di] [ɾozən]
Heimlich erzählen die Rosen
Secretly, tell the roses

[zɪç] [dʊftendə] [mɛɾçən] [ɪns] [oɾ]
Sich duftende Märchen in's Ohr,
Themselves fragrant fairy-tales in the ear,

[ɛs] [hʏpfən] [hɛɾbae] [ʊnt] [laoʃən]
Es Hüpfen herbei und lauschen
It hops here and listens

[di] [fɾɔmən] [klugən] [gatsɛln]
Die frommen, klugen Gazell'n;
The devout, clever Gazelles;

[ʊnt] [ɪn] [deɾ] [fɛɾnə] [ɾaoʃən]
Und in der Ferne rauschen
And in the distance rustles

[dɛs] [haelgən] [ʃtɾoməs] [vɛln]
Des heil'gen Stromes Well'n,
The holy stream waves,

[dɔɾt] [vɔlən] [viɾ] [nidəɾzɪŋkən]
Dort wollen wir niedersinken
There want we to low-sink

[ʊntəɾ] [dem] [palmənbaom]
Unter dem Palmenbaum,
Under the palm tree,

[ʊnt] [lip] [ʊnt] [ɾuə] [tɾɪŋkən]
Und Lieb' und Ruhe trinken
And love and silence drink

[ʊnt] [tɾɔimən] [zelɪgən] [tɾaom]
Und träumen seligen Traum
And dreams blissful dream

Bitte [bɪtə] (p. 206)
Plea

[vael] [aof] [miɾ] [du] [dʊŋkləs] [aogə]
Weil auf mir, du dunkles Auge,
Be (linger) on me you dark eye,

[ybə] [daenə] [gantsə] [maxt] [ɛɾnstə] [mɪldə]
übe deine ganze Macht, ernste, milde,
practice your entire power serious mild,

[tɾɔimərɪʃə] [ʊnɛɾgɾʏntlɪç] [zysə] [naxt]
traümerische, unergründlich süsse Nacht.
dream-like unfathomably sweet night.

[nɪm] [mɪt] [daenəm] [tsaobəɾdʊnkəl] [dizə] [vɛlt] [fɔn] [hɪnən] [miɾ]
Nimm mit deinem Zauberdunkel diese Welt von hinnen mir,
Take with your magic darkness this world from me,

[das] [du] [ybəɾ] [maenəm] [lebən] [aenzɑm] [ʃvebəst] [fyr] [ʊnt] [fyr]
Dass du über meinem Leben einsam schwebest für und für.
that you above my life alone hovers forever and ever.

Con amores, la mi madre (p. 218)
With love in my heart, my mother
(Castillian Spanish)

[kon] [amoɾes] [la] [mi] [madɾe] [kon] [amoɾes] [me] [doɾmi]
Con amores, la mi madre, con amores me dormi;
With love, the mine mother, with love I slept;

[asi] [doɾmiða] [soɲaβa] [lo] [kel] [koɾaθon] [belaβa]
Asi dormida soñaba lo que‿el corazon velaba
This way sleeping I dreamed that the (one) heart it veiled

[kel] [amor] [me] [konsolaβa]
Que‿el amor me consolaba
That the love me consoled

[kon] [mas] [bjen] [ke] [meɾeθi]
con mas bien que mereci.
with more goodness than merited.

[adoɾmeθjome] [el] [favoɾ] [ke] [amoɾ] [me] [djo] [kon] [amoɾ]
Adormeciome el favor que amor me dio con amor;
It put me to sleep the favor that love me gave with love;

[djo] [deskanso] [a] [mi] [doloɾ] [la] [fe] [kon] [ke] [le] [seɾβi]
Dio descanso a mi dolor, la fe con que le servi
(He) gave rest to my pain the faith with that him I served

Dona Nobis Pacem (p. 45)
Give Us Peace

[dɔnɑ] [nɔbis] [pɑtʃɛm]
Dona nobis pacem.
Give to us peace.

Donzelle, fuggite (p. 189)
Damsels, run away

[dontsɛlle] [fuddʒitte] [prrokaʃe] [bɛlta]
Donzelle, fuggitte procace beltà!
Damsels, run away from provocative beauty!

[fuddʒitte] [fuddʒitte] [fuddʒitte]
Fuggitte, fuggitte, fuggitte!
Run away, run away, run away!

[se] [luʃido] [zgwarrdo] [vi] [penɛtrrail] [kɔre]
Se lucido sguardo vi pénetra il core,
If lucid glances (you) penetrate the heart

[laʃate] [kwel] [darrdo] [del] [perrfidoamoɾe]
Lasciate quel dardo del perfido amore,
Abandon that arrow of perfidious (treacherous) love*

[keinsidje] skaltrrite] [trramando] [vi] [sta]
Che insidie scaltrite tramando vi sta!
Which trap shrewd passes on you

*Cupid's arrow

Dubinushka* (p. 95)

[εx] [dubinuʃka] [uxnjεm]
Ex, Dubinushka, uhnem!
Oh, green stick, away (heave-ho)

[εx] [zεlɔnaja] [sama] [paidjɔt] [sama] [paidjɔt]
Ex, zelyonaya sama pojdot, sama poydyot!
Oh, it will yield if you push (strike) hard, push (strike) hard!

[padjɔrrnεm] [da] [uxnjεm]
Podyornem, Da uhnem!
Push, yes away (heave-ho)

**Dubinushka* is a large wooden club or sledgehammer. (Russian translation and pronunciation by Alex Pudov.)

Ego Sum Pauper (p. 45)
I Am a Pauper

[εgɔ] [sum] [pɑupεɾ]
Ego sum pauper
I am pauper

[nihil] [abεɔ]
Nihil habeo
Nothing possess

[kɔɾ] [mεum] [dabɔ]
Cor meum dabo
Heart of mine I offer

El majo* timido [el] [maxo] [timido] (p. 216)
The Timid Suitor
(Castillian Spanish)

[ʎega] [a] [mi] [rreha] [i] [me] [miɾa]
Llega á mi reja y me mira**
He arrives at my (window) grille and at me he looks

[poɾ] [la] [notʃe] [un] [maxo]
por la noche un majo
for the night a majo.

[ken] [kwanto] [me] [βe] [i] [suspiɾa] [se]
que‿en cuanto me ve y suspira se
That in as much as me you see and sighs

[ba] [kaʎe] [abaxo]
vá calle abajo.
he goes street down.

[ai] [ke] [tio] [mas] [taɾðio]
¡Ay! que tío más tardio!
Oh that man more slow (dull)

[si] [asi] [se] [pasa] [la] [biða]
Si asi se pasa la vida,
If this way he spends his life,

[estoi] [dibeɾtiða]
Estoy divertida.
I am amused.

**majo* is an untranslatable word for a handsome young man.
**In Castillian Spanish, double ll is pronounced [ʎ], like "million."

Gaudeamus Igitur (p. 41)
Rejoice Therefore

[gɑudeamus] [idʒituɾ]
Gaudeamus igitur,
Rejoice therefore,

[juvɛnɛs] [dum] [sumus]
Juvenes dum sumus;
Youth as long as is;

[pɔst] [jukundum] [juvɛntutɛm]
Post jucundum juventutem
After delightful the age of youth,

[pɔst] [mɔlɛstɑm] [sɛnɛktutɛm]
Post molestam senectutem
After annoying old age

[nɔs] [ɑbɛbit] [umus]
Nos habebit humus
We dwell in earth

Ici-bas (p. 208)
Here Below

[isibɑ] [tu] [le] [lilɑ] [mœɾə]
Ici-bas tous les lilas meurent,
Here below all the lilacs die,

[tu] [le] [ʃɑ̃] [dezwazo] [sɔ̃] [kuɾ]
Tous les chants des oiseaux sont courts.
All the songs of the birds are short.

[ʒə] [ɾɛvozete] [ki] [dəmœɾə] [tuʒuɾ]
Je rêve aux été qui demeurent Toujours!
I dream of summers that live forever!

[isibɑ] [le] [lɛvɾəzeflœɾə]
Ici-bas les levres effleurent
Here below the lips brush against

[sɑ̃] [rjɛ̃] [lɛse] [də] [lœɾ] [vəluɾ]
Sans rien laisser de leur velours,
Without anything to let go of their velvet,

[ʒə] [ɾɛvo] [bɛze] [ki] [dəmœɾə] [tuʒuɾ]
Je rêve aux baisers qui demerurent Toujours!
I dream of kisses that live forever!

[isibɑ] [tu] [lezɔmə] [plœɾə]
Ici-bas, tous les hommes pleurent
Here below, all the men (people) weep for

[lœɾzamitje] [u] [lœɾzamuɾ]
Leurs amitiés ou leurs amours,
Their friends or their loves,

[ʒə] [ɾɛvo] [kuplə] [ki] [dəmœɾə] [tuʒuɾ]
Je rêve aux couples qui demeurent, Toujours!
I dream of couples who live forever!

Mi caballo blanco (p. 91)
My White Horse
(Latin American Spanish)

Verse 1:
[es] [mi] [kabajo] [blanko] [komo] [un] [amaneseɾ]
Es mi caballo blanco como un amanecer,
It is my horse white as a dawn,

[sjempɾe] [huntitos] [vamos] [es] [mi] [amigo] [mas] [fjel]
siempre juntitos vamos, es mi amigo mas fiel.
Always together we go, it is my friend the most faithful.

Refrain:
[mi] [kabajo] [mi] [kabajo] [galapando] [va]
Mi caballo, mi caballo galopando va.
My horse, my horse galloping he goes.

[mi] [kabajo] [mi] [kabajo] [se] [va] [i] [se] [va]
Mi caballo, mi caballo se va y se va.
My horse, my horse he goes and he goes.

Verse 2:
[en] [alas] [de] [una] [ditʃa] [mi] [kabajo] [korrio]
En alas de una dicha mi caballo corrio
In wings of a happiness my horse he ran

[i] [en] [bɾasos] [de] [una] [pena] [tambjen] [el] [me] [jevo]
y en brazos de una pena tambien el me llevo.
and in arms of a pain also he me took.

Verse 3:
[asta] [ke] [a] [djos] [le] [pido] [ke] [lo] [teŋga] [muj] [bjen]
Hasta que a Dios le pido, que lo tenga muy bien,
Until that to God him I request, that him have very well,

[si] [a][su] [lado] [me] [jama] [en] [mi] [blankito] [iɾe]
Si a su lado me llama, en mi blanquito ire.
If to its side me he calls in my little white (horse) I will go.

Niño precioso (p. 88)
Precious Child
(Latin American Spanish)

[niɲo] [pɾesjoso] [mas] [kel] [armiɲo]
Niño precioso, mas que el armiño,
Child precious, more that the cloth,

[rrisweɲo] [niɲo] [djos] [del] [amoɾ]
risueño niño Dios del amor.
Smiling boy God of love.

[dweɾme] [trankilo] [dweɾme] [entɾetanto]
Duerme tranquilo, duerme entretanto,
Sleep calmly, sleep meanwhile,

[eleva] [un] [kanto] [mi] [umilde] [vos]
Eleva un canto mi humilde voz.
Raises a song (to) my humble voice.

[dweɾme] [tʃikitito] [ke] [oi] [ase] [fɾio]
Duerme, chiquitito que hoy hace frio.
Sleep, little boy that today is cold.

[dweɾme] [tʃikitito] [jo] [βelaɾe]
Duerme, chiquitito yo velaré
Sleep, little boy, I will cover him.

Ombra mai fù (p. 195)
Shade mine never was

[ombrra] [mai] [fu] [di] [vedʒetabile]
Ombra mai fù di vegetabile
Shade mine never was any plant

[kaɾa] [ɛd] [amabilɛ] [soavɛ] [pju]
cara ed amabile, soave più
dear and sweet, gentle more

Paun I Kolo [paun i kolo] (p. 84)
*Peacock and Dance**

[paun] [pasɛ] [tɾava] [ɾastɛ] [paun] [moj]
Paun pase, trava raste, paun moj!
Peacock grazes, grass is growing, peacock mine!

[pauna] [nam] [nogɛ] [bolɛ] [paun] [moj]
Pauna nam, noge bole, paun moj!
Peacock's legs ail, peacock mine!

[pauna] [nam] [otsi] [bolɛ] [paun] [moj]
Pauna nam oci bole, paun moj!
Peacock's eyes ail, peacock mine!

Note: The word "moj" rhymes with our English word "toy." Also, the letter "c" in Bosnian is pronounced "ts." Be sure to flip the "r"s.
*Translation by Nenja Hasanic (http://boslang.tripod.com). Pronunciation guide: *Bosnian-English/English-Bosnian Dictionary and Phrasebook,* Susan Kroll, Hippocrene Books, NY, 1998.

Santa Lucia (p. 81)
Saint Lucia

[sul] [maɾe] [luttʃika] [lastrro] [darrdʒɛnto]
Sul mare luccica l'astro d'argento
On the sea sparkles the star of silver

[platʃida] [e] [londa] [prrɔspeɾo] [e] [il] [vɛnto]
Placida è l'onda, prospero è il vento.
Placid are the waves, prosperous is the wind.

[venite] [alladʒile] [barrketta] [mia] [santa] [lutʃia]
Venite all'agile barchetta mia! Santa Lucia!
Come to the agile small boat mine! Saint Lucia!

[kon] [kwesto] [dzeffiro] [kozi] [soave]
con questo zeffiro così soave.
with this zephyr so sweet.*

[o] [kome] [bɛllo] [starr] [sulla] [nave]
Oh, com'è bello star sulla nave!
Oh, how it is beautiful to be on the ship!

Note: It is important to observe the double consonants in Italian (luccica, barchetta, zeffiro, bello, sulla. . . .) Give the double consonants a little extra time.

*A zephyr is a warm, gentle breeze.

Shalom,* Chaverim (p. 46)
Farewell, Friends

[ʃalɔm] [xavɛɾim] [ʃalɔm] [xavɛɾim]
Shalom, chaverim, shalom chaverim,
Farewell, friends, farewell, friends,

[ʃalɔm] [ʃalɔm]
shalom, shalom.
farwell, farewell.

[lə] [xit] [ɾaot] [lə] [xit] [ɾaot]
Le hit raot, le hit raot.
Until we meet again, until we meet again.

[ʃalɔm] [ʃalɔm]
Shalom, shalom.
Farewell, farewell.

**Shalom* can mean hello or goodbye. (Hebrew translation and pronunciation by Cynthia Lee Fox.)

APPENDIX C

Additional Vocal Exercises

Just as athletes do specific warm-ups, stretches, and exercises to strengthen certain muscle groups, singers can choose specific exercises to target vocal technique. Some target areas for singers are *body, breath, resonance, flexibility,* and *range.*

Body

For full-body exercises, refer to the alignment and physical stretching exercises in Part I.

Breath

The vocal sighs, buzzes, raspberries, and trills introduced in Part I are excellent exercises for improving your breathing technique.

Exercise 1

Place the backs of your hands at the back of your lower ribs. With your best body alignment, inhale deeply and release the breath without deliberately pulling in your abs as you "chant" the alphabet from A to Z (or as far as you comfortably get). Think of chanting as fluid speaking—somewhere between speech and song. As you chant, be aware of a full body stretch. Avoid holding your breath between the inhalation and exhalation.

Resonance

Any exercise that uses hums [m][n][ŋ] and glides [j] is helpful for creating a more resonant vibrant tone. Start with this very gentle [m] hum. Lips are lightly closed, top and bottom teeth are apart, tip of the tongue is forward, with a slight lift of the soft palate. Hum very softly on this descending pattern and notice the vibrations throughout your face and head. If you hum too loudly, you will feel vibrations mainly in your mouth. This soothing exercise is also a great "cool down" after you have finished your daily vocal practice time or a choral rehearsal.

Exercise 2

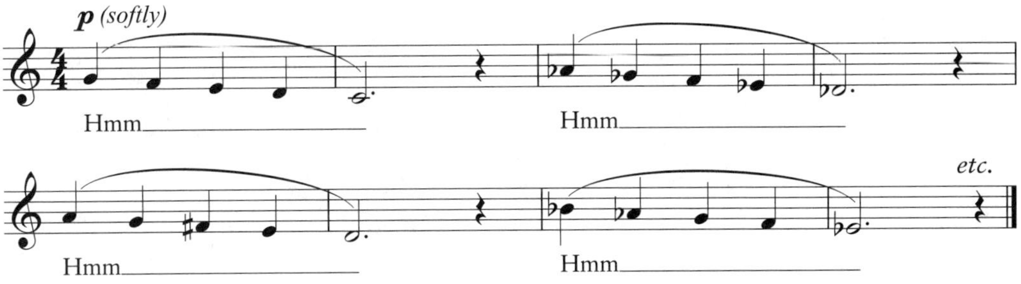
p (softly)
Hmm
Hmm
etc.
Hmm
Hmm

Once you have found an easy "ringing" sound, experiment with this simple 5-note descending pattern on a variety of texts, rhythms, dynamics, and moods. Be creative and have fun. You can sing words from your textbook, from your songs, from anywhere.

Exercise 3

mf
etc.
ma - ma - ma
ma - ma - ma
ma - ma - ma

Exercise 4

mf
etc.
mee - meh - ma
she - sheh - sha
thee - theh - tha
(with an unvoiced "th" like "thanks")

Exercise 5

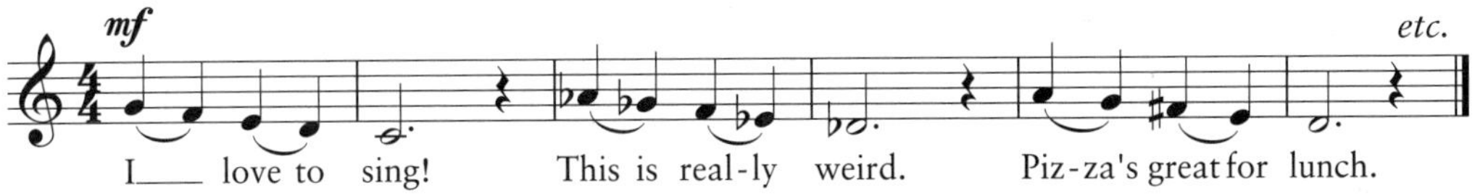
mf
etc.
I love to sing!
This is real-ly weird.
Piz-za's great for lunch.

Exercise 6

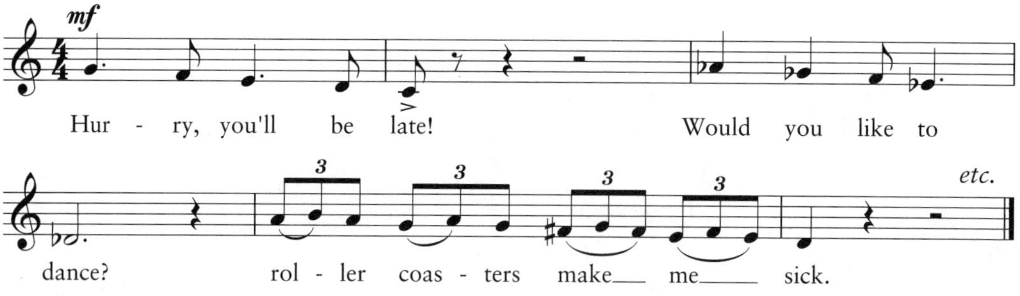
mf
Hur - ry, you'll be late!
Would you like to
dance?
rol - ler coas - ters make___ me___ sick.
3
etc.

RANGE

Now experiment with various vowels, words, dynamics, and moods on a descending octave *arpeggio*. Remember to modify or open the vowels on higher pitches.

Exercise 7

mf
etc.
Ah___
[a]
Oh___
[o]
Oo___
[u]

Exercise 8

p
f
mf
etc.
Qui - e - tly now.
I'm ve - ry MAD!
Oh, what a mess...

Sing some ascending arpeggios now, both legato (smooth and connected) and staccato (light and detached). Take it as low and as high as you are comfortable.

Exercise 9

legato (smoothly)
mf
etc.
ah___
ah___
ah___

Exercise 10

staccato (detached)
mf
etc.
ah
ah
ah

FLEXIBILITY

Start these vocal aerobics slowly, then gradually increase your speed. Have a friend watch (or use a mirror or video) to make sure that you aren't bobbing your chin and head as the pitches rise and fall.

Exercise 11

mf
etc.
ee
ah
eh
eh
ah
ee

Exercise 12

mf
etc.
ah
ee
eh
ah

Choosing different exercises every day will keep your vocalizing fresh. The goal is to apply the vocal skills (breath management, resonance, smooth registers, flexibility) to your songs. You can even create exercises from problem spots in your songs:

Example from "He Shall Feed His Flock," Handel

mp
mf
Ah
Thah - lah
The lambs with his arm.

Spending a few minutes daily to exercise target areas in your vocal technique will make a big difference in how easily and healthily you sing your songs.

APPENDIX D

Making Sense of a Music Manuscript

The language of music has its own special symbols or alphabet. While they may look like hieroglyphics to the uninitiated, each symbol has very specific meanings to musicians. Following are some basic guidelines for looking at a musical score and beginning to make sense of it. We can do this by looking at the way a songwriter might approach notating a song. Where would the composer begin? The answer is with some manuscript paper. (For the purposes of this exercise, we will pretend this composer has no music writing facilities on his computer.)

NOTATION

Manuscript paper is full of horizontal lines that are grouped into patterns of five. Each of these five-line and four space groups is called a *staff or stave.*

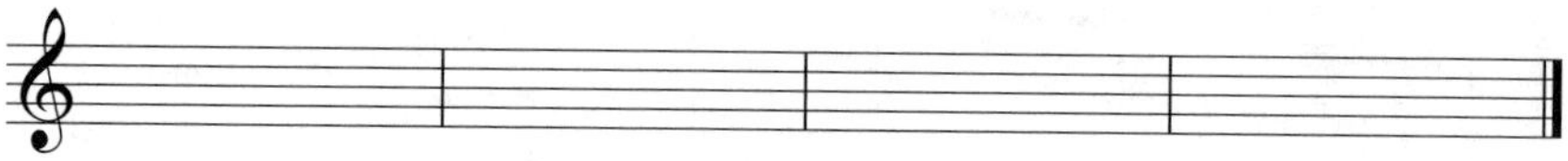

Several staffs joined to each other, as they are in the songs in this text, form a *system.*

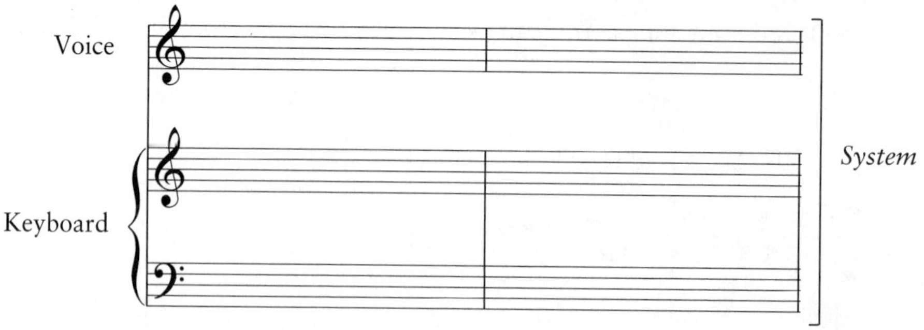
Voice
Keyboard
System

The staff is the scaffolding for the notes, or pitches, of the song. Each line and space represents a different note. Our system of notation uses the letters A, B, C, D, E, F, G as the names of the notes. They are repeated over and over again in different pitch ranges in units called octaves.

Staves are divided by vertical lines, or *bar lines,* into sections, called *measures:*

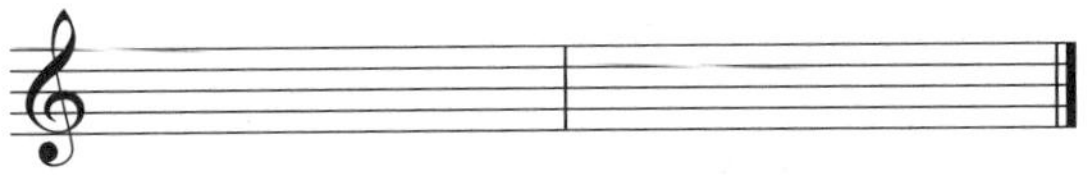

Their purpose is to group units of musical time. This ensures a regular accent or beat throughout the song. The value of these units is indicated by a *time signature* (see below) at the beginning of the composition.

However, before a composer puts the time signature on the lines, he has to denote whether the staff is designated for higher or lower pitches. Marking the staff with *clef signs* does this. The treble, or G clef, looks like this 𝄞 and the bass, or F clef, looks like this 𝄢

Note that the curled part of the treble clef is around the second line from the bottom of the staff. This tells you that the second line is the G above Middle C (C_4). Once you know the location of this single note, you can then figure out the rest of the notes.

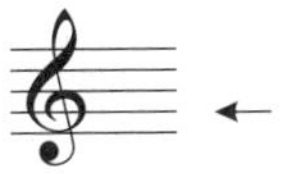

The bass clef has one dot above and one below the second line from the top. This tells you the location of the F below Middle C.

Notes are placed on the staff to tell you their duration and the correct pitches to sing or play. Below is an illustration of a piano keyboard, the names of the notes on it, and their relationship to the musical staff.

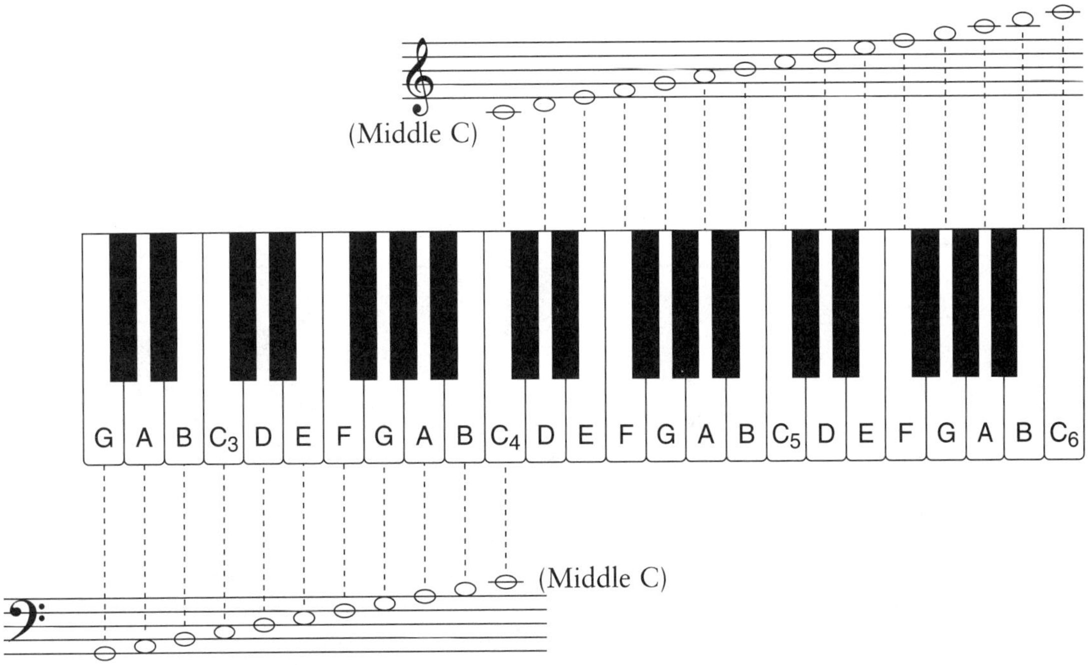
(Middle C)
G A B C3 D E F G A B C4 D E F G A B C5 D E F G A B C6
(Middle C)

RHYTHM

The *time signature* tells us the meter of the song—

whether it is a waltz, a march, or a lullaby.

Time signatures can be thought of as a form of musical math. If you have a time signature of $\frac{3}{4}$ it means that in each measure there must be the equivalent of 3 one-quarter notes or beats. Mathematically, you may have any combination of musical notes or rests in each measure as long as they add up to three quarter notes. You will know the value of a note or rest by its appearance. (See table below.)

Note values		Rest values
𝅝	Whole	𝄻
𝅗𝅥	Half	𝄼
♩	Quarter	𝄽
♪	Eighth	𝄾
𝅘𝅥𝅯	Sixteenth	𝄿
𝅘𝅥𝅰	Thirty-second	𝅀
𝅘𝅥𝅱	Sixty-fourth	𝅁

A dot after a note increases the value by one half of its original value.

For example, dotted half note (𝅗𝅥.) is the equivalent of 3 quarter notes (♩♩♩).

Exercise

Look at two or three folksongs in Part II.

1. Notice that the solo vocal part has its own staff, and it is connected by a line to the two staffs of the accompaniment. There is a treble clef sign for the singer and both treble and bass for the accompanist. Often the treble clef is used for both male and female singers. The male is expected to sing an octave lower than the music is written.

2. Look at several measures and notice how many different ways the value of the notes adds up to the amount indicated by the time signature. For example, in measures of $\frac{3}{4}$ time, you might have the following combinations that all add up to three quarters:

   a. Three quarter notes (♩♩♩)

   b. One quarter note, two eighth notes, and one quarter rest (♩ ♫ 𝄽)
   (Rests are an integral part of a composition, not a very quick holiday.)

   c. One half note and one quarter note (𝅗𝅥 ♩)

PITCH, SCALES, AND KEY

Look at the illustration of the keyboard again. You will see that the same pattern of white and black keys is repeated many times. Each of these patterns is grouped into 7 white keys and 5 black keys making up 12 equal semitones or half steps. This is because the Western musical systems use a tuning system that is called *equal temperament.* Without this system, playing an instrument like the piano would be very cacophonic.

Acoustically what this means is that each pitch exhibits a certain frequency of vibrations. Find Middle C: 256 Hertz (cycles per second) is the frequency of vibrations that gives us the sound of Middle C. The C an octave below is half that frequency, or 128 Hertz; the C above is double, or 512. Every octave the frequency is doubled. This provides the basis for Western harmony.

Different scales have been used throughout music history. However, we will confine this discussion to those that you will commonly encounter. The twelve semitones or half steps become very important when we start to build a scale. They are combined with whole steps to create scale patterns. A whole step is the distance of two half steps between any two pitches. The *chromatic* scale uses all twelve semitones. For the music in Part II, major and minor scales are used. A major scale is identified by a pattern of eight whole and half steps in specific places. The song "Do-re-mi" from *The Sound of Music* is based on the major scale and musical *solfège,* or singing names given to the notes. You know them as do, re, mi, fa, sol, la, ti, and do. If we use numbers, rather than names for the notes from 1 to 8, you will find the half steps fall between 3 and 4, and 7 and 8. Knowing this you can construct a major scale beginning with any note by keeping this pattern of whole and half steps.

C MAJOR SCALE: Half steps between 3–4 and 7–8

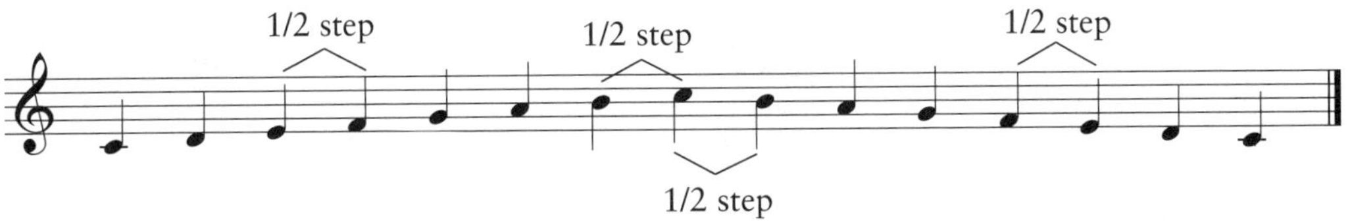
1/2 step
1/2 step
1/2 step
1/2 step

There are several versions of minor scales in use. Each of these versions has a particular pattern of whole and half steps as well. Composers use minor keys to add a different tonal color or to create melancholic moods in a song. Minor patterns look like this:

C natural minor scale: Half steps between 2–3 and 5–6

1/2 step
1/2 step
1/2 step
1/2 step

C harmonic minor scale: Half steps between 2–3, 5–6, and 7–8 ascending and descending

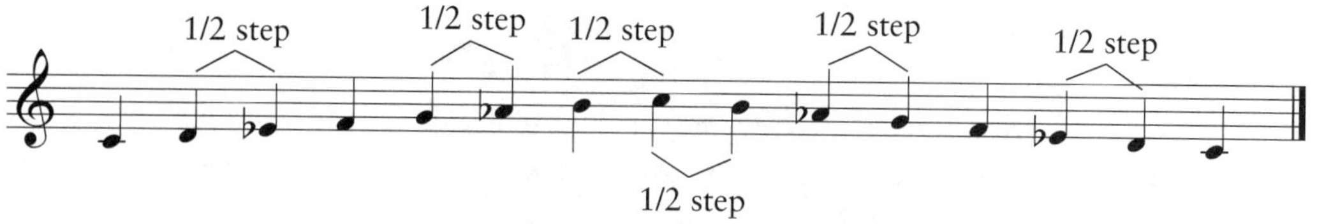
1/2 step
1/2 step
1/2 step
1/2 step
1/2 step
1/2 step

C melodic minor scale: Half steps between 2–3 and 7–8 ascending, and between 2–3 and 5–6 descending

1/2 step
1/2 step
1/2 step
1/2 step

Songs in minor keys are listed in Appendix E.

blues scale: A variation of the minor *pentatonic* scale (all 5 black notes). See "Swingin' in Minor Blues," Part II, p. 31.

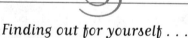

Finding out for yourself . . .

- Use a real piano or the drawing on page 319 to construct a major scale. First find Middle C.
- Now add up whole and half steps to match the scale pattern of half steps between 3–4 and 7–8. Remember that each key of the piano is separated by a semitone or half step. So you need to move from C to the next black key, then to the next white key, and so on.
- What happens when you get to the note marked E? There is no black key next. So the half step is to a white key.
- Now you know that the C major scale uses only white keys.
- Now repeat the exercise beginning on the note G. How is it different?

- Now try your hand at constructing a natural minor scale from the note E.
- You can work with these concepts creating scales on any pitches of your choice.

You have found that the C major scale can be played without using any black keys. However, any other major scale is going to require the use of black keys in order to maintain the pattern. You found that in the key of G major there is a half step between F and the black key above it. That note would be called F-sharp. So that you would not have to keep writing a sharp sign in front of all the F's in the song, it is easier to give it a *key signature* next to the clef sign. That way, the musician would know that every F was to be played as an F-sharp unless otherwise directed.

 or 

Note: In general, the black note just above the white key takes its name and adds to it the word *sharp*. The note below the white key takes the name of *flat*. So what's the difference between F-sharp and G-flat? On the keyboard there is no difference. It has the same sound. However, in a song written in sharps, you would confuse things by calling F-sharp G-flat. For instrumentalists, there can be slight differences between F-sharp and G-flat. Most instruments have more leeway with pitches than the piano.

We have talked about time signatures. There are also key signatures that are located between the clef sign and the time signatures. Key signatures use two sets of symbols, sharps (♯) and flats (♭). A shortcut to knowing what major key the composition is written in is to look at the last sharp on the staff and go to the next note name. For example, if there are four sharps, the last sharp is D-sharp. The next note up is E. The key is then E major. For major flat keys there is a different shortcut; the key will be that of the next to last flat. For example, if there are five flats—B, E, A, D, G—the next to last flat is D-flat and the key is D-flat major.

Common key signatures found in this book:

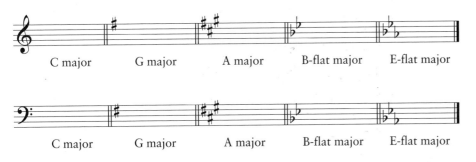

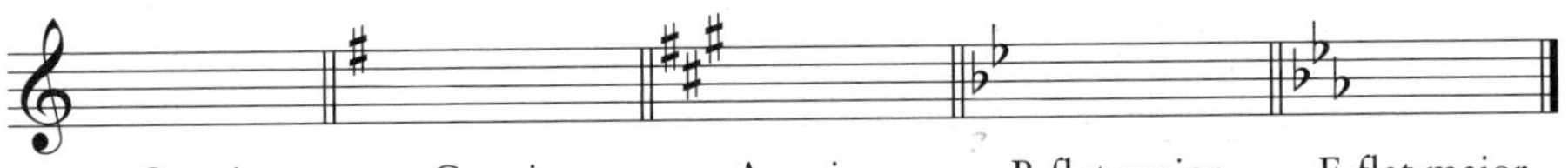

C major G major A major B-flat major E-flat major

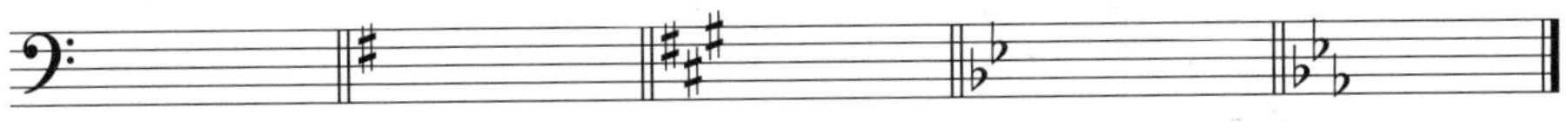

C major G major A major B-flat major E-flat major

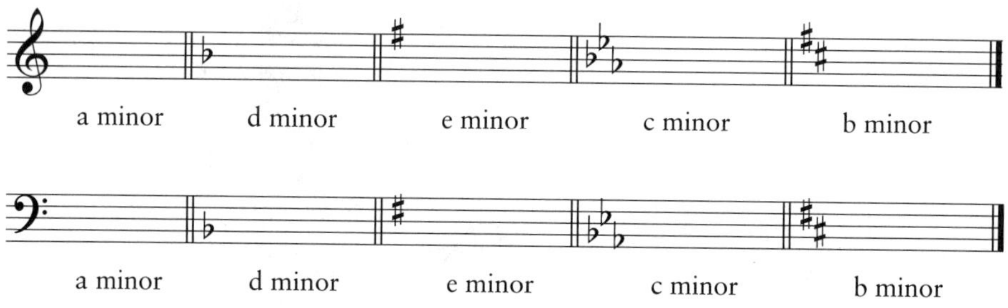
a minor
d minor
e minor
c minor
b minor
a minor
d minor
e minor
c minor
b minor

> ### *Finding out for yourself . . .*
>
> Look at the key signatures of three or four songs in Part II. In which keys are they written?
>
> *Hint:* Look at the beginning and ending bass notes—particularly the last one. Appendix E has a list of songs in major and minor keys.

The key of a song is chosen by the composer for its ease or difficulty of playing or of singing, and sometimes for mood. Keys are consistent musical patterns that tend to center around one main note. For example, when a song is written in the key of C, its "home base" or *tonic note* is considered C. With C as the tonic it will feel uncomfortable or unresolved if the song ends on another sound. Contemporary and modern music tends to be less restricted by these patterns, and there is often less feeling of "key."

With the information you have now, it is possible to compose your own melody. What if you want to add harmony or chords to that melody? More information is necessary. What follows is some general information, not a complete scholarly description. For that, you need a course in music theory or a good book on the subject. You can also find information on the Internet.

Harmony

Harmony is based on combining several notes at once to make chords. Melody usually refers to a single musical line and harmony to multiple notes being heard at the same time.

> ### *Finding out for yourself . . .*
>
> Now that you are somewhat familiar with the keyboard, you can create chords for yourself. We have numbered the notes of a scale from 1 to 8.

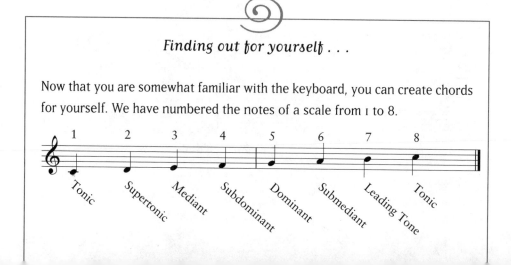

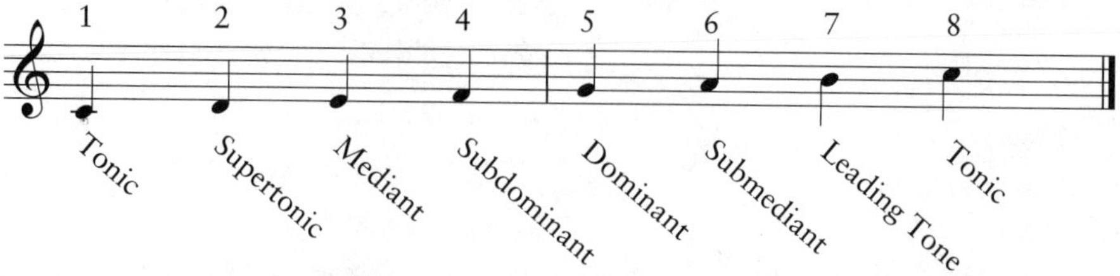
1
2
3
4
5
6
7
8
Tonic
Supertonic
Mediant
Subdominant
Dominant
Submediant
Leading Tone
Tonic

Beginning with Middle C, play notes 1, 3, and 5 together. You will find you have a chord.

Now play notes 2, 4, and 6 together. This is a chord with a different sound.

Play the following notes, and say the specific name of each chord while playing:

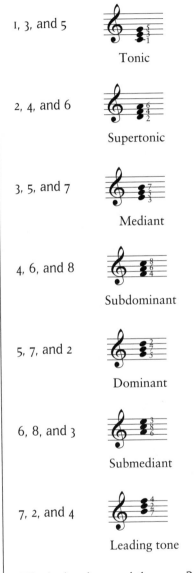

1, 3, and 5

5
3
1

Tonic

2, 4, and 6

6
4
2

Supertonic

3, 5, and 7

7
5
3

Mediant

4, 6, and 8

8
6
4

Subdominant

5, 7, and 2

2
7
5

Dominant

6, 8, and 3

3
8
6

Submediant

7, 2, and 4

4
2
7

Leading tone

Which chords sound the same? Which ones sound different?

Now play chords with four notes together.

For example, play 1, 3, 5, and 7, or 5, 7, 2, 4.

Congratulations! You are almost playing jazz.

You can build a chord on any note of the scale. However, for our purposes, it is important to stick with the correct notes of the scale. For example, if you are in the key of G Major, you must remember that there is an F-sharp in that key.

I hope you noticed that all the chords you composed had different qualities of sound. Each chord that you played was made up of intervals of a third. Some of those chords had a "major" quality and some of them had a "minor" quality. Every key has a variety of chord qualities. However, it is the predominant sound of the key that determines whether it is called major or minor. If the chord built on the first note of the key or scale has a major quality, the key is then determined to be major. A minor chord built on the first note of a scale implies that the key will be minor. Play a variety of chords at the keyboard and you will soon develop a sense of major and minor.

Look at the beginning of a song. Determine the key and then look at the chords. Notice the beginning and ending chords of the song. Usually you will find that they are both the tonic. The lowest bass note at the end of the song will usually be the tonic note of the key. You may notice also that the notes of any given chord can be placed in a variety of ways. For example, rather than playing 1, 3, and 5, play 3, 5, and 1(8) or 5, 8, and 3. These are all still the tonic chord, but in rearranged positions, or *inversions*. Create some time to play around with chords on a keyboard or at the piano.

The Internet has many music theory links. The music department at your school may have a list of links they find helpful. Music programs for computers (e.g., Finale or Sibelius) will write melodies, play and write chords, create an orchestra, and do many other wonderful musical things for you. In fact, there are programs that allow a pianist to play the music and the computer will turn it into a musical score.

However, it is important to know what you are doing. Knowledge stops panic in its tracks. The more you know about music, rhythm, and notes, the more confidently you can perform. It is easy to lose your confidence and trust if you are dependent on rote memory. "Fake it until you make it" is not particularly useful where musicianship is concerned.

Classification of Songs

Songs Best Suited for Men

Modern Major-General
If You've Only Got a Moustache
Salley Gardens
Wand'rin' Star
The Angler's Song (duet)

Songs Best Suited for Women

Civil War Medley
Con amores, la mi madre
El majo timido
Goodnight, My Someone
He Shall Feed His Flock
Into the Night
No Other Love
Summertime

Songs for Men or Women

Most songs in The Singing Book *are suited for either gender. Some songs have alternate text so that men or women may sing them.*

Songs for Low Voice

The Angler's Song (duet)
Evening Prayer (duet)
The Hippopotamus
Night and Day
Wand'rin' Star

Duets

Ah, Poor Bird/Shalom
The Angler's Song
Banana Boat Song
Evening Prayer
Somewhere Out There

Songs for High Voice

The Angler's Song (duet)
Con amores la mi madre
Evening Prayer (duet)
Gentle Annie
If You've Only Got a Moustache
Into the Night
I Never Knew
No Other Love
Over the Rainbow
Somewhere Out There (duet)
Summertime

Songs for Medium Voice

Most songs in The Singing Book *are for medium voice. Multiple keys are available for many songs on* The Singing Book *Web site*

Songs with a Limited Range (octave or less)*

Banana Boat Song (C4-A5)
Mi caballo blanco (E4-C5)
My Country 'Tis of Thee (F4-E5)
My Lord, What a Mornin'! (F4-C5)
Oh, How Lovely Is the Evening (D4-B5)

**The lowest notes on a piano are designated A1, B1, C1, D1, E1, F1, and G1. Middle C is C4.*

Songs with an Extended Range (10th or more)*

Con amores, la mi madre (D4-optional F#5)
Danny Boy (B4-E5)
Ev'ry Time I Feel the Spirit (A4-D5)
Goodnight, My Someone (B♭4-E5)
The Hippopotamus (G3-D5)
I Never Knew (B4-F♯5)
Into the Night (E4-G5)
Night and Day (G3-C4)
No Other Love (D4-optionalG5)
Over the Rainbow (C4-F5)
Shalom, Chaverim (A4-D5)
Shenandoah (A4-D5)
Skylark (C4-F5)
Somewhere Out There (duet: E4-A6/A♭4-E5)
A Time for Us (C4-F5)
Wand'rin' Star (A4-C5)

**The lowest notes on a piano are designated A1, B1, C1, D1, E1, F1, and G1. Middle C is C4.*

Songs in a Minor Key

Ah, Poor Bird
Ah, Poor Bird/Shalom
Bitte
Babylon
Civil War Medley
Con amores, la mi madre
Dubinushka
Ici-bas
Swingin' in Minor Blues
Mi caballo blanco
Niño precioso
Scarborough Fair
Shalom, Chaverim
Westryn Wynde

Humorous Songs

The Frog in the Bog
The Hippopotamus
Modern Major-General
If You've Only Got a Moustache

Songs for Improvisation

Ballad Improvisation
Swingin' in Minor Blues
Blue Skies
Ev'ry Time I Feel the Spirit
God Bless' the Child
My Lord, What a Mornin'!
Night and Day
Skylark
They Can't Take That Away from Me
When I Fall in Love

Songs in French

Ah! si mon moine voulait danser!
Ici-bas

Songs in German

Auf flügeln des Gesanges
Bitte

Songs in Italian

Donzelle, fuggite
Ombra mai fù
Santa Lucia

Songs in Latin

Alleluia #I, #II, #III
Dona Nobis Pacem
Ego Sum Pauper
Gaudeamus Igitur

Songs in Spanish

Con amores, la mi madre
El majo timido
Mi caballo blanco
Niño precioso

Vocal Challenges

Rhythm
Dubinushka
El majo timido
Mi caballo blanco
Night and Day
Skylark
They Can't Take That Away from Me

Breath/long phrases
America the Beautiful
Dona Nobis Pacem
He Shall Feed His Flock
Into the Night
My Country 'Tis of Thee
My Lord, What a Mornin'!
Over the Rainbow
Summertime

Leaps (intervals of a fourth or more)
Danny Boy
Dona Nobis Pacem
Evening Prayer
Gentle Annie
Goodnight, My Someone
My Country 'Tis of Thee
Over the Rainbow
Santa Lucia
Scarborough Fair

Articulation/flexibility
Alleluia #II and #III
Donzelle, fuggite
El majo timido
The Frog in the Bog
Modern Major-General
If You've Only Got a Moustache
Niño precioso

Further Reading

Adams, David. *A Handbook of Diction for Singers: Italian, German, French.* New York: Oxford University Press, 1999.

Bunch, M. *Dynamics of the Singing Voice.* New York: Springer-Verlag, 1997.

Calain-Germain, B. *Anatomy of Movement.* Seattle, WA: Eastland Press, 1993.

Caldwell, Robert. *The Performer Prepares.* Redland, WA: Caldwell Publishing, 1990.

Conable, Barbara. *The Structures and Movement of Breathing.* Chicago: GIA Publications, 2000.

Craig, David. *A Performer Prepares: A Guide to Song Preparation for Actors, Singers and Dancers.* New York: Applause Theatre Book Publishers, 1999.

Dennison, P. *Brain-Gym,* Ventura, CA: Edu-Kinesthetics, 1986.

Emmons, S., and Thomas A. *Power Performance for Singers: Transcending the Barriers.* New York: Oxford University Press, 1998.

Goldsmith, Joan Oliver. *How Can We Keep from Singing: Music and the Passionate Life.* New York: W. W. Norton, 2001.

Kimball, Carol. *SONG: A Guide to Style and Literature.* Redland, WA: Caldwell Publishing, 1996.

Macdonald, Glynn. *Illustrated Elements of Alexander Technique.* London: Element, 2002.

Nelson, S., and Blades-Zeller, E. *Singing with Your Whole Self: The Feldenkrais Method and Voice.* Rochester, NY: Inspiration Press, 2000.

Ristad, E. *A Soprano on Her Head.* Moab, UT: Real People Press, 1982.

Sataloff, R. *Vocal Health and Pedagogy.* San Diego, CA: Singular Publishing Group, 1998.

Zander, R., and Zander, B. *The Art of Possibility: Transforming Professional and Personal Life.* Boston, MA: Harvard Business School Press, 2000.

Recommended Web Sites

The Singing Book has an easy-to-use Web site, described below:

***The Singing Book* Web site: wwnorton.com/web/singing**
Using the registration code provided with *The Singing Book* CD set, students and teachers can access music in additional keys for the folk songs, group songs, and rounds in the anthology. Users can listen to songs in various keys and print them as performance-ready sheet music.

National Association of Teachers of Singing (www.nats.org)
A list of related links on this Web site provides access to many useful resources for singers and teachers of singing. The site also includes student message boards and a "Find a Teacher Directory."

Song Texts and Lieder Page (www.recmusic.org/lieder)
This Web site contains an extensive database with thousands of foreign and English song texts and translations.

The Diction Domain (www.scaredofthat.com/dictiondomain)
Everything you always wanted to know about the International Phonetic Alphabet and singing in foreign languages is available on this easy-to-use Web site.

Music Theory (www.music-mind.com/Music/indexlrm.HTM)
This site is excellent for explaining the basics of music.

Index

Recordings to Accompany *The Singing Book*

The 2-CD set gives you three listening options for learning and practicing all of the songs in *The Singing Book*. Tracks 20 to 43 on CD 1 and all of the tracks on CD 2 are recorded in split-track stereo, with melody and guide rhythm on the right track and piano accompaniment on the left track. Using a computer or any CD player equipped with balance controls, you can adjust the speaker balance to hear either the melody/rhythm or piano accompaniment alone, or to hear both tracks played together. Stereos without balance controls will play both tracks simultaneously.

CD 1

1 Ballad Improvisation
2 Swingin' in Minor Blues
3 My Country 'Tis of Thee
4 America the Beautiful
5 There's Music in the Air
6 The Frog in the Bog
7 Gaudeamus Igitur
8 Banana Boat Song
9 Music Alone Shall Live
10 Oh, How Lovely Is the Evening
11 Babylon
12 Dona Nobis Pacem
13 Ego Sum Pauper
14 Ah, Poor Bird
15 Shalom, Chaverim
16 Ah, Poor Bird/Shalom
17 Alleluia I
18 Alleluia II
19 Alleluia III
20 Shenandoah
21 Scarborough Fair
22 Danny Boy
23 Civil War Medley
24 The Water Is Wide
25 The Lark in the Clear Air
26 Salley Gardens
27 Westryn Wynde
28 Santa Lucia
29 Paun I Kolo
30 Ah! si mon moine voulait danser!
31 Niño precioso
32 Mi caballo blanco
33 Dubinushka
34 Dance of Youth
35 My Lord, What a Mornin'!
36 Ev'ry Time I Feel the Spirit
37 Amazing Grace
38 How Can I Keep from Singing?
39 I Move On
40 Wand'rin' Star
41 Goodnight, My Someone
42 No Other Love
43 I Got the Sun in the Morning

CD 2

1 Where Is Love?
2 Over the Rainbow (high key)
3 Over the Rainbow (low key)
4 Sing!
5 Somewhere Out There
6 A Time for Us
7 Blue Skies
8 When I Fall in Love
9 They Can't Take That Away from Me
10 Skylark
11 Night and Day
12 God Bless' the Child
13 Come Again, Sweet Love
14 The Angler's Song
15 Donzelle, fuggite
16 He Shall Feed His Flock
17 Ombra mai fù (high key)
18 Ombra mai fù (low key)
19 Auf Flugeln des Gesanges
20 Bitte
21 Içi-bas
22 Gentle Annie
23 If You've Only Got a Moustache
24 El majo timido
25 Con amores, la mi madre
26 Evening Prayer
27 Summertime (high key)
28 Summertime (low key)
29 Modern Major-General
30 Into the Night
31 The Hippopotamus
32 I Never Knew